MW01670858

DIARY OF A VAGABOND

By

Mustansar Hussain Tarar

SANG-E-MEEL PUBLICATIONS
25, SHAHRAH-E-PAKISTAN (LOWER MALL) LAHORE.

070.442 Tarar, Mustansar Hussain
Diary of a Vagabond/ Mustansar Hussain
Tarar.-Lahore: Sang-e-Meel Publications, 2018.
288pp.
1. Columns. I. Title.

2018
Published by:
Afzaal Ahmad
Sang-e-Meel Publications,
Lahore.

ISBN-10: 969-35-3061-6
ISBN-13: 978-969-35-3061-2

Sang-e-Meel Publications
25 Shahrah-e-Pakistan (Lower Mall), Lahore-54000 PAKISTAN
Phones: 92-423-722-0100 / 92-423-722-8143 Fax: 92-423-724-5101
http://www.sangemeel.com e-mail: smp@sangemeel.com
PRINTED AT: HAJI HANIF & SONS PRINTERS, LAHORE.

Contents

Shaking the long arm....5
Morality is the name of the game....9
The snake game....13
It's time to go to sleep....16
K-2 Kahani....20
The coming of senior age....24
The tree that was murdered....29
An old hunter's tales....33
Arabian horses or mules?....37
An eventful journey....41
"Flower hill" was the motivation....43
Rattled in Kaghan....46
Spellbound in paradise....50
Of dreamlands and nightmares....54
A dream within a dream....56
The visa saga....59
Wells of Madina....63
Farewell, Madina....67
Rasul Hamzatof's Daghistan....71
Spectacular Athenian results....75
A mystical experience....79
The fairies of Nanga Parbat....83
The fairies of Nanga Parbat....86
Will ye no, come back again....89
I dreamt of Shah Gori....93
The survivor of Michni Post....97
Roaming the heavenly Harlem....102
Black is beautiful....105
Black is our beloved....109
Who is on the right track?....113
The Jews and the Muslims....116
King Solomon's Temple....120
Beggars of New York....124
The village that is Greenwich....128
The bitter Rice....132
The egg merchant and the moon....135
The Idiot Box....138
Beware, my dear birds....141
The hawk speaks....145

Tears of Shiva 149
A stroll in heaven 152
Enchanting Dudiput 156
A resplendent lake, indeed 160
Ballet in the mountains 163
The dream lake 166
The Day of Judgment 169
The journey continues 172
In search of daffodils 175
The road to Paris 179
Far, far from the maddening crowd 183
Tourism tamasha 187
Cutting a lonely furrow 190
Dubai chalo 194
An Arab with a Pakistani soul 198
Saving Gandhara treasures 201
Back from the Yellow Devil 205
Yajuj and Majuj in India 209
City of the golden owl 213
A tear on the cheek of eternity 218
Lost in Rajisthan 222
Farewell to New Delhi 226
Go, camel kids, go! 230
Believing in reincarnation 235
Dreamland and wasteland 238
The gates of Babylon 242
Literary wanderings 245
The politicians of New York 249
Of mice and men 253
Our dogs and their dogs 257
Hangman's noose 261
The city of the yellow devil 265
The American royalty 269
The houses of my dream 272
In defence of Pakistani films 275
Dasvidania, Moscow 279
Dancing in the desert 282
In the black robes of sorrow 285

Shaking the long arm

Yesterday I was in a state of severe depression due to some unknown reasons. And the remedy I normally apply under such conditions could not be applied due to the presence of my family.

At this age, your kids in particular do not leave you alone for a moment and will even knock at the bathroom door if your stay is prolonged, fearing the worst. They will barge into my study frequently to a make sure that I have not slumped on my seat due to stroke or something. I do appreciate their concern for my health, but this love and affection of my off-springs robs me of my privacy, although at this age of incompetence, privacy is of no use. Even then I do want to be all by myself at times.

However, I had to cure this fit of depression so I used a time-tested ploy to achieve my ignoble ends. I offered to finance a dinner in one of the most exclusive and, naturally, expensive restaurants of the town, provided they take along their mother too. As expected, they readily agreed and after giving me instructions to contact them on cell phone immediately if I felt strange in anyway, they left me in peace, securing my wallet first, naturally.

As soon I was alone, I switched on the television and started searching for the remedy of my depression i.e. navel-jerking Indian damsels who are in distress due to their strict moral code. The poor things have to adorn themselves with two strips which tease them so much that they jerk and shake all the time to get rid of them. Mind you, these properly dressed damsels have to be Indian; the European flesh leaves me cold because it reminds me of my colonial past.

I desperately kept on pushing the remote button but could not find the only antidote of my depression on the TV screen; perhaps the ladies had reformed and gone on a tableeghi mission as some of our actresses had declared.

However, during this futile search I came upon a hitherto unknown Timbuktu Channel, which was broadcasting a current affairs discussion programme. The host was interviewing Mr Jhootani and Mr Badkalami, the disinformation chief and the outlaw chief of Timbuktu, respectively, about some muddle in the judiciary in which a judge and the emperor were at daggers drawn at that time.

As this channel is rarely watched in Pakistan, I would like to reproduce the discussion so that we may realize how very fortunate we are in this part of the world where true democracy is flourishing, the judiciary is respected, the media is free and safe, the law enforcing agencies respect the rights of citizens and our ministers utter the truth and nothing but the truth, so help them God, so here goes.

Host: "I am truly grateful to you two gentlemen that you have readily accepted my request to participate in this discussion programme to express your august opinions about the present crisis raging in the country. Actually, your eagerness was such that you were here in the studio while I was still in the bathroom combing my sparse hair. Mr Jhootani, we hear that the chief justice...."

Jhootnai: "Please correct yourself. He is not a chief justice, but weak justice because his judgments weakened us."

Host: "Well the chief judge...."

Jhootnai: "Please correct yourself again! He is not a judge anymore, we are the judges...."

Host: "Sorry sir. Let us agree upon the weak justice then. We hear that he is virtually under house arrest and even his children are not allowed to go to school to continue their education."

Jhootani: "Well, who can deny the importance of education? Children must be educated and if they are not educated how can our country progress. In fact, I am also thinking of getting some education."

Host: "But sir, the children of the weak justice are not allowed to go to school for education."

Jhootani: "Ah, The children! They are the future of Timbuktu. They must be educated, it is their right and I will sacrifice my life to defend that right."

Host: "But sir they cannot go to school."

Badkalami: "Oh look here! What rubbish are you talking about? So what if they cannot go to school? I never went to any school and even then became the outlaw minister."

Host: "Sir, would you like to tell the people of Timbuktu how you achieved this greatness. I mean you never went to school and even then became outlaw minister?"

Badkalami: "Why should I tell the people anything? They did not elect me, the emperor appointed me."

Host: "Then please tell me, I will not tell the people."

Badkalami: "Well, I had a lot of in-laws, brothers-in-laws and sisters-in-law and I was fed up with them. So I thought if they were in-law, I would become outlaw. That is how I became an outlaw minister."

Host: "Sir, you are the long arm of law..."

Badkalami: "Oi, two-paisa worth journalist! What did you say? Long arm? I will give long arm to your family."

Host: "Sir I did not mean that long arm."

Badkalami: "If you did not mean that long arm then I did not mean that long arm to your family also, so the matter is finished."

Host: "You are short-tempered, sir."

Badkalami: "I am short on everything, you rascal. And understand one thing, you are harping on the same subject of weak justice and how he has refused to resign. I tell you if we really wanted his resignation, we could get it with long arm in no time."

Host: "Did you say the long army, sir?"

Badkalami: "Long arm, you fool, the real one. Moreover, if you keep on parroting this justice and media freedom thing you will get it."

Host: "Mr Jhootani, you are the minister for disinformation, during the present crisis the arm of the media was also twisted...."

Badkalami: "Oh! Again this arm business. I think I will have to do something to you."

Jhootani: "Well, Mr Host you know that we believe in the freedom of media sincerely, if we did not would we be answering your stupid and insolent questions? Would we tolerate these two-paisa worth journalists, would we?"

(In the meantime, during this live broadcast some uniformed personnel barge inside the studios and start ransacking the premises and roughing up studio employees, the host naturally gets nervous).

Host: "What is happening? Who are these people, Mr, Jhootani, what is going on?"

Jhotani: "Nothing is happening, nothing is going on. I do not see anything."

Host: "But sir these people right in front of your eyes are smashing windows and terrorizing the staff."

Jhootani: "Oh these people? I thought this channel was recording some drama and these were your actors performing with a rare vengeance."

Host: "Sir, don't you recognize them? They are your actors!"

Jhootani: "In that case I condemn this attack on media's freedom and I will personally order an enquiry and punish the culprits."

Host: "But sir, why don't you stop them? You are a minister!"

Jhootani: "How can I stop them, it is a free country and everybody is free to do whatever he deems fit. Besides, if I stop them right now the case against them will be become very weak, so let them do their job and then I will order an enquiry." (Mr Jhootani starts sobbing and wipes a tear).

Host: "Mr Jhootani I hope you are feeling all right?"

Jhootani: "My heart is shedding tears of blood. This is an attack on media's freedom and I condemn it wholeheartedly, leave me alone with my sorrows."

Host: "Mr Badkalami, do you have anything to say?

Badkalami: "Long arm."

Morality is the name of the game

Some years back I was sitting in a transporter's office in Gilgit trying to arrange a jeep for Tarshing, which in my opinion is the most spectacular and breathtaking village in Pakistan, surrounded by the snows of killer mountain Nanga Parbat. In the meantime a German tourist arrived who booked a jeep for the Khunjrab Pass. He paid the advance money and said, "Please make sure that the driver is competent as the mountain road is rather precarious."

"All the mountain drivers are competent, otherwise they would have perished a long time ago," Mr Baig, the transporter, assured him smilingly.

"Then make sure that the driver is not very young," the German was also amused and while getting up to leave he said, "I want the jeep at my hotel exactly at six clock in the morning."

"InshaAllah," Mr Baig muttered.

The German, slightly taken aback, pointed a finger at Mr Baig and said in a somber tone, "No InshaAllah, I want my jeep at six in the morning."

"Sir, it will be there at six, InshaAllah."

The German was agitated, "Look here I have told you that I want my jeep at six in the morning without an InshaAllah."

When I intervened to settle the matter, the German disclosed that it is his experience in Pakistan that when an InshaAllah is added to a statement it means maybe or maybe not, so he wants his jeep at six in the morning without it.

When the Pakistan cricket team was leaving to compete in the World Cup, the captain and most of the players declared that they will win the World Cup, adding InshaAllah. After all I am also a true believer of sorts, having penned a travelogue of Haj and a night spent in Ghar-e-Hira and truly believe in InshaAllah, but there were so many of them that I had my doubts. It was less of a maybe and more of a maybe not, so I was not disappointed by their dismal performance at all. However, the rest of the nation wondered that if the female students of Hafsa Madrassa are still not out, how come our equally pious and bearded players got out.

Whenever our cricket or hockey teams come back after winning some prestigious tournament which used to happen quite frequently in the distant past, they always declared they owed their success to the prayers of qaum. Now if they come back rather ignobly defeated, it is the qaum who should be reprimanded for not praying hard enough. The players are not to be blamed at all.

During the benevolent reign of Ziaul Haq, the Pakistani contingent after "competing" in the Olympics returned empty-handed, without winning even a bronze to console the grieving nation. They were invited for a presidential dinner during which Ziaul Haq very kindly enquired from each team member as to what was the main cause of their total failure.

The hockey wallas complained about the hockey sticks which had somehow shrunk due to the weather conditions. The athletes said that the other competing athletes were so ill-mannered that they just kept running while they were catching their breath and they did not wait for them to catch up. Besides, their meters were longer than Pakistani meters, etc., and then the President asked the manager of swimming contingent as to why they had not won any event.

He replied grudgingly, "Mr President, you are talking about winning a swimming event. You should thank God that all of us are back alive and none of us was drowned there."

Therefore, we should also thank Almighty that the cricket team has come back alive. Look what happened to Woolmer.

But seriously, who are these nuts who are burning effigies of the players and stoning their houses and abusing them left, right and centre. What are their credentials as a nation? One of the most corrupt nations in the world – is that the credential? What have they achieved on the world level except notoriety and religious bigotry, and they expect their team to win the World Cup?

They have never burut a single effigy of a person who was responsible for the loss of half of their country, nor of those rolling stone lotas who gather a lot of moss while rolling from one party to the other without any shame. No sir, they do not indulge in such dignified reactions, instead they hurl stones at the helpless players who were definitely, but temporarily, inefficient to say the most.

Mind you, it is easier to become a minister in this country than to achieve a national and international status in the cricket field. You have to have exceptional talent and lifelong devotion to achieve that. You do fail at times, and who does not.

However, there was this ray of sunshine in this dark episode, the failure of the boys was not attributed for once to their lecherous morals as most of the team is supposed to be very pious and "thanks to Allah" type. Nevertheless, the question is, do our brand of morals matter to achieve a victory in the field of sports or war? The Australian players, from our standards, are the most lecherous and immoral to say the least. Every other day some lady of questionable virtue walks into the hotel where the Australians are staying, with a baby in her lap and enquiring where the father is or maybe who amongst them is the father. And even then they are unbeatable on the cricket field.

Mr Shane Warne, easily the most outstanding bowler of our age, has a reputation which, at least, I envy very much. I doubt if any of them has even peeped inside a church during their present immoral life. It holds true for South Africans, Kiwis and the Brits.

It will be interesting to note that in years gone by, the Pakistani cricket teams which won laurels for their country were also slightly 'immoral'. Without naming anyone, there was this cavalier dashing batsman of Pakistan who was totally merry when he went in to bat.

Then another star batsman, very popular with the crowd, would puff away at a cigarette refilled with some sort of grass while waiting for his turn. And when his turn came, he would get up, take a few steps towards the pitch and then come back and request his friend, who would be holding his cigarette, "Yaar aik soota aur lagwado". And he always performed.

About our dear Imran Khan, now reformed perhaps, the less said the better. Our cricket team, which created history by leveling the series on their first tour of England by winning the Oval Test, created another record. When they returned home, three of them were accompanied by their recently acquired English wives. At least one of them was married in a church ceremony.

I am sure people of my age remember a photograph of Fazal Mehmud, without doubt the most dashing and handsome cricketer the like of which was never seen again, holding and hoisting a glass of bubbly champagne after the Oval victory. It is another matter that afterwards he turned towards religion, not out of fashion but out of conviction, and wrote some very thought provoking books about religion. This only happened when his cricketing days were over, so no harm was done.

I do sympathise with the much-abused Pakistani cricket team because after a dismal failure, they do not have the options of politicians to roll over and change sides by establishing their patriotism and their empires. If we can forgive the politicians and the generals, why can't we forgive these poor souls?

The snake game

I am a self-styled vagabond and why shouldn't I be when everybody around me is self-styled, including the politicians, mullas and generals. And in this capacity I have roamed the world, spending nights in unknown jungles, camping on the banks of wild rivers and unknown lakes, and tramping in deserts.

During those days of gay abandon, I never had the slightest fear that I will encounter some wild animal and at times I did, but there was one thing which I really dreaded – the snakes. I will perhaps readily agree to put my hand into the jaw of a crocodile or a tiger or meet a lota politician but I will not touch a dead, venom-less water snake with a stick even if I am offered a million dollars. I start shivering and stuttering with fright when I see a slithering snake on the National Geographic channel and, naturally, I grab the remote to change the channel, although with shivering hands it becomes an ordeal.

I remember a certain hot summer day when as a child I was bathing in a shallow water channel in a far off village, Duniyapur, and noticed that the waters of the channel were seeping through and flooding a field of cotton. The water was being soaked up by the thirsty and dusty earth, and at times filled a deep hole in the ground. In due time you saw the thin moustaches of a field rat emerging from the hole, where he had resided so far, and then jump out of this hole to save his dear life from flooding.

This spectacle of jumping rats amused me a great deal, so I forgot about bathing and instead busied myself in pouring water with my cupped hands into the holes, which were still some distance away from the creeping water. Soon enough my efforts bore fruit in the shape of a field rat, first his moustaches appeared and then the terrified animal, seeing my glittering expectant eyes hovering over him, fled in panic. This was indeed great fun for a city lad and I busied myself with great devotion in pouring water into those rat holes.

Then something entirely unexpected happened. As usual the moustaches of a rat appeared on the edge of the hole and, by the look of it, it was a huge rat but the damn thing was too frightened to come out so I goaded him with a stick and maybe pulled one of his thin hair or something. These endeavours bore result and the thing emerged from the hole and kept on emerging without an end in sight. I was paralysed.

It was a huge king cobra whose abode I had flooded and it kept on slithering and passing right beside my feet almost touching them with its warm body. However, it did not harm me (I would not be writing this column if it did), just gave me a dirty look and then disappeared in the thick cotton field. This experience shattered me completely and from then onwards I have been extremely scared of snakes.

A few years back I was camping by a stream on the highest plateau in the world, the Deosai, and while sipping a cup of coffee outside my tent on an enchanting evening descending slowly on its hills and grasslands, I noticed a small hole nearby and I could clearly see some thing with moustaches peeping from it. I gave a loud yell that echoed throughout Deosai and ran towards the tents of my porters. I again yelled at my guide Ali who had assured me that there were no snakes to be found on Deosai.

Ali smilingly went up to that hole and instead of a snake a loveable brown marmot emerged from the hole. He did have moustaches and then he just sat there on the edge of his abode, whistled at us for a while and then went back to his underground quarters.

While canoeing on an ancient Red Indian river Wakaiwa in Florida, my son-in-law Bilal duly informed me that there were twenty-seven different varities of snakes found in the area, however, only four of them were poisonous, including the Moksin which normally hung on the trees looking like a dead branch and then would suddenly fall on its unsuspecting prey. It was also called the flying snake. This information completely unnerved me and I immediately abandoned the canoeing expedition.

Until recently, we in Pakistan did not have flying snakes, just the usual snakes that came out in dozens from their holes and joined some recently arrived king cobra to terrify the masses for some time to come.

These snakes very dutifully abandoned the king cobra as soon as they felt that its grip was loosening, people had had enough of him and they wanted another king cobra in its place. Now these flying snakes, recently introduced, naturally flew into the country when the going was good and then flew out when the going got tough. During their tenure, they will give us sermons on patriotism, Islam and the Pakistan movement. It was a normal practice that a cobra will arrive and declare himself the king, and it was a normal practice that lesser snakes with a lust to bite would gather around him.

A foreign reporter asked an ordinary mortal, "Do you support your cobra?"

The reply he got was, "If it is our fate to be ruled by cobras I prefer the present cobra."

It is a strange phenomenon that every few years the public wants a new cobra. They do not enjoy the poison injected in their veins by the old cobra any more and want a more lethal dose. They think that the new arrival will solve all their problems in a jiffy, but they always end up with a worst deal as experienced in the past.

I have another snake tale to prove my point. The tale was narrated to me by my grandmother who was a master storyteller. There was this innocent weaver who was going to another village to attend a marriage ceremony, and on his way he encountered two snakes entwined with each other, supposedly making love. The weaver, thus frightened, killed one of them with his shoe but the other snake escaped his wrath.

Next year exactly on the same date when the weaver had killed his companion on a night with a full moon, the other snake appeared, bit him and sped away. The weaver's body was full of poison but he recovered somehow. Then for the next few years it became a routine but with a difference – a few days before the appearance of the snake the weaver would get lethargic, would not sleep at nights and actually waited anxiously for the snake to appear and inject venom into his body. This welcome dose would rejuvenate him and he would go back to his normal life like a new man.

However, there is a difference between our plight and the weaver's lethargy. He always waited for the same snake but we, after a while, get fed up with the same old snake and do not enjoy his poison any more. We want a new cobra every time with much more lethal venom to stir our bodies. We celebrate his arrival, support him and make him a king. The weaver's snake appeared on the same date on a full moon night, whereas our new cobra can appear any time of the year but only on dark nights. The waiting game may have begun, we are feeling lethargic and lazy, and we cannot sleep at nights and are hoping naturally in vain that the newcomer will solve all our problems.

What would you name this snake opera? "Waiting for the new cobra", perhaps?

It's time to go to sleep

They, all seven of them, woke up after centuries from their deep slumber and saw that there was light at the end of the cave.

"For how many centuries have we slept?" the seventh one asked his companions.

"Do you think we were wide awake counting the centuries while you were sleeping? Stupid! How should we know?"

"Well, I would like to know. Do you have any suggestions?"

"Why don't you go out and find who the king is these days and what currency is in circulation? The second one is a history buff and he will calculate the century we are in."

"I will go outside the cave but not alone. At least two of you should accompany me, I cannot venture into an unknown world. Who knows what dangers are lurking out there?"

"All right, you coward," said the fifth and the sixth got up lethargically, "we will accompany you."

And as they were going out of the cave to find out how many centuries they had slept, the first one said, "Please do not forget to bring us some food, we have been hungry for centuries. A roast lamb and four legs of a camel with some bread will do. And if some non-alcoholic beer is available, fetch a few dozen pitchers."

"Supposing the non-alcoholic stuff is not available, then what would your majesties like to drink?" the seventh asked sarcastically.

"Then we are helpless. And if it is a matter of life and death, the haram also becomes halal. So alcoholic beer it would be."

"But it is not a matter of life and death!"

"For me it is."

All three of them stepped out of the cave into an unknown world. The four remaining waited and waited, and then to while away their time, they started sketching on the walls of the cave, creating cave paintings of those who were their first love. One of them painted a nude woman and he was admonished so he immediately clothed the figure. The other one painted a young boy and he was not admonished because this was the "sin of saints," piously overlooked. Finally, when they thought that all three of their companions had met some tragic fate, the seventh one entered the cave and he was laughing his head off like a maniac.

"What happened? What happened? What did you see outside the cave?" all four of them asked in unison.

"Outside, my friends, it is a mad, mad world, you can't imagine how comic it is that is why I cannot stop laughing."

"Where is my beer and roast lamb?" the first one moaned.

"Why don't you shut up, you glutton! Let him narrate what he saw outside the cave. Please, the seventh one, tell us what you saw."

"Well, there seems to be a row between the king and the chief qazi and they are at daggers drawn. Although it is due to the legal shield which the previous and present qazi provided to the illegal kings, including the present one, that these kings walk in and place themselves on the throne with immunity. The public, it seems, is siding with the qazi, showering kisses on the tires of his jeep, convinced that he is the new messiah who will carry them across troubled waters."

"Do you think he will do that?"

"How can I say that? I am still sane. Actually, the public every now and then gets fed up with the present king and whosoever comes their way, they take him for a messiah. And then after a few years the same messiah is turned into a traitor, and the game of messiahs and traitors goes on."

"These sorts of games are played all over the world, specially in our countries. They are funny, but the way you are laughing it seems that you have seen something much more funny and ridiculous."

"Well, the continuous sleep of the centuries seems to have enhanced the number of your brain cells and you rightly point out that there is yet something funnier. Another messiah, a financial wizard, has appeared on the scene and, can you believe it, he doubles your money within 70 days through some method henceforth unknown to the human mind. He is a very pious man, a Syed in fact, and promises to pay all those billions which he has accumulated if he is released."

"Did they arrest this messiah?"

"Yes, they did. And do you know that the whole nation is rallying around this man called 'Double Shah'. They want him to be released, there are huge demonstrations in his favour, people are praying for him and cursing the law authorities who arrested him."

"In a way they are right. They could make him the finance minister of the country, amass every penny of the national exchequer in front of him and he could double the money in 70 days and then again double the doubled money and within a year or two this country would be the richest nation in the world. They will not need any factories or businesses; they would just sit back and relax while Double Shah will keep on doubling. But, seriously, do these people really believe that money can be doubled within 70 days?"

"That is the funny part of it – they do!"

"What sort of nation are they?"

"The funny sort, and that is not all. There are these black robed chicks with the sticks who are threatening to become suicide bombers if their demands are not met."

"What are their demands?"

"They don't know as yet."

"And they are threatening to attack their own country and people?"

"That's what I heard."

"It is a funny country indeed. So let us have a good laugh because they say that laughter is the best medicine."

All of them laughed their heads off and the cave echoed with their mad laughter and then suddenly one of them said, "Oh, we forgot to ask, where are the fifth and the sixth ones."

"Well that is a sad story. The fifth one has become the law minister of the country."

"But he does not know anything about the law."

"Neither did the previous one."

"And the sixth one?"

"He has joined a madrassa and intends to go to heaven directly from there."

They, the remaining five, sat in silence for a while and then the seventh said, "Brothers, these are no times to go out of the cave. We are much safer and sane here so let us again go to sleep for some centuries."

They fell into a deep slumber and soon the walls of the cave decorated with drawings of their sweethearts reverberated with their snoring.

K-2 Kahani

I asked Ashraf Aman the same old question, what were your emotions when you stood on top of the second highest mountain in the world?

The first Pakistani to ascend K-2, Ashraf not only related, but also recreated the experience with his wild gesturing, smiles and a lot of pride. From his facial expression one could see that he was transported back in time and at that very moment was standing on top of K-2, experiencing the same joy and pride, waving the Pakistani flag as he had done years ago.

K-2, like all the great mountains, has had its share of tragedies and tales of sorrow. While we celebrate those who came back, we must remember those who never did.

What about Lashkar Khan whose frozen body still adorns the eternal snows of K-2? Framed in a upright position he is there near the summit, his face blackened with the impact of winds and blizzards. Almost twenty years ago he was accompanying a French mountaineer as a high-porter. They came across a thin gallery of ice, over an abyss and while they were trying to cross it, Lashkar Khan's lungs suddenly collapsed due to the height and he died then and there. It was impossible for the French mountaineer to bring back his body to the base camp and the only alternate was to push it into the abyss below. The French gentleman did not have the heart to do that as Lashkar Khan was not only a high-porter but a dear friend as well. So he covered the frozen body of Lashkar Khan with a terpal, left the face open and then secured it with nails. After so many years he still stands erect, framed within the snows of K-2. Even today, when a porter or a mountaineer comes across Lashkar Khan and pays his tribute to the frozen man who has become a legend.

I fondly remember John Smolich who led an American expedition during a particularly dangerous year when K-2 claimed dozens of lives and some of the Balti porters abandoned the base camp fearing the wrath of the mountain. My younger brother, Lt Col Mubasshir Hussain Tarar was appointed the liaison officer to this American expedition and I went to Rawalpindi to see him off.

There in a large room of colonial Flashman Hotel I met John Smolich, feverishly packing and organizing hundreds of cartons contain mountain equipment and food to be carried to the base camp of K-2. He was rather boyish and very handsome. I jokingly requested him to take care of my kid brother who was a dashing young captain at that time and John replied with a huge grin, "Well, I will do that, provided the captain takes care of me as well."

Upon his return, Mubasshir, shattered by the tragic experience, narrated the fate of smiling John. "He had gone up to Camp Three, along with a team member to supervise the transportation of equipment and they were coming down quite effortlessly. From the base camp we were keeping an eye on their movements through our binoculars, when all of sudden a huge mass of ice, that had been hanging there for centuries, collapsed on them. Immediately a rescue team was dispatched and when they reached the spot, they could only see an arm of John protruding from the now frozen ice mass; the rest of his body was buried in it."

He was brought back to the base camp and that evening we finally buried him in the crevices below the Gilky memorial. The rocks on the Gilky Memorial, underneath K-2 are adorned with pots and pans bearing the name of those mountaineers who rest forever underneath its snows. The expedition was abandoned.

Then there was great Hiroshima, whose love for Pakistan verged on madness; a Japanese who took pride in calling himself an adopted Pakistani. Hardly a year went by when Hiroshima did not visit his adopted country. He trekked and climbed, and upon his return lectured and propagated the beauties of Pakistani mountains. Once when the Indians organized an expedition to climb K-2 from the Chinese side, it was Hiroshima who led a campaign against it, claiming that it was a Pakistani mountain. I missed a chance of meeting the great man while I was leading a trekking expedition into the Pamirs, beyond Lake Kromber. Hiroshima was there in the valley of Broghil and he sent me an invitation to dine with him that evening. Unfortunately, despite the offer of rice wine, I could not accept it as I had to push on to cross Darkut Glacier.

About four years ago, Hiroshima along with some of his Japanese friends scaled a minor peak next to K-2 and on his way back, an unexpected avalanche engulfed the team and six of them died on the spot, including Hiroshima. I happened to be in Skardu at that time and met a shattered Nazir Sabir who was very close to Hiroshima.

A special plane brought the families of dead mountaineers from Japan so that they could see the bodies of their dear ones and bury them. But they could not proceed to the base camp of K-2 for that purpose as the roads were blocked and the weather did not permit helicopter flights. Finally the Japanese families gathered at the banks of Braldo River that flows down the snows of K-2. Lit candles and and dropped handwritten messages in its waters in the memory of their dear departed. So the adopted son of Pakistan, Hiroshima, came to rest in the snows near K-2, never to leave again.

But amongst all these tales of sorrows, the story of Alison Hargreaves reads like a Greek tragedy. Alison a mother of two, a housewife from England, the most daring climber after the Polish Wanda, scaled the Everest summit solo and then headed straight for K-2 to create an unbelievable record. Solo Everest and the solo K-2 in the same go. But records require you to summit a mountain and then come back alive, and she did not. It is said that she did conquer K-2, but was buried in a snowstorm on her way back.

Next year her husband arrived with their two kids who wanted to see "Mummy's Mountain". They reached the base camp of K-2 under the expert guidance of Ashraf Aman, where the kids sketched and painted "Mummy's Mountain" hoping to preserve the snows in their sketchbooks, underneath which lay their dear mummy.

On Ashkole Road, beyond which lies the king of mountains, across a bridge on Braldo, near the camp site of Thungle, you can still see a plaque on a rock placed by her husband and kids which reads as follows;

Mother of mountains, Such wonder you conceive, how can one so small,

Dream of measuring their scale?

In fond memory of ALISON HARGREAVES

Who died on her way down after successfully scaling

The summit of Chogori, Mount Godwin Austin (K-2) on August, 13, 1995.

The last tale I am going to tell, is not that tragic, but of an event that took place right on the top of K-2 summit. Well not exactly on the summit, but slightly higher than that -- in the sky above it.

My travelogue about the trek up to Concordia K-2 Kahani had recently hit the stalls when Tariq Anwar of PIA, during an official dinner came up to me. "Tarar Sahib, would you be interested in a launching ceremony of your book K-2 Kahani?

I told him that normally I do not indulge in this activity; instead of launching my books in ceremonies, I launch them directly to my readers.

"But it will not be a run of the mill usual launching ceremony," he said enthusiastically. "Your book is about K-2, right. We will arrange a launching in a PIA jet while flying right over the K-2 summit. Are you interested?"

Was I interested?

A special Safari flight left Islamabad airport with hordes of journalists and television crews from all over the world, including BBC, German and Greek television teams. The jet flew over the same route that I had traversed in days and spotted some of the camping sights below, including Paiyo and Urdukus. Finally flying over the Concordian glaciers, we saw the great K-2 looming large and rushing toward us in the pilot's cabin. In a few moments we were on top of the summit.

I presented a copy of K-2 Kahani to the pilot in full view of king of mountains, a bridge between the earth and heavens and we were flying in those heavens.

"Tarar Sahib", the pilot thanked me and said "You have exactly six minutes to launch your book while I keep circling the K-2 over its summit."

The PIA MD of those days presided over the ceremony, the speakers had only one minute each to express their opinions about the book. I was too overcharged with emotions to say anything; I could never in my wildest dreams imagine that my K-2 book will be launched right over the summit of K-2.

Tariq Anwar planned to send the details of this unheard of book launching to the Guinness Book of Records people, I am not aware of the fate of this dispatch if at all it was executed.

Those were the days when I dreamt of Shah Gori and had the strength to fulfil my dream. But now I can only dream, until of course another PIA jet or army helicopter takes my aging body to my beloved, Shah Gori.

The coming of senior age

From the buxom young singer, to the gate-keeper at the Lahore zoo, old-age seems to be in the eyes of the beholder

PRESENTLY I am in a severe state of depression and melancholy and I know exactly the root cause of it.

It's not the Wana Operation, nor the smile of Condoleezza Rice, prose, poetry or my bathroom's permanently leaking taps. Rather, it's a recent visit to the Lahore Zoo. It has got nothing to do with the animals residing peacefully there, as a matter of fact the elephant Suzi, the African gray parrot and the magnificent Royal Bengal tiger gave me a rousing reception, so much so that the huge chimpanzee definitely gave me a broad smile of recognition and offered me a half eaten banana in the bargain.

So what caused me to go into a state of depression and melancholy. Simple, it is the entry ticket to the zoo, which my children very dutifully bought for me.

I know I am being slightly abstract but what can I do, as I have gone abstract since the procurement of that fateful ticket; perhaps I should elaborate a little and go back to last month when suddenly I felt that for the very first time in my life I was being treated with respect and reverence. It was a pleasant surprise indeed and I thought that finally my genius has been recognized by the masses and in consequence I was being accredited with respect. For instance, during my morning walk in the nearby park, the joggers will slow down and give me the right of way. If a literary function is being held in some hotel and I enter the hall, immediately the people sitting in the front row will get-up and offer me a seat. So much so that when at times I politely tried to refuse their kind offer, they almost pushed me into a vacant seat.

While standing in a long queue to pay my utility bills, the bank clerk will come out of his cabin to facilitate me. It was all very embarrassing but to tell you the truth I was overjoyed to be treated as a celebrity for once; after all it was not their fault. My great contribution towards the Pakistani literature and television had forced them to honour me in this way.

During one of those days, I happened to visit the Lahore television station A, for a recording and lo and behold, surprises waited for me there as well. As I was walking down the corridor, a well-known actor approached me, shook my hands and ... well, he kept on shaking it! He just wouldn't let go.

He then bowed and reverently kissed my hands profusely, saying, "Sirjee, we have learut a lot from you, you are our senior and thank God you are still around."

"Well I am around and why shouldn't I be around?" I was slightly puzzled by the "Thank God" thing.

He ignored my query and said, "Sirjee, please remember me in your prayers."

"Unfortunately I don't pray that regularly, but exactly in which prayer?"

Once again he ignored my question and leaned towards me, "Please give me a pat on my shoulder for blessing." I patted but failed to understand the implication of blessing.

There was a short break in the recording and I was puffing away in a "No Smoking" area when a buxom young singer rushed towards me, puffing and pouting and in consequence her contours also puffed.

"Sirjee, I was recording a ghazal in Studio B, when Ustadjee told me that Tarar Sahib is here and I rushed out to meet you. It is not every day that we have the good fortune of having a Didar of a senior artist like you."

I was overwhelmed with emotions. Here was this relatively new pretty singer who was dying to Didar me, whereas in normal life a lot of people could not have her Didar because she is a very expensive commodity.

"Well I am grateful Bibi, what can I do for you?"

She immediately bowed her head and with her outstretched hands grabbed both my knees, "Sir I need your blessings."

Now this knee grabbing business shook me a little but I applied my self-control and freed my knees with a jerk.

"Sure, but how do I go about it Bibi?"

The bashful Bibi came dangerously close to me and bowed her head, "Sirji, please piyar me a little on the head and I will be blessed."

I performed the needful and in a sombre voice said, "May Allah bless you with the sur of Ustad Barkat Ali Khan and the melody of Noor Jehan; go your way and conquer the hearts of masses."

The Bibi almost cried and while thanking me profusely produced a Rs10 note from her dainty purse and presented it to me saying, "Sirji a little Nazrana from your humble junior."

Before I could protest she puffed away. Now this was the limit. People asking for my blessings and presenting offerings in cash? But in my heart of hearts I was rather flattered and decided then and there that if ever a financial situation arose and I could not make both ends meet by my writings, I will immediately become a Pir of sorts.

Perhaps you are fed up of me by now, I am elaborating too much, beating about the bush so to speak. But dear reader, bear with me for a little while more because great tragedies need a little bit of elaborating and dramatization before the climax, in this case the tragedy which ensued from buying a zoo ticket.

Some years back my daughter, Annie, all of a sudden demanded that we should visit the local zoo as was done very frequently in the days when she was Little Annie. Actually she wanted to relive her childhood days. Although it was an innocent enough desire, but somehow or the other the visit did not materialize due to my engagements and laziness. Then she got married and left for the distant shores. Last month she came back for a visit after a period of two years and upon her arrival she presented a list of demands.

"Abbu first of all I would love to gobble a few gol gappas and dahi bhallas, no more chicken please, serve me the vegetables, bhindi, shuljum, ghia tori, tinda and above all karelas with onions.

"For breakfast, first of all Lohari ki nihari and then hulwa puri from Royal Park along with lassi and — take me to the zoo after this."

So after completing this menu in one week, we headed for the zoo along with my younger son Sumair. Both of them were very excited about it and exchanged their childhood memories when they were no bigger than the monkeys of the zoo and would gaze for hours at their counterparts.

Upon reaching the zoo, Sumair went to obtain the entrance ticket while I parked the car. Upon entering the zoo gates our tickets were checked by the gate keeper but I had a vague feeling that the gate keeper holding one particular ticket looked at me with dubious eyes. He would glance at the ticket and then again observe my face and then finally allowed us to go in.

"Why was this keeper-thing looking at me so dubiously, as if I was a criminal of some sort?" I asked Sumair.

"Perhaps he is your fan!"

"Fans don't look at you like that and how can a zoo keeper be a fan of mine, he has better choices," I laughed.

It was indeed a treat to be with the animals after such a long time. The only difference was that in those days I managed the kids, and now the kids were managing me, "Be careful dad, the steps are steep. Don't go near the cage Abbaji, the lion is not in a good mood and he does not watch television and cannot be a fan of yours" etc.

Upon our return, as soon as we entered our home the kids burst out laughing. Sumair was waving a zoo ticket and was grinning cheek-to-cheek, "Abbaji do you know why that keeper was looking at you so closely?"

"Why?"

"Because he wanted to make sure that you deserved that ticket. The normal entry fee to the zoo is Rs10 per person, but for the senior citizens there is a concessional ticket for Rs2 only so Abba, we have saved Rs8 today because you are a senior citizen now." "Just to save Rs8 you bought a senior citizen's concessional ticket for me?" I controlled my rage.

"And why not, you are a senior citizen Abbaji and deserve this concession." "But you spent Rs20 for the bananas to feed the monkeys and gave another Rs20 to Suzy the she-elephant just because she saluted you with her raised trunk and you could not spend a mere Rs8 to buy me a regular zoo ticket?"

The kids could not see my point and looked at me as if I had gone bananas. I protested to my wife and she also instead of sympathizing, started laughing.

"I will suggest it to the kids that they should buy you a seasonal ticket and then you can visit the zoo daily; naturally the special senior citizen seasonal ticket."

So that is the root cause of my depression and moroseness, just by obtaining a concessional zoo ticket my senior citizenship has been confirmed officially that I had been avoiding for so long, never boarding a flight when the first announcement invited the families and senior citizens to board the aircraft first.

Now I realize why the morning joggers gave way, why people offered me seats and why everybody was after my blessings because they felt that I won't be around for long.

The respect and the Pir status, which I was commanding recently, was not due to my contributions towards literature and arts, but entirely due to my old age and now my kids had turned against me.

So my sincere advice to fellow senior citizens is — never ever go to the zoo with your kids.

The tree that was murdered

I DESPERATELY want to make a confession; until and unless I make it I cannot get rid of that sense of guilt and remorse, which has been haunting me day and night. My confession is not at par with good old Rousseau, it is much more painful and regrettable.

Let me confess that I have wilfully and intentionally committed two murders, one of a living breathing soul, a twenty-two-year-old araucaria tree which is native of New Zealand, and the other of a small pond in which reflected the green branches of the Araucaria. At this very moment the slaughtered trunk of the Araucaria is lying in a filth dump and the debris of the pond is scattered in my backyard like the aftermath of Bam's earthquake.

Why did I commit these ghastly acts, you may ask. Simply because I wanted to modernize my backyard with tiles and to create enough space for garden chairs and a barbecue setup. And now when the araucaria and pond are a thing of the past I am like that Prince in War and Peace who loses his entire state and worldly belongings on the gambling table and then curses himself and wishes that time should go back to the moment when he sat at that table and he would not sit on it and he will have all that he possessed, and now lost for ever.

Maybe right now there is a smile on your lips that I am mourning the loss of a mere araucaria tree and a dirty pond. Let me narrate in short their life span and then decide for yourself whether my mourning and depression is justified or not.

About twenty-two years back, I built in parts, my present small but functional house. And after spending my last penny, I realized that the windows are without glass panes, the roof has not been tiled, and no main door, and above all no electricity connection, simply because I had no money left, not even for the dozen electric bulbs required.

As I did not foresee any money coming my way for the next two years or so, I shifted in with some candles to celebrate. However, there was a small consolation. The famed white haired architect Javed Najam had designed a very small pond in a corner of the backyard in which floated lotus plants, two green tortoises and some water plants. Lovingly I planted different varieties of tropical ferns and a small cute araucaria of green frills.

Living in an unfinished structure this was the only corner where I sat on a cement bench writing reading and dreaming, dreaming that I was in a tropical forest where pink lotus flowers abound, wild ferns swayed in the mist and green tortoises sat on the wide lotus leaves sunning themselves. But above all, the magical form of araucaria in my imagination grew to such heights that the tropical parrots sat on every branch and chirped in unison. The fantasy of this small corner made me forget the unfinished house through which the winter winds howled, not finding any hindrance of a door or a window and at times extinguishing the few candles which we lit as soon as the evening approached.

During hot summers, my three kids splashed in this pond turning it into a small swimming pool, disturbing the tortoises and swaying the lotus flowers. Afterwards they dipped into many a posh and swanky pools, but never did I see on their faces that innocent glowing happiness which the small muddy pond generated. At times they floated their little paper boats in it and were amused vastly when a tortoise tried to hitch a ride on one of them.

However, the pond did present some unforeseen problems. When the rainy season came it became the abode of big fat frogs fit for a once in a life time delicious French dinner. During the day these frogs were in deep meditation contemplating Darwin's theory of evolution and wondering as to why it applied to apes only, while they were left out. But it was during the night that they decided to become full-throated, testing our patience and their lungs to the full. At times in the middle of the night, they blasted our ears like air-raid sirens. Ofter tossing in my bed trying to sleep, and unable to do so, I would get up and with clenched fists and teeth, barge out of my bedroom holding a cricket bat hoping to beat the hell out of them. The problem was, I could not. Due to the pitch darkness I could not pinpoint their position and in desperation would thrash the whole pond, wetting myself in the process. Hoping that I had squashed them once and for all, I would go back to bed and fall asleep.

However, just a wink or two and then again, the orchestra would become operational. Again the cricket bat and me boiling with rage and attacking the unseen cowardly enemy. This became a regular exercise in rainy seasons. During summers, the stagnant water of the pond was the greatest mosquito-breeding farm in the world. Still, despite these froggy problems, the pond was a favourite rendezvous for morning teas and afternoon naps in the sun, even after the completion of our little house.

The very first day at school of my one and only daughter, Annie, was documented in the shape of a photograph in which one can see a rolly-polly pretty child, sitting beside the pond holding her nursery books and smiling like a rose bud. And now that very child is Dr Quratulann, MD in Orlando, USA, and I don't have the heart to inform her that her pond has gone, where she frolicked in the water, and started her first day at school.

There is another photograph in which my son, Sumair at the age of five, is standing beside the newly planted Araucaria, which is way below his shoulders. Both of them grew tall but the araucaria surpassed the six-feet height of Sumair and entangled itself in the branches of a neighbouring tree. The pond and the Araucaria grew and matured with my children. Even then I slaughtered both of them callously.

Many years back, twenty to be exact, I committed another folly. I bought my very first car and discarded my run down motorbike. As there were no buyers of a motorbike, which was ten years old, totally rusted, without guards or lights, I just pushed it in my side garden and forgot all about it. After some time, when per chance I went there, the bike was engulfed in creepers and there was nest of humming birds on its worn-down saddle. That day, the motorbike almost groaned and sighed at my forgetfulness. It had carried me and my wife along with three kids for ages, became a celebrity when I used it in a television serial, kept all my secrets as to who ever shared the back-seat with me. Finally my wife sold it to a scrap dealer and a chunk of my past was scrapped from my life. Somehow or the other I felt guilty as hell for a long time.

Granted I had to discard the useless motorbike but what was the crime of this pond and Araucaria that I, with my own consent, had them killed? Just for a wider space, for the sake of a few garden chairs and a barbecue spot? Without thinking I had them removed. The remorse and horror came when the evil deed was done, debris and broken branches littered the back yard came under my feet and literally moaned, groaned like a patient on its deathbed. Then I realized what I had done. But now it was too late. The empty space where a few moments ago stood the Royal araucaria and the lotus pond, stared at me blankly, accusing me of robbing it of God's gifts of greenery and water.

The debris of the pond and the lifeless trunk of the araucaria lying in a rubbish dump torment me and torture me.

If you ever decide to renovate your old house, my advice is DON'T. If at all it is necessary do not uproot even a small plant or remove an old structure to create more space. If you do you will never forgive yourself.

Just to atone for my horrible deed I have decided to plant another araucaria tree in my backyard, and, with apologies to it, I will never uproot it till my dying days. That is a promise.

An old hunter's tales

We sat under the shadows of the Pamir Mountains, in the far-flung valley of Sokhtarabad, by a glacier stream and listened attentively to the tales of bygone exploits of Abdul Latif, an old hunter who sat cross-legged in front of us.

The old gentleman could not converse in Urdu, hence his nephew Ahad, who was also our trek guide to the Kromber Lake and Darkut Glacier, translated his tales of the past.

"Almost seventy years ago we descended from those mountains and entered the valley of Sokhtarabad," the old hunter pointed towards a high pass situated on the top of little Pamirs.

"I sat terrified on the back of my father's horse as the animal almost out of control came tumbling down from the Pamirs. We just had one look at this valley and decided that this is where we will stay and make it our new home. There was plenty of water and thick grass and the mountains were teeming with wild animals."

"So you came down from Russia?" someone inquired.

"No-No", the old man shook his beard violently. "We came from our own ancestral land, Uzbekistan. We lived in a small town, Uzgin, which has been renamed Osh. My father Qazi Jani Beg was the Emir of Uzgin. Then the red Cossacks invaded our town and made an offer to my father; you can remain the Emir of Uzgin if you accept the authority of Soviet Union. My father refused the offer and escaped into the high Pamirs and there waged a war against the Russians for ten years. But he could not fight an Empire with his few horses and old swords, for long. So, he crossed the Afghan Wakhan corridor and little Pamirs and entered the realm of the then British empire."

"So your whole family settled in Sokhtarabad seventy years ago?"

"No, my brother Adalat Khan crossed the mountains of Caucasia and went to Turkey; Mohammad Ibrahim did not have a heart to abandon his ancestral land and stayed there; Mohammad Ismail settled in Gilgit and I chose this valley."

"Sir, what kind of food do you relish most?" the formal interview started.

"Whatever is available I thank Allah for that".

"But is there anything particular for which you thank Allah most?"

"Milk, yogurt and meat — and tea."

"What kind of meat?" I asked smilingly. "Lamb, goat and specially the wild markhor sheep if available."

"Do you hunt the markhor yourself?"

"Not any more," the old hunter said gloomily. "Although I can still climb vertical rocks and reach the heights where markhors are found, but my sons forbid me to do so. They say I am too old for such pursuits, you know your sons; just to prove their youth (they) forcibly declare you old and out of wits." Every body laughed heartily including the old hunter's sons.

"Now my sons, Saat Beg, Tulan Bai and Kainja Bai do the job. Kainja Bai is best of them all, his eyes are like binoculars and he can see during the night also."

Kainja Bai's Mongol eyes lit up by this compliment. That evening under the shadows of the Pamirs, how could we ever imagine that the same Kainja Bai would slip from a rock and fall to his death while pursuing a markhor.

"Sir, how many markhors have you hunted during your lifetime?" a banker trekker inquired.

"I don't remember. They must be in hundreds, but I did not kill them just for fun, as some cruel people do. I only went after markhors when we were short of meat. However, I remember that I killed at least thirteen ferocious wolves."

This was alarming news for us. "Sir, there are wolves around here, near our camp site perhaps?"

"Yes they are around, but never come down in the valley. Oh yes, I also killed a bear, the size of Pamir mountains. But it's a long story and I will narrate it some other time."

He was not too keen on sharing his exploits with us.

"Uncle sir, rest assured we have no intention of risking our lives again to reach Sokhtarabad and we can safely say that you will never come all the way to Lahore. You don't even fancy going to Gilgit, so this is now or never. Tarar Sahib bores us to death by narrating his cooked up travel adventures. We are sure your stories will be much more interesting," a trekker friend said, as his meanness reached its limit.

"I was thirty-years old," the aging hunter went back in time. "He was huge. A brown bear whose face strangely looked like a human came upon me while I was climbing a rock to go up to a meadow. In those days guns were not very common and I had an old sword to defend myself. It was purely for self-defence that I had to attack him, he was wounded and from the gash that I inflicted blood poured like a mountain spring. He retreated to a safe distance and with his snout started uprooting the grass; he was trying to stem the flow of blood by putting the grass on his wound.

"He knew that I would not attack him in this critical condition because in this environment, by living together, we know the animals and the animals know our behaviour. Then he got up and started walking away from me and I followed him. I had to kill him at all cost otherwise he would have traced me right back to my abode and killed me to take his revenge. Finally he took refuge in a dark cave and I knew he was playing with me, luring me inside to kill me so I sat outside the mouth of the cave with the sword in hand. The night came and then the next day dawned and I sat there without having any food or water, I could hear his growls challenging me to come inside. Then another night came and the next day due to weakness I became delirious and started talking to him."

"You mean you were talking to a bear? In which language did he reply? What did he say?" the excited trekkers asked in unison.

"As I have told you we live in the same world so we understand each others language. Many times a markhor would look at you and say it with his beseeching eyes that 'please spare me in the name of your children' and we will oblige and lower the barrel of the gun.

"Once in the high Pamir, a snow tiger suddenly appeared in front of me. I was totally unarmed and he could easily tear me apart. I just started talking to him, telling him that I am not his enemy and please let me go back to my children and he spared me."

"What about the bear, what did you say to him?"

"Oh, the brown bear in the cave. Well I challenged him to come out in the open and face me like a man. 'You coward hiding in a cave like a woman, come out, you mouse hearted brown hunk, son of a doubtful mother'. The whole day I kept on insulting him and I could hear his angry growls in reaction. Finally as the third evening of our conflict approached, he suddenly emerged from the cave without a sound and fell upon me.

"It is not easy to kill a beast of that size with a sword especially if you had been starving for the last three days and nights. I really felt very sorry after killing him and wept for him because he was a brave bear. We believe that a beast does not die until and unless it is his fate. So fate killed the brown bear, not me."

That evening in the remote valley of Sokhtarabad underneath the little Pamirs hunter Abdul Latif honoured us by inviting all of us for dinner in his mountain home. His aging wife, Afghan Bibi and their daughters prepared the classic Uzbek pulao and a roasted leg of markhor.

After dinner, talk again revolved around the tales of the old hunter. All of us were interested in the mythical snow tiger, which was still found high above the Pamirs.

"I never killed a single snow leopard for the pleasure of it or to prove my bravery. At times I have to defend my flock and family and sometime I had to save myself."

"There are certain heartless and cruel people who are involved in this heinous crime. They sell the hide in Gilgit to foreigners who pay a huge sum to procure it."

During the night Kainja Bai left the valley to climb the vertical rocks to reach a small meadow by early next morning where during the day, through his binoculars (eyes), he had spotted two markhors. It was during such an expedition that he never returned to his aged father Abdul Latif. He was buried underneath the same cliffs which he used to climb during the night like a markhor.

Arabian horses or mules?

LONG before the advent of the hippy culture, Lahore had its fair share of very genuine hippies who were dubbed Bohemians in those days, of which the famed poet and revolutionary Zaheer Kashmiri was one of the most obvious.

He lived on Beadon Road adjacent to Laxmi Mansions, hawk nosed, with bright red shoulder-length hair and a French cut goatee. Wearing a matching communist red tie he would emerge from his abode quickly on a 50 CC German bike and frighten the wits out of us kids because the engine of the motorbike made such awesome noises, made even more intimidating by the man with flowing hair whom some contemporaries called the red Shakespeare due to his attire. Later on Munir Niazi who had a knack of calling people names according to their idiosyncrasies lovingly dubbed him "The Golden Scorpion".

Baba Zaheer Kashmiri was very staunch in his progressive views and as was the fashion in those days he believed that religion was the opium of the masses. One day as he emerged from Beadon Road some zealots of Jamat-e-Islami who were protesting against the Ahmadis confronted him, and asked what they were asking every body, "Do you believe that our Prophet (Peace be upon him) was the last Prophet sent by Allah?" To this, Zaheer Kashmiri very casually answered "You are talking about the Prophet, I don't even believe in Allah".

The agitators could not believe their ears and instead of thrashing him they smiled and said to each other "The man is raving mad, let him go".

The same flamboyant Zaheer Kashmiri who spent his last days in a dingy street and in great misery, wrote his most famous couplet in my autograph book:

Hamain khabar hai ke hum hain chiraghe Akhre shub

Humarey baad andehra nahin ujala hai.

The generation of the Fifties venerated and loved three poets amongst all, Sahir Ludhyanvi, Akhtar Shirani and Abdul Hamid Adam. Their couplets and nazams vibrated in our youthful innocence and their poetry represented each and every emotion we felt, however, it was beyond my teenage resources and my Raleigh bicycle to reach these favourites. But Faiz Sahib was upcoming and I decided to obtain his autograph.

In Lahore's scorching sun, I stationed myself outside the offices of The Pakistan Times. After a number of hours, I saw Faiz Sahib descend the stairs of Progressive Papers Ltd; I approached him and presented my autograph book hoping that he would write my favourite, Rat Yun Dill Main Teri Khoi Hui Yad Aai. But much to my disappointment he wrote:

Hum Parverishe Loho Qalam Karte Rahain Ge, and that too in his abominable handwriting.

"Sir, please honour me with your rubai, Rat Yun ..." I begged.

It was very hot under the mid-day sun and Faiz sahib wanting to get rid of me as soon as possible, scratched his balding head and said:

"Bhai woh to hamain yad nahin" and left.

I was not going to give up that easily so I remembered that particular rubai by heart and the very next day when Faiz sahib was coming down from his office I was there to greet him, grinning from cheek-to-cheek.

I presented my autograph book to him almost without his consent and said, "Sir if you do not remember your own kalam I will help your memory, now please write down my favourite rubai, Rat Yun Dill main ... while I recite it to you."

Faiz sahib meekly obliged.

Many a years later, during an exclusive sitting after dinner that lasted till the early hours of the morning I narrated this incidence to Faiz sahib who had come to know me rather well by then, and claimed that I was the person who made him write poetry. Faiz sahib, who very rarely went beyond a smile, laughed like a child and then said, "Well Tarar sahib, now I remember that rubai, would you like me to recite it?" It was indeed a memorable moment.

I was also fortunate enough that there came a time in my life when some of those literati who adorned my autograph book personally, read papers about my meagre contribution in literature. What more could a person want in a lifetime?

The politician part of my autograph book is rather feeble because the gentlemen playing the game of politics then and now are not my favourites; only Mushtaq Ahmad Gurmani and Feroz Khan Noon add a little spice. However, it is the cricketers part of it which is still very precious to me, most of the cricket legends of those days are enshrined in my little book, including Pakistan's Fazal Mahmud, Mian Saeed, M.Jahangir Khan, Hanif Mohammad, Shakoor Ahmad, Shujauddin (of the Lukky Kabootri fame) Imtiaz Ahmad, Wazir Mohammad, Alimuddin, Wallis Mathais, Khan Mohammad, Maqsood Ahmad, Zulifqar Ahmad, Mahmud Hussain and Miran Bux.

I was a witness to that "tragic" incidence when, during an India-Pakistan Test match, at Bagh-e-Jinnah, Lahore, our dear Maqsood Ahmad went out of his crease to hit Gupta at the score of ninety nine and was stumped by wicket-keeper Tamhane. The hearts of the Lahoris stopped, how mean of a Hindu not to allow a Muslim to complete his century? Everybody hated Tamhane for this meanness. Rumours say that our Merry Max was always merry while maxing, I mean batting.

Although the ink is fading, I can still make out some of the names of those in the Indian cricket team, Lala Amarnath, Poly Umarigar, Roy, Borde, Patel, Bhandari, Gupta, Tamhane Ramchand and the spin wizard, Ghulam Ahmad. I had the opportunity of meeting the great cricket commentator Maharaj Kumar of Vizzianagram who signed my autograph book as "Vizzy".

There is another cocktail of Test cricketers including Brian Close, John Reid, F. Titmus, Thompson, Tony Lock, Jim Laker etc. If you want to find out the year and the series detail, kindly contact the cricket guru Mr Omar Qureshi.

However, it was my "English Hunt" that provided me with great trophies to decorate my autograph book.

In the summer of 1957 the West Indian cricket team arrived in England while I had arrived the previous summer. When they came to Nottingham to play a Test match, I dressed myself properly in a recently acquired tuxedo, if you please, equipped with my German camera, flash gun and two dozen flash bulbs, I presented myself at the desk of hotel where both the teams were staying "I am the sports correspondent of daily 'The Pakistan Times' from Lahore and would like to cover the English and West Indian teams," I boldly declared.

The desk clerk was duly impressed although he did not have the foggiest idea as to which newspaper I was representing or where on earth this Lahore was. I was, however, ushered in.

Most of the English team was in the bar where I chatted with them, shared a drink (orange juice, perhaps) and took their photographs. Amongst my victims were Sir Len Hutton who was bowled by Khan Mohammad for a duck in Oval; Peter May, Tom Graveney, Godfrey Evans and many others. The West Indian team was rather scattered and even then I bagged the three W's i.e.; Walcot, Weeks and Worrel. Besides them, I found Mr Garfield Sobers, who was not very sober. The famous pair of Ramadin and Valentine was there who, sadly, died recently. Rohan Kanhai became a friend and invited me as a personal guest to the Test match where bands of Calypso singers sang in chorus "Ramadin And Valentine" and I also joined them. We exchanged a few letters and then Kanhai and I lost touch with each other.

Now, after almost fifty years what do I do with my autograph book? The ink is fading and with it the names of all those greats who once ruled the world of cinema, sports and literature because fame is a mistress of doubtful character. "An autograph book is like a stable where along with Arabian horses, mules are also found" wrote Ibrahim Jalees in my autograph book dated 13.7.56. Do you think I have some mules in my collection? Even if there were, with the passage of time, they have become Arabian horses for me.

An eventful journey

ONCE upon a time I flew to England and literally "flew" like a bird and took as much time to land in London as a bird would do. Well, the simple reason is because in those days jet aircraft were far from anybody's mind. Hence nobody thought of inventing them.

The super constellation that I was travelling in, really took its time in reaching England and that was because the plane did not pass a single airstrip on its way, without landing on it.

From Karachi it went to Tehran where it was perhaps refuelled. After a three hour stop it was onwards to Gamal Abdul Nasir's Cairo, where in the middle of the night, a coach took us to a shameful nightclub or restaurant for a meal.

Here, for the first time in my life, I saw most parts of the female anatomy in the form of belly dancing. You can first imagine dear readers, the plight of a simple kid from Lahore who very easily got excited by the mere sight of a female ankle back home. And lo and behold, if you can, there was this female slithering like an eel who had a patch here and a patch there on her body. But in the haze of excitement, to me she simply seemed without any patch whatsoever!

I could hardly gulp my food which was heaped on our table by "Turkey Topi" clad Egyptian waiters. From a wall a photograph of Gamal Nasir smiled on the plight of this innocent kid from Pakistan. And kindly note that Nasir had very recently bade farewell to King Farooq and General Najib in the same order very recently. Good old King Farooq, who upon hearing a passionate lecture on Islam by a Pakistani, had commented that it seems Islam was bestowed on us as recently as 14th of August 1947.

From Cairo with flushed faces, courtesy the semi-clad belly dancers, we again flew and flew, and finally reached eternal Rome. Alas we did not have enough time for a "Roman Holiday" and search for a petite princess like Audrey Hepburn. Instead we were ushered into the airport restaurant for lunch. And by the way, throughout this long journey a simple minded

Maulana was my constant companion who was on a mission to convert the heathen of Europe. Although he was totally oblivious to the existence of English language but according to him, the heathen, would understand his sermons in whatever language he chose to speak as God would be his interpreter.

As I was ordering a chicken dish for myself in the restaurant, the maulana asked me whether the chicken ordered was halal or not? I pleaded ignorance and he asked me to order for him some vegetable not fried but boiled. After half an hour's wait, our lunch appeared, on a trolley, a steaming roast chicken which was as big as a turkey, and beside that in a small saucer were three potatoes, a carrot and few peas, properly boiled.

When I was devouring my chicken with relish, the maulana was gloomily trying to catch his elusive pea with a fork. Suddenly he declared, "This chicken of yours looks halal to me. Ask the waitress to bring me the same."

After the Roman "halal" chicken, we flew into Dusseldorf, and then onward to Amsterdam where we had to change planes. To while away the interim period, we were provided with a coach to roam around the canal city Amsterdam. This was my first face to face meeting with a European city and I was thunderstruck as it looked like a dream. The sights, buildings, canals and aroma was surely the stuff of dreams. For me, an inexperienced teenage Lahori, all females, no matter of what age, looked devastatingly pretty and delicious.

When all the world is young lad, and every tree is green and every goose a swan lad...

Thy world was young and even the geese looked the swans to me. In the streets of Amsterdam there were echoes of that ancient Dutch song, which went something like this...

When its spring again I will bring again Tulip from Amsterdam With a heart that, true I will bring to you Tulip, from Amsterdam...

I detached myself from the charms of Amsterdam with a heavy heart and finally reached my destination London. It looked drab, dull and slow after Amsterdam. Even the girls seemed overdressed in comparison to the Egyptian belly dancer.

"Flower hill" was the motivation

CALL it an article, a column or a semi-autobiographical note. Call it what you may, but let me explain the title, Diary of a Vagabond. You, my dear reader, are totally justified in objecting to it, as vagabonds do not keep dairies, dispatch clerks mostly do. Frankly, I was at a complete loss as to what the title should be, and then I remembered the Diary of a Madman. Lo and behold, the problem was solved. Like Nutha Singh and Prem Singh are one and the same, madmen and a vagabond are also one and, thus, the same.

Let me spend a bit of time going into the root cause of this madness that went into the making of the vagabond, and how did it all start. Where did this travel bug come from? From my blue-eyed six-feet tall father who could have been a heartthrob of the fifties no less than Gary Cooper if he had migrated to Hollywood. But, alas, he had a humble farming background of limited means. He ploughed fields, looked after the buffaloes and almost daily swam across the romantic river Chenab to deliver a breakfast of lassi and tanur ki roti to his father, who use to tend his buffaloes and cattle in the greener pasture of Bela, where Mahinwal in the days gone by did the same for his Sohni.

My father then swam back and walked a mere ten miles to his school to pursue his studies. My grandfather's tribe of Tarar Jats always looked down upon him for allowing his son to be educated, as Jats had no business to study, only the Mullahs and the Hindus opted for such a low profession.

My father, Chaudhry Rehmat Khan Tarar, was in love with nature. Give him a handful of soil, and just by smelling and feeling it lovingly he would tell you whether it belonged to Punjab or Sindh, and had the capability of growing sugarcane, cotton and fruits with equal competence. An ear of wheat, a bud, a flower, a butterfly would send him into ecstasy. He wrote more than two dozen books about horticulture, and published a monthly agricultural magazine for over 30 years till he almost went bankrupt.

Once on his way to Srinagar where he was cultivating dahlia flowers, he saw a hillock which was totally barren. Just by smelling the soil he knew that it could give birth to vegetation, so he single-handedly, like a madman, planted seeds of flowers on the whole length and breadth of the barren hillock. And by the next spring, passengers travelling towards the vale of Kashmir could not believe their eyes as the barren hillock, by some miracle, was covered with flowers of all the colours of the rainbow.

From then onwards, it was called "the flower hill of Chaudhry Sahib". Before I cross over into eternity, I wish I would have an opportunity to set my dim and aging eyes on that hillock, the "flower mountain" of my father.

Sorry, I know I have rambled on and on about my father, but then, he was a father, and every father is to be rambled on. I inherited that love of nature and freedom of spirit from him, but could not inherit his humble nature and greatness. He had sown in me the seed of adventure and the love of the wild.

In 1956 — almost half-a-century ago — the first opportunity came my way to test my mettle. Do I declare myself that ancient? Let's face it. I am that ancient. The venue was the fabled Government College, Lahore, where I got admitted not because of securing high marks in Matric, but due to my faulty, but fluent English which was the end result of my watching — naturally without my family's permission — almost thirty English-language movies every month.

During one of those days, we saw behind a mesh of wires on the notice board a notice typed on a vintage typewriter, salvaged from the debris of World War II, no doubt. It read:

"Kishan Gunga Valley Expedition

"The Govt College Hiking and Mountaineering Club is planning to take an expedition to Kishan Gunga Valley in Kashmir and scaling the summit of Ratti Gali peak, via Abbottabad and Kaghan. We will be pleased to consider the applications of such volunteers who are physically fit and do not shy away from the dangers of adventure. Kindly contact Khawaja Sahib for further information."

Now this Khawaja Sahib was a burly, rather elderly, physical instructor who took pleasure in torturing us students by ordering us to do push-ups and such other things whenever we had the misfortune of coming across him. So we avoided him like the plague. I, needless to say, hadn't then the faintest idea as to where this Kishan Gunga Valley was, but if it was in Kashmir, it was somewhere near my father's "flower mountain". So I had to go.

The next day, rather hesitantly, I presented myself to Khawaja Sahib. I was encouraged to see other volunteers there too. He ordered us to stand in a line, and then, to our utter surprise and shame, he told us to strip. Being a decent soul, he allowed us to keep our underpants on, but how many in those days wore this "uncomfortable, senseless attire"? None, I am afraid.

The expedition was still a long way off, and if this was the beginning, I wondered if it would be worth it.

Rattled in Kaghan

PICKING up the thread from where we had left it a fortnight ago, as it happened, all the boys who were silly enough to volunteer for the hiking trip to Kishan Gunga Valley were selected. We were instructed to climb the hillocks of Lawrence Garden every day to prepare for the assault on Ratti Gali Mountain. We were handed over a list of gear that was required for the expedition.

Most of the items listed were rather strange. Do remember we are talking of the '50s. For instance, 'a rucksack' — now, for heavens sake, what sort of sack was it and from where could we obtain it? 'An ice axe' — for what and why, we were not ice-cutters. 'A pair of army boots, brown trousers, woollen army socks, a Gorkha hat, mufflers, walking sticks, a lota' and God knows what.

We were told to look for these things in Lahore's Lunda Bazar, where in those days you could buy such remnants of World War II. I knew this Lunda Bazar because a young and fashionable Khalajan of mine used to buy parachutes from there, and fashion her dresses as these parachutes were made of pure silk and were called "kulian". In those days, these parachute kulian were a rage amongst the ladies of Lahore.

We collected the required gear, most of which belonged to the dead Brits, and then collected ourselves in the gym before the burly Khawaja Sahib. Prior to this, there was a heated debate in our family as to why I was opting to go into the wilderness where wild animals abound. After all, I was a mere baby. At this point, my father came to my rescue, and told my mother to stop crying and "let the boy go to Kashmir".

The boys who were present in front of Khawaja Sahib had their apprehensions, and wanted to know where exactly we were going.

A dialogue ensued:

Q: Sir, where exactly is this valley of Kishan Gunga?

A: Somewhere in Kashmir, I think.

Q: If you are not sure, how will we find it?

A: We have maps and a cook who claims he knows the area.

Q: But, Sir, the name of the valley sounds rather Hinduish — Kishan Gunga. It must be in India and we don't have passports.

A: It should be in Azad Kashmir.

Q: Do we have to climb this Ratti Gali Mountain to reach this valley?

A: Most probably...

Q: Will there be snow on this mountain?

A: Perhaps.

Q: Sir, how can we walk on snow, we have never seen the thing and we will slip.

A: You will make way with your ice axes and climb, my boys, and no more questions.

Q: How will we manage, Sir, if there are no toilets around?

A: Shut up. Now carry your full load on your back and make ten rounds of the cricket ground. Yes, you have to carry your own gear and from now on you are not dear students, but dear hikers.

The D-Day arrived, and the "dear hikers" arrived at the Lahore Railway Station in whatever mode of transportation available, including tongas and bicycles. Only Shafique emerged from an ancient black Opel and astounded everybody, that Opel being the only car seen on the railway station that day.

Along with the required gear, the boys who were suddenly elevated to the status of "hikers", deemed it necessary to bring along quilts, tiffin carriers, water pitchers, holdalls and sugarcane to munch during this journey up to Havelian, the last railway station before the mountain range began. From Havelian, we made use of public transport to reach Balakot, via Abbotabad and Mansehra.

The village of Balakot by the River Kunhar was the gateway to the valley of Kaghan, which was rather unknown in those times. After spending a night in Balakot, we offered Fateha at the mazar of Syed Ahmad Shaheed, and then rattled on jeeps towards Naran. We thought that we would just rattle on like this to Ratti Gali, Kishan Gunga Valley, on jeeps, and then onwards to Lahore rattling on. We were, in the days to come, rattled all right, not on jeeps but on other accounts.

Naran in those days was not even a sleepy old town, as there was no town, only some huts by the River Kunhar, a Tanoor Hotel whose menu started and ended with aloo shorba, a Dak bungalow and a newly-built youth hostel in which we stayed and had the honour of being the first hikers to sleep under its roof.

Naran, indeed, was picturesque, lush green and of pleasant clime, but it was so remote and far away from Lahore, incredibly pitch dark and cold after sunset. Whenever we ventured out of the youth hostel for a walk, we huddled together holding hands lest we get lost in the darkness.

Then we were told by the chowkidar that it was dangerous to step outside after sunset, as a certain species of bear deluded from the mountains during the night and gobbled up whatever came their way. They were specially fond of devouring young kids and strangers, or so we were told! This piece of information terrified us, and that night we shivered not only due to the cold, but also due to a slight noise from outside that resulted in us calling out to our mothers in fear and crying wholeheartedly. We should have saved some of those tears for the days ahead when better opportunities would come our way.

But it was not all that bad. There was this unforgettable evening in the old Dak bungalow by the river where we were served a dinner of fried trout in candlelight, and, mind you, on proper tables. The khansama who served us was yet unaware of the fact that the British had left, and spoke only in English and addressed us as sahib.

But the most memorable event was our day hike to the fairy-tale Lake Saif-ul-Muluk, which hadn't become too well-known and was not polluted by a mass of tourists in those days. It was almost unspoiled and virgin. Needless to say, we were the only visitors bowing our heads in front of this blue goddess of the mountains that day, perhaps that month.

Come to think of it, we were also virgins, unspoiled and yet-to-be-polluted by life as it is. There is a black-and-white photograph somewhere ... on the banks of Saif-ul-Muluk, an immature lad of seventeen in army boots, a Gorkha hat carelessly adorned, a broad forehead littered with black curly hair, gazing at the horizon, not knowing what the future holds for him, a lifetime of vagabonding, perhaps.

From Naran, a couple of jeeps took us to a place called Burawai, situated in a plain lush area surrounded by high mountains and yet again by the River Kunhar. That was the end of our jeep days and the start of our miseries.

Burawai was again on a road to nowhere, desolate beyond description, decrepit and Godforsaken. Burawai was just a one-room ancient Dak bungalow, a typical lantern-bearing old chowkidar who roamed the premises during night, muttering to himself. In the Burawai Dak Bungalow, an old visitor register still existed in 1956, pages of which bore testimony to some Gora Sahib's presence, who had ventured this far and spent a night in this wilderness.

After so many years you cannot expect me to quote the contents of that register exactly, but in the foggy vagueness of the years gone by, there are impressions of a Burawai of 1914 or 1920s when a John White, or somebody, writes: "My pony has died, how will I reach Gilgit where Patricia is waiting for me?" Or "I fear the native chowkidar who lurks around, I think I will go back to Peshawar first thing in the morning."

Does this forlorn, lonely outpost still exist? I cannot say as I have never been that way since.

The next morning was the real D-Day when we abandoned the Burawai Dak Bungalow, leaving the road to Babusar Pass and turned right towards the mythical goal of Ratti Gali glacier and the peak beyond.

Some mules were hired for the heavy equipment and food supplies, but we were really shocked when Khawaja Sahib ordered us to carry our personal belongings. The boys who had brought huge quilts and water pitchers were the real victims. And this was the day when we realized that we should have saved at least some of the tears that were shed in Naran, but, by then, it was too late.

Spellbound in paradise

PLODDING on with our heavy loads, slipping on rocks, falling and cursing the day when we volunteered for this horrid expedition, we struggled towards the unknown destination of Kishan Gunga valley. Blisters bloomed, scratches appeared and we were sure that some bones were broken during the falls. We had, in the meanwhile, entered a sprawling lush green valley, crisscrossed by streams and surrounded by misty mountains — but we were totally oblivious of its charms. As luck would have it, Shafique, who had only a few days back emerged from his Royal Opel car, slipped while crossing a mountain torrent and fell into the fast flowing water, hitting the stones. finally When rescued, he was badly bruised, shivering and no other sound came from his blue lips except the whimper: "I am dead, Ammiji."

This episode shattered us completely as from then onwards he was carried on the back of a mule. We calculated immediately and found out that there were not enough mules to match our numbers so the rest of us would have to keep on walking. The master plan of the expedition indicated that during the hike we will spend our nights in Dak bungalows wherever available, and in the wilds a friendly village would be looked for, to provide us with shelter. We did not carry any tents simply because in those days these present day light and easy-to-erect tents were not forthcoming. The only "tents" which were available were the shamianas erected for the purpose of weddings and funerals.

On this trek, the villages, usually comprising a few huts, that we came across did not show any sign of friendliness as the whole populace, the two or three dozen souls, would abandon their village as soon as they saw us appearing on the horizon. Mind you, we were attired in army boots and khakis, and they mistook us for soldiers because only the army roamed around these areas near the border of India. They fled as soon as they saw us because they were afraid that we would confiscate their chicken and goats in the name of patriotism, pay a meagre price and then march on to confront the infidels.

Finally, we halted on the outskirts of a village, waited for the dark to come and then crept in before anybody could flee. We assured the simple souls that we had nothing to do with the army and only wanted to spend the cold night in the one-room mosque and then march on the next morning. If we were not the army, then they could not fathom what we were doing in this desolation. However, they offered us two chickens free of charge.

The one-room mosque — the wall comprising stones plied one on top of the other and with hay on the floor — was a heaven, but the valiant hikers, including the burly Khawaja Sahib, moaned and sighed throughout the cold night.

The next morning was misty and in the mist this unknown village looked mysterious, the cattle moving slowly and villagers walking in slow motion. Faraway one could see the Ratti Gali peak covered with pure snow, glistening in the first golden rays of the rising sun. The sight refreshed us beyond description as it was the first time in our teenage life that our eyes were witnessing such a white spectacle. However, in this surge of ecstasy, there was a streak of gloom because Shafique, who had fallen into the icy stream, was not only badly bruised but running a high fever too. He was carried back to Naran on a makeshift stretcher by two porters. Like the first casualty in a war, his departure saddened us. This could happen to any of us, was the thought in everybody's mind.

When the second day of our actual trek began, most of the boys simply refused to carry their personal loads which was duly transferred on the backs of the poor mules. Although we were lighter now, the blisters had ripened and the scratches on our bodies throbbed with unbearable pain. We walked and walked alongside our mule train without respite.

My agony was double-fold because the secondhand army boot I had bought from Lunda Bazar did not complement each other in size — my left boot was of size nine and the right one turned out to be of size eleven. So my walk was akin to Lord Byron hopping and at times dragging my feet.

The evening approached and from the distant heights of Ratti Gali peak descended a chill which almost paralyzed us. The mules also became sluggish and that was the moment when we entered a paradise lost, a magical valley of deep green hues, almost plain and in the lush green plains rose small rocks here and there as if they were placed there for decoration. These rocks, the like of which I never saw again, were like miniature hills of a Chinese painting and amongst them were pitched a few tents of nomad Gujjars, while the sheep grazed lazily around them. But the most heartwarming sight was that of half a dozen or so lit up fires. The light of these fires gave the landscape a very unearthly look.

If I say that we were spellbound, it will be an understatement. The nomads, at seeing us, a haggard and tired bunch of city dwellers dragging their feet and entering their private abode, rushed towards their tents and disappeared in them. However, pretty soon curiosity got the better of them and they started peeping from the flaps of their tents.

Finally when we started unloading our mules, they realized that we were here to stay and came out sheepishly. They proved to be a very friendly lot and soon we were sharing their fires. They offered us fresh goat milk which was a treat under the circumstances, but tasted like a goat which had not bathed for years.

"How come you Sahib (Loag) from distant Lahore have come to this desolation? We hear you eat rotis made of wheat and have plenty of ghee down there," we were asked.

Now this was a tricky question if there was one. We had learned from our past experience that if we told them the truth — that is we came out for a bit of trekking and adventure — they will not believe us. They will not believe that anybody in his right mind can abandon the pleasures of Lahore and willingly tramp in these desolate valleys. A pin drop silence followed in which only the crackle of logs in the fire could be heard.

Then our good old burly Khawaja Sahib came up with an amazing explanation: "Dear brothers, we are also devout Muslims like you and we had heard in our city that if one goes to the valley of Kaghan and then turn right from Burawai, there, under the massive snows of Ratti Gali, a pir-e-kamil is buried and we have travelled this far only to pay tribute to this Pir sahib, offer our Salam, pray and then go back to our city. This is the sole purpose of our sojourn."

Upon hearing this story, we paid tribute to Khawaja Sahib's craftiness in our hearts. He had heard in Naran of some Pir sahib up there and had come up with this appropriate answer. Naturally, it was news for us too. The nomads were stunned. It so happened that this particular Pir sahib was their patron saint too and here were some young devotees who had come all the way from Lahore just to pay their respects to him. Thus, to them, we were their "Pir bhais" and from then on they treated us as if we were minor pirs ourselves, offering us the best place in front of the fires to warm our bodies. Not only that, they insisted on massaging our tired bodies. During this ritual, some of the boys started laughing because they were ticklish and one or two of the boys felt threatened.

All this was going on while the fattest lamb in their stock was specially slaughtered in our honour and was being roasted on the fires. Being massaged and pampered in a distant valley, lying under the stars with the aroma of roasted lamb rising in the cold air, — these things could happen only in a paradise and we had found it. Almost 50 years have passed since then, but I can still feel the purity of that air and in it the aroma of a lamb being roasted, the fire burning and the rocks looming.

Of dreamlands and nightmares

Finally the day came when we walked into the promised Kishan Gunga Valley, with the river Kishan Gunga flowing thousands of meters below us and the dark unfriendly rocks all above us. It was the valley after which our expedition was named — and it was a drab valley that was nothing short of a nightmare after the captivating Ratti Gali dream sceneries that we had passed to reach this place. We felt cheated.

Nothing exciting happened that day except that two of our boys crossed a bridge and landed right in the middle of an Indian Army base and were duly arrested on the charges of being Pakistani spies. There was no obvious demarcation of borders in those days to warn people that they were straying on the wrong side of the divide. It just so happened that a certain Major Shah of the Pakistan Army appeared on the scene, riding a chestnut horse and twirling his brown and bushy moustaches. He was kind enough to take pity on the boys and the good chap went over to his Indian counterpart and secured the release of those "spies". Needless to say, the two boys were shaken from their misadventure as they had thought that they would probably never see their homes again and will rot in some enemy jail for years.

We trudged along the river Kishan Gunga which was later to be baptised and renamed Neelam. A chowkidar of a deserted dak bungalow informed us about a myth that was related to the said river. There was, in ancient times, a giant of dubious character who poured all the water which flowed in the streams and rivers into a huge pitcher, carried it on his giant head and walked away. The people of the valley were left without a drop to drink, they approached one of the lords, perhaps Rama or Krishna, and he sent a two-pronged arrow flying towards the pitcher and pierced it. Out came two streams from the pitcher, hence the name Kishan Gunga valley.

Moving onwards, we trudged along by the river, stayed in different Godforsaken rest houses and army huts during the nights. At last, one fine morning there was a real wagon in front of us in which we loaded ourselves and it took us an hour or two to reach Muzaffarabad of 1956, a proper hovel to be sure and it has maintained this dubious distinction to this day.

However, I would like to narrate a small but chilling incident which could have resulted in a fatal accident before the wagon ride.

We were walking along on a dirt road with Kishan Gunga on our left, down below somewhere and the gloomy black mountains up above. We were tired and fed up beyond description, a long treacherous day was coming to an end and our abode for the night was nowhere in sight. In the descending darkness, I walked way behind the team along with the expedition cook, he being in a sombre mood was discussing life, death and fate, when right in front of us, maybe a yard or two away, a huge boulder, rather a titanic size rock, rolled down from the mountains above and fell. Yes, right in front of us two, maybe a yard or two away, it blocked our view of the dirt road for a while and then bounced like a tennis ball and went down into the depths of river Kishan Gunga! A few steps more and we would have been unwilling mashed potatoes for sure, perhaps worste. That is fate.

From Muzaffarabd, our Lahore seemed a stone's throw away but certainly not that stone which fell right in front of us. As I have mentioned repeatedly, this journey took place almost 50 long years ago, so if I have erred in the description of places and distances I may be forgiven as the memory dims in so many years and dreams take over. Many things take on a more fabulous aura than they really deserve, and some unappealing ones are blocked out from the memory.

Upon our safe and successful return, our families offered shukrana ke nafal and prepared some zarda daigs to be distributed in our locality. As for the Government College, it also chipped in by awarding all of us the college colour of mountaineering, which, alas, I never received in person or wore as I left for England soon afterwards.

Ashraf Aman, the famed mountaineer who has the honour of being the first Pakistani to climb the peak of K2, is a friend and always jests that I am his senior in the matter of mountains because of this undeserved and per chance colour of mountaineering bestowed upon me by Government College in 1956.

So dear readers, (if you are still reading), these were the first seeds of adventure sown in me by the trip to the Ratti Gali peak and those dreamy lakes. The roots went deep into my body and soul and from then onwards, for the rest of my life, it blossomed, tortured and tormented me. However, I must confess, this torture and torment made my life worth living — and it may be an abnormal life, but worth living all the same.

A dream within a dream

NOW we were very close to our destination of the formidable Ratti Gali peak, for which we had been travelling under all kinds of conditions all these past many days. Though very excited, we slept like logs that night snuggled inside the nomad tents, what with the warmth of roast meat in our stomachs and fires burning all around. Amazingly, when the morning came the magic of the valley was still there, only the fires were not there. Instead, a mist full of secrets engulfed the nomad tents and rocks.

The nomads insisted that we should give them the honour of staying with them for another night and we insisted that we could not wait to present ourself at the grave of the great Pir sahib. To begin with, the whole tribe was ready to escort us to their Pir sahib's grave, we were slightly reluctant because Pir sahib's eternal abode was in the opposite direction of our destination. Finally, it was decided that only one of them would guide us to Pir sahib.

This devout guide had the shock of his life when, after putting as safe a distance between the nomad abode and us, we almost threatened him to get lost. He, in turn, threatened us with dire consequences, and went back muttering vengeance. I was sure that lamb which was slaughtered the night before belonged to his stock.

We resumed our trek. The Ratti Gali glacier loomed right in front of us, as if threatening to crash down and bury us good and proper. Then came a point when we understood the reason why we were carrying those useless ice axes. The eternal snows were under our feet and we had to slash them with our axes to make a way and climb. When the evening descended, and it descended rather suddenly, there emerged a small hut perched on the snows of the glacier. Khawaja Sahib ordered a halt and decided to spend the night in this stone hut. This was to be a base camp for next morning's onslaught on Ratti Gali peak.

That night was horrid, freezing, uncomfortable and unbearable beyond words. No roasted lamb or fires burning to warm our chilled bodies, just a chappati or two with aaloo shorba in which the potatoes were harder than the rocks of the valley.

A senior by the name of Javed Asar complained that he was forced by the call of nature to venture outside the hut and due to the non-availability of water, he had utilized the snow. Hence, he felt absolutely paralysed in the lower parts of his fragile body.

During the night, the winds howled like mad wolves and our bodies shivered like eels out of water. We also feared the attack of disgruntled nomads. It was late night rather than early morning when we came out of the hut for the final assault on the mountain, flashing our torches on the glacier which was at that moment solid and negotiable. In the next hour or so, with the warmth of early rays of the sun, it was to turn into slush. It was not a difficult climb and our ice axes helped us in maintaining our balance. Finally, we were there — Ratti Gali peak almost 17 thousand feet high, shrouded in mist and eternal snow. It was rather flat at the top.

Khawaja Sahib raised his hand and shouted: "Hip, hip, hurray!"

We followed in equal excitement. Soon we were breathless not because of excitement but due to the height and our "hurrays" dwindled. Out came my baby Brownie Kodak camera which I had bought for the princely sum of Rs26 and I took some snaps. We celebrated our achievement with a cup of tea and then started descending on the other side of peak into Azad Kashmir, where the valley of Kishan Gunga awaited us.

Soon, we left the eternal snows behind and then an unbelievable sight unfolded right before us as we were descending and all of us suddenly stopped. There lay under our feet a valley that seemed right out of a fairy tale, remembrance of which still haunts me and I am still not sure whether I actually saw it or it was a fabrication of my youthful imagination. I do declare and swear that in my almost 50 years of wandering, I have never set eyes upon such a fairy tale landscape and a dreamlike vista, such a breathtaking panorama of nature's wonders. It is futile to describe it but then life too is futile, so why not give it a try.

As we were going down on the other side of Ratti Gali summit, the snow gave way to a lush green carpet with thousands upon thousands of flowers rolled out in front of us. We tried not to trample them but it couldn't be and we kept on descending into a valley of wonders which was carpeted with poppies as far as the eye could see. And amidst the colours of a Khalid Iqbal painting, deep greens and flaming reds, there glistened a mountain stream flowing as if it was mercury.

But the best was yet to come — beyond this amazing valley and its stunning beauty, there was a wall of unbelievable blue mountains, standing guard over this hidden Shangrila, lest its beauty and purity be vandalized or molested.

There was another dream within this dream — in the midst of these blue mountains, partly shrouded in the mist, were two sapphire blue lakes, appearing still and stunning from where we saw them. And in one of these lakes a white wonder floated majestically, a small glacier which swam in the lake, languidly like a snow swan. Was it not a wonder of wonders that a small waterfall emerging from the heart of the blue mountains was falling right into this lake? We kept on gazing mesmerized, the snow swan floating came under the waters of this fall and its pressure forced it to glide away.

"Sir," I addressed our leader Khawaja Sahib, who was puffing, "can't we head for these lakes, one of these lakes, preferably the one with the snow swan, spend the night there and then move forward tomorrow morning?"

There were other voices which rose in support of my suggestion but Khawaja Sahib, not as young and romantic as we were, was a practical man and he smiled, fully understanding our teenage desires. "No my boys, we don't know the proper way to reach those lakes and they are not as near as you imagine. We might get lost and who knows if those lakes are there or not there?"

"They are there!" we shouted.

"Who knows?"

I have yet to come across a hiker or a vagabond of mountains who has seen those lakes and described them to me. Perhaps they were not there and I was under the influence of Shafiqur Rehman's Neeli Jheel. So we resumed our journey, kept on going down till the lakes disappeared in the distant mist, the lush green grass and riot of flowers gave way to stony and dangerous paths.

Once again we were labouring, puffing and cursing our fate, but not so loudly as we had just come out of a dream within a dream. The terrain was treacherous beyond description. We were treading on razor sharp pathways which bore kinship to pule sarat, and during one of these crossings one of our mules slipped and disappeared in the abyss, never to be recovered.

We mourned the loss of our luggage and then the loss of the mule. Needless to say it was a harrowing experience and the thought that was foremost in everyone's mind was: "What if instead of the mule it was me?"

The visa saga

"I AM the son-in-law of America," he declared and grinned. I was sitting on a rickety wobbly wooden bench underneath a tree which was providing me a sunny shade — sunny because the tree was devoid of any foliage so it was a psychological shade which I was enjoying right in front of the American Embassy in the hot Islamabad afternoon, waiting for three hours for my nervous wife who had gone inside the embassy for a visa interview.

I was not alone. There was an assortment of people littered all over the place waiting for their near and dear ones who had entered the holy premises for the procurement of the elusive American visa; worried fathers, praying mothers, fidgety relatives and bored husbands, including myself.

I noticed that there was this middle-aged gentleman with a leathery face dressed in shalwar qameez but wearing a cowboy hat on his bald head. He was a gentleman because he abhorred any kind of shade and was standing in the midday sun gazing at the embassy lovingly. He recognized me and smiled, some of his teeth were missing, I smiled back. This encouraged him and he approached me.

"Tarar sahib, nice to meet you. Why are you sitting here?"

"Well I love open spaces and especially picnics in the midday sun, so I am enjoying myself," I was irritated by his stupid question.

"Ha ha you joke."

"Yes I joke." I wanted this conversation to be over.

"You know I am the son-in-law of America and even then they are not granting me a visa." This declaration bowled me over and I immediately got interested; you don't meet a son-in-law of America every day. "No I did not know, it must be a very daunting task to become the son-in-law of America, how did you manage it?"

"I was in America for two years you know."

"You went there on a tourist visa and stayed on, is that it?" Now it was his turn to be irritated. "What does it matter how I got there, I was in America and I married a young beautiful American girl and we lived happily. Then my mother died and I had to come back to Pakistan, now they won't let me go back to my legally wedded wife, look I have all the proof."

I had noticed that he was clutching a huge photo album which he was kind enough to open and show me the proof. "Look, this is my American wife in our drawing room and these are her parents."

I was really amazed, his wife was indeed pretty although a few hundred pounds off her would have helped and her parents were rather decent considering their son-in-law. He showed me all the relevant documents pertaining to his marriage which looked convincing enough.

"Have you shown these documents and photographs to the embassy people?"

"No, the guards won't let me in, I keep telling them that I am America's son-in-law but they laugh, can you help me?"

"Have you applied for the visa?"

"Why should I? I am their son-in-law, they should come out and receive me if they have any dignity. This is no way to treat a son-in-law."

"Indeed it is not."

The case was complicated; he closed his album, grinned again and went back to his sunny location. Pakistani guards of the embassy came towards the waiting crowd and handed over a few bottles of cold water, which was welcome in that heat. However, they requested that the plastic bottles are to be returned as some people casually carry them away.

If I was having a wonderful picnic feeling hungry and thirsty at the same time and my wife was inside the embassy for the last four hours, it was entirely due to my one and only daughter Dr Annie who presently resides in Orlando, USA. She was going to have her first baby and had sent an SOS to her "mama" to be with her during the delivery and afterwards to look after the baby as only desi mamas can do.

Twice a day, she would call and all she said was "Mama, Mama, Mama", like a lost duckling. My wife applied for the visa through proper channels. When the interview call came I accompanied her and was allowed to chaperon her inside the visa section, a small comfortable room with four windows behind which sat the lords who decided the fate of the applicant. The third window lord, however, was more benevolent than the others as the rest of them were refusing profusely. So the remaining applicants immediately became pious and started praying that on their turn they should be lucky enough to present themselves at that particular benevolent window.

In the meantime an ex-chief minister of Punjab entered the visa room. Dressed in his sherwani and past glory, he stood their as there were no seats available and waited patiently. He heaved a sigh of relief when his turn came to present himself in front of the visa officer. His name, like that of all others, was called on the address system and I remembered the way an under trial prisoner is called by the bailiff of the court: "Such and such, son of such, hazir ho." It was heartening to see that the Americans treated the beggars and princes alike.

Outside, an old lady, standing in the queue like everyone else, had requested for a chair as she could not stand any more. The request was refused, despite the fact that she declared that she was the wife of an ex-commander-in-chief of Pakistan Army, now deceased. The applicants whose visa requests were accepted came back beaming as if they had hit the million dollar jackpot and they were few in number; the unlucky ones came with long drawn faces clutching their passports in a state of shock.

I saw a woman, demure and pretty with streaked golden hair who had come for a visa extension from the USA. Her request was turned down. She was almost begging the visa officer and crying. I am sure her circumstances were such that this refusal was going to destroy her entire life, otherwise she was too dignified to stoop so low.

Another old lady, very rustic and very simple was asking the Pakistani interpreter to tell the sahib that she had not seen her son for many a year and all she wanted was to look at his face and hug him. To the sahib this argument was ridiculous because in his culture it was unthinkable that a mother should travel through half of the world just to look at the face of her son or to hug him. They lady was turned back in tears.

Finally my wife's name was announced, she went to the appointed window and came back. All she said was "Annie is waiting and I can't go." The reason for refusing her a visa was that it was feared that she won't come back from America, settling there permanently abandoning her home, kids and a good for nothing husband and will perhaps at this age work on some gas station and who knows might join the firefighters of New York! She was inconsolable. Upon hearing the news of refusal Annie cried on the phone for hours, very expensive crying.

Fortunately there was a provision that she could re-apply provided the visa fee is paid all over again which she did. And that is the reason why I had been sitting here for the last four hours, waiting for her to emerge from the embassy, either smiling or with a morose face because she does not cry easily.

In the meantime I observed the spectacle of sorrow, ambition, disillusionment and boundless joy writ large on the faces of those who waited and those who came out of the embassy one by one. I saw an elderly woman dressed in a sari weeping loudly, her husband staggered up to receive her but she refused his hand, totally shaken she sat there right on the pavement in the burning sun. No matter how hard he pleaded she refused to come in the shade. Finally the husband left her alone to mourn her loss. Then there was this very pretty young woman, unfortunately stricken with polio, carrying with great difficulty her documents and files, she was the happiest person on earth; she contacted her mother on the cell and told her the good news. Everybody congratulated her profusely. But where was my wife?

I had given up and thought that the Americans had abducted her and taken her to Guantanamo Bay, when finally she emerged, composed, but smiling: "I am going to Annie, they say I will get the visa within the next three days. You must be bored to death by now."

"No, the son-in-law of America was keeping me company," and as I waved towards him he was still wearing his cowboy hat and sitting in the sun.

The visa did not take three days but almost three months to come; it was issued on the 9th of September and I know why. The Americans made sure that she won' reach New York on 11th of September and I don't blame them. I have always considered my wife a terrorist, terrorizing me for the last thirty-four years. Clever Americans, they found out within a few minutes.

But in Orlando my grandson Noffel was too impatient to see this world and did not wait for his grandmother and decided to appear almost three weeks before the expected date. His grandmother arrived rather late but fully equipped with all sorts of desi araks, lungots and punjeeris to groom this newborn American. I do sincerely hope that she will not get a job as a gas station attendant and come back to me in due time.

Wells of Madina

Do you know that on the day when the waters of a newly dug well spout out for the first time, dozens of midgets leave their underground abode, jump out of the well and disappear before you can catch one of them? If you don't then you are definitely not a kid from a rural background.

Almost sixty years ago my maternal uncle Cheema sahib decided that on a tract of barren land so that it could be brought under plow. For this purpose a clan of famous well diggers was approached who had specialized in the digging business for generations. As soon as the news of a new well being dug reached the population of village urchins, and I was certainly one of them, the whole lot of them stationed themselves on the magical spot. In the sizzling summer days beneath the burning sun we sat on the mound of earth and peeped inside the pit where the well diggers worked soaked in mud looking like creatures of some other world. Besides, digging they were building a brick sphere which was to be finally lowered in the pit forming the walls of the well.

Then, after weeks of this tremendous entertainment, came the day when hopefully the water would emerge from the bottom of the well for the first time. We were waiting for the midgets. Not only the kids, but the elders of the village also firmly believed in the myth that whenever a new well was dug, the earth and the underworld were connected and the midgets who lived down below came out with the first splash of water. When the magical moment approached we sat shoulder-to-shoulder so the emerging midgets would not escape and we could at least catch one midget each for a rainy day. We craned our necks to catch the first glimpse of the little creatures and held our breath.

The first waters did gush out but at least I did not see a single midget. However, every other kid swore that he had seen at least a couple of them scurrying past and disappearing in the nearby cane field. Now it was an utter disgrace if I admitted that I had not seen any, the shame of it could last till my dying days. So I also declared that yes I swear I saw at least a couple of them, one with dark glasses and in his Sunday's best actually winked at me before disappearing! Perhaps that was the start of my storytelling career, I saw midgets where there were none!

Midgets or no midgets my fascination with wells lasted throughout my life, be it in Andalusia, Iran, Damascus or Turkey. A well, along with a bridge, and they both connect two different worlds represent best of the human spirit. The cylindrical walls of Mohenjodaro's well prove my point.

I was in Madina again, in the city of my Prophet (Peace be upon him) and it was my desire to locate some of those ancient wells whose waters had the honour of quenching the thirst of a person who quenched the spiritual thirst of the whole humanity.

I was in Madina again How does it feel to be in Madina

Like on the crumbling walls of Alhambra a couplet of Mexican poet Akaza is displayed. He saw a blind beggar in the streets of Granada and told his ladylove:

O, woman — give alms to this beggar,

Because to be in Granada.

And to be blind,

Is the biggest misfortune of this life

And Granada was an ordinary offshoot of this giant blossoming tree that is Madina. In a city like Madina if you are totally blind, even then you are the luckiest person on earth — that is how it feels to be in Madina.

There was good old Maula Bux, the Pakistan Consulate driver, at my disposal and Baba Faqir an old resident of Madina to show me around. We headed for "Bair Usman", the well of Hazrat Usman.

Far from the hectic traffic of Madina in a semi-deserted locality we stopped near a totally deserted house. The gate was locked.

"That is the historical well which was bought by Hazrat Usman from a local Jew and then he donated it to the Muslims who were facing a shortage of drinking water."

There was an abandoned rusty tube well in the wilderness of a small lawn beyond the locked gate but I could not see any well.

"Baba, where is the well of Usman?"

"It used to be here and then the authorities erected a tube well on it, you know the pilgrims came and drank its water and took it away in bottles and that was shirk."

"But Babaji water is meant for drinking, what's wrong with it?"

"Ordinary water yes, but if you consider it holy then it is shirk to drink it."

"The waters of Zamzam are considered holy, people not only drink it but take it home and immerse their shrouds in it, isn't that shirk?"

Baba glared at me. I could see he was towing the official policy. "Those are Allah's waters but these...". Far from touching just one of its ancient bricks I could not even go near it. It could easily be an abandoned Model Town bungalow with a rusty tube well structure, which did not betray the historical well on which it was squatting.

I was disappointed to say the least. I went near the locked gate and as soon as I peeped inside baba Faqir warned, "Don't try to go near it, it is not permitted."

I drew back.

Our next stop was "Bair Garas", an ancient well where the Holy Prophet rested and drank its water while on his way to Quba from Madina. The well was not visible from the roadside and it was Baba Faqir who led me to a cylindrical wall on which rested a rusted tin roof. Two Pakistani teachers who were on the staff of the Pakistani school situated next to the wall of this well, happened to pass by and with their help I was able to peep inside for a few moments. I have given a full description of "Bair Garas" in my column, Farewell, Madina. However, I had missed out in that particular write-up one of the most famous wells belonging to the revered Sahabi, Hazrat Salman Farsi.

These wells along with most of the sites connected with the Holy Prophet are in danger of being obliterated and this is being done very methodically. Hence my humble write-up may someday serve as a reference to the wells gone by.

Bagh-e-Salman Farsi, the unique garden of date trees of Salman the Persian is now no more. There is a piece of barren ground on which only a few years back, some date trees of the unique orchard existed. But they too came under the axe of Shirk and were cut down. The trouble with date trees is that their roots go deep into the soil and even if the trunks are cut down, with the passage of time they again sprout and refuse to die. To thwart this unwelcome possibility, it is rumoured that the roots were finally burnt.

This orchard along with a well, was a gift from the Holy Prophet to his only foreign Sahabi.

The unique orchard belonging to the same Salman survived for fourteen centuries and then recently, was cut down and burnt. However, his well still remains, for how long, it is anybody's guess.

The well is almost of the same size and construction as "Bair Gharas". It has a huge circumference and is built with rectangular lava stones. The building material of a huge structure has engulfed it already and when the construction is complete the well will disappear forever underneath its foundations. I could not reach the edge of it to peep inside because of the iron girders and bags of cement that were suffocating it but one could hear its laments "I am the gift of the Holy Prophet, I am the personal well of Salman of Faris who saved this city. Let me live so that in times to come people may see in my water the reflections of the Holy Prophet and his dear Salman Farsi."

Perhaps it was due to his being a fire worshipper once that his orchard was put to torch and burnt and as far as his well is concerned it will soon follow the burnt orchard.

Farewell, Madina

BABA Faqir emerged from a narrow street of Madina, like a biblical character dressed in long white robes and a staff in his trembling hand with a toothless smile. That smile disappeared as soon as our driver told him that we were not VIPs. Baba Faqir made it very clear that normally he only took around VVIPs.

"What would you like to see?" he asked arrogantly.

"Babaji just take us to the places and spots which were honoured with the presence of our Prophet (Peace be upon him), that's all."

Babaji originally belonged to Multan area and had been staying in Madina for the last thirty years or so. He earned his living by taking the guests of Pakistan embassy and consulate around the historical sights of Madina and in turn was paid for his services. And this time, he reluctantly became our guide.

Our first stop was an ancient graveyard which is famed to be the site of Um-ul-Momnin, Hazrat Maria Qibtia's house. She was the only wife of the Holy Prophet who did not reside in the hujras adjacent to Masjid-e-Nabvi. Rather, she had separate lodging on the outskirts of Madina. She had the honour of giving birth to the Prophet's last son, Hazrat Ibrahim who died at a very young age leaving the Prophet shattered, as he loved him to the limits.

Our next stop was Bagh-e-Salman Farsi. This unique garden of date trees is now no more. Only a few years back, there were some fruit bearing trees from the times of our Prophet but these were chopped down because people revered their fruit and wood.

The well of Hazrat Usman cannot be visited now because it is inside a municipal building and a tube well has been installed to draw its ancient water. It is the same historical well, which Hazrat Usman Ghani had bought from the local Jews and presented it to the fellow Muslims who were facing shortage of drinking water.

Most of these sites are well known and are visited by the pilgrims. But it was only due to Baba Faqir that we were able to reach some very unknown and historically very important sights. One of them was the castle of Kaab Bin Ashraf.

The ruins are situated on the outskirts of Madina and a few walls, a courtyard and a disused well still exist. It is on record that our Prophet used to come here to negotiate with the Jews and on one of his visits they tried to kill him by pushing a rock onto him. Later on the Muslims laid siege to this castle and the incident is quoted in Holy Quran.

The ruins hardly cover an area comprising three or four kanal of land. But the word "castle" conjures up different images in different lands. In Arabia, a castle was in fact a big haveli or a residential area whereas in our part of the world, it is something as big as the Lahore Fort. It is exactly due to this disparity that I am in favour of preserving these historical ruins because once they disappear, every mind will visualize a castle according to his environment. Beside that without a reference, gradually the fact turns into a myth; without the present ruins of Kaab bin Ashraf's castle, with the passage of time it will grow bigger in people's imaginations, the doors will touch the skies, the walls will become higher and higher and reality will turn into fiction.

To my simple mind the basic difference between Islam and other religions lies in the fact that its history can be proved by the villages, cities and spots where it happened. Whereas in most of the other religions it is based on myths which cannot be proven by references. The need is to protect and preserve these and other ruins so as to save our history from turning into a myth.

When I asked our driver, Maula Bux as to why the locals are disinterested in preserving the reference points of Islamic history and the Prophet's life, he came out with a very philosophical explanation, "Sain Tarar these people are well fed, whereas we are the thirsty ones, the hungry ones. Why should they bother because they have had enough of it and we will never have enough of it."

Later we saw the sights where once lived the Jews of Madina, including Banu Nuzair and Banu Qariza.

Baba Faqir by now had softened up and asked us, "Would you like to see an ancient well where the Prophet rested while going to Quba from Madina?"

The sun was scorching. Beside a deserted road we could see the building of a school and underneath the outer walls there was a structure piled with stones and a corrugated metallic sheet. I could see certain roundness in the structure but there was no way I could peep inside, it was totally blocked. In the meantime two young Pakistanis emerged from the school building and approached us, they were part of the teaching staff there. Fortunately they recognized me and offered me a cup of tea. However, I was interested in drinking from the well of my Prophet.

"There used to be a small hole in the wall through which one could peep inside but that has been filled", said one of them.

"Anyway let us be a little illegal." He carried a small rock from a nearby pile, placed it beside the structure and then with a little effort displaced a small stone.

"You can peep inside from here but don't take too long, somebody might report us".

I stood on the shaky rock, craned my head inside and tried to see inside. It took me sometime to get used to the eternal darkness of ages and then the darkness thinned and I could clearly see a large well built of huge lava rocks. But unfortunately my position was such that I could not see the water level, just the musty ancient stones and some wild plants protruding from the cracks. Now you must visualize my position, my head was inside the hole where there was coolness of ages and the rest of my body was exposed to the sun and present age. I felt as though I had gone back to the times of the Prophet and breathing the same air. This certainly was the well that was situated in between Madina and Quba. The Prophet broke the journey here and quenched his thirst with its water. I have read that a certain well was the favourite of my Prophet and often he would sit on its edge, dangling his legs inside to feel the cool of it. It is also said that he wished to be bathed after his departure with the waters of the same well and Hazrat Ali fulfilled his desire. However, I am not sure if it is the same well. Still, I would like to be enlightened if any of the readers have historical information in this regard.

While we were on our way back, Baba Faqir told Maula Bux, "You see that orchard of date palms, right in the middle of it are ruins of a mosque which was called Hiranuna and the Prophet said whosoever prays in this mosque, his prayers are answered. Let's go there."

"Baba Faqir there is no such mosque there, I have been here in Madina for the last so many years and I have never heard of such a mosque," Maula Bux did not obey his instructions.

"Yes there is a mosque." Babaji thundered.

"No there is not," Maula Bux was quite adamant, "If there was one I would know."

"Alright, you win, there is no mosque," Babaji sulked.

"Maula Bux there is no harm in checking," I suggested.

There was a fence around the date orchard, which was rather sprawling and the iron gate was locked. We could see a few young men tending the orchard. Maula Bux rightly guessed that they were from Sindh, Pakistan and addressed them in their language; they came running, opened the gate for us and took us inside. And Baba Faqir was right.

In the middle of the orchard there were ruins of a mosque and one could spot the remains of a Mihrab, piles of dates were drying in the ruins.

"Please leave quickly, if our sheikh comes back and sees you, he will turn us out for letting you in," one of the young men requested urgently and we hurried out. However, before leaving, those brothers presented us with fresh Madina dates. As we were putting the bags in the back of the car, one of them requested my wife, "Begum sahiba, please do not place the Ajwa dates in the back of the car, they are the favourite dates of our Prophet and from a tree whose ancestors provided the fruit for our Prophet; put them in your lap."

My wife almost cried while putting the Ajwa dates in her lap and guarded them as she would her other valuables.

Thus ended our visit to Madina with a present of the same dates, which were favourites of the Prophet.

Rasul Hamzatof's Daghistan

And if no one is in love with you

And you are forlorn and lonely,

Then be sure somewhere on the high mountains, Rasul Hamzatof is dead

MANY summers ago, Ahmed Daud the master story-teller, during a literary chit-chat asked me, "Tarar have you read Rasul Hamzatof Mera Daghistan?

"Rasul Hamzatof whose poetry was translated by Faiz sahib and included in his Sar-i-Wadieye Sina? yes I read the book mentioned by you some years back"

"How was it?" he asked with his high cheekbones and restless wolf eyes.

I hesitated, "Well it was a long time ago but the book was interesting enough."

On our next meeting, like a magician he produced Mera Daghistan from the inner-pocket of his jacket.

"You should read it again, it is not an interesting enough book, as you put it very casually, but a great book".

Ahmed Daud was wrong, it was not a great book but one of the greatest masterpieces ever written, fables, folk wisdom and tales from Daghistan written in a prose, which soared beyond the heights of Mount Olympus. It changed my whole concept of creative prose. In short I was not the same man after reading Mera Daghistan. There is hardly a single line which cannot be quoted as a quotable quote. It simply starts with a request from an editor of a Moscow literary journal, to the Lenin prize winner poet, to write an essay, short story or a sketch about his homeland, Daghistan, but it should not exceed more than nine typed pages. It exceeded far beyond nine pages i.e.; three hundred and fifty pages to be exact and resulted in the creation of a masterpiece which was Mera Daghistan. Some random quotes won't be out of place.

"If you can't narrate a story, turn it into song and if you can't sing, make a story out of it."

"My land is my favourite subject. We do not choose to love our land but it's the land, which chooses us. There is no eagle without his own sky, every mountain goat has its own rock, if there is a trout, there will be a clear water stream where it swims, every aeroplane has a landing strip and there is, not a creative writer who does not have his own land. If an eagle walks along the chicken in a poultry farm, he is no more an eagle. If a bull chooses to graze grass along with sheep, he will become a sheep. An aeroplane displayed in a museum is no more an aeroplane and a writer who does not have a country to sing about is no more a writer. A person who does not have command over the language and decides to be a poet is a madman who jumps into a river but does not know how to swim."

"They say a chicken dreamed that he has turned into an eagle and tried to fly from a rock and lost his wings."

"A small stream dreamed that it was a river, it flowed towards a desert and dried up forever."

"Don't jump out of your bed as soon as you wake up, first of all think about the dream you had last night."

Rasul's love for his mother-tongue, Avar, that is spoken by only seventy-thousand people, is fathomless. He narrates that once he travelled to Paris for a literary conference and an Avar painter came to visit him. The painter had left Daghistan many years ago and was settled in France, married to a French girl. They had a full afternoon to themselves, eating, drinking and reminiscing about their native land. The Avar, painter requested Rasul to go to his mountain village, if possible, and find out if any of his relatives are still alive.

Upon his return, Rasul travelled into the mountains and with great difficulty found this small village of a few huts and to his great surprise, the mother of that Avar painter, although very feeble and nearing blindness, was still alive. She had given up any hope of ever seeing her son again because she was sure that he had died somewhere in the distant lands. Upon hearing that he was still alive and very prosperous in Paris, tears of joy rushed out of her dimming eyes. But then suddenly she composed herself and asked Rasul, "You spent a whole afternoon conversing with him, tell me in which language were you talking to each other?"

"In French," Rasul replied "because he has absolutely forgotten Avar."

The mother upon hearing this, covered her head with a scarf and pulled it in front of her face, as was the custom when an Avar woman hears the news of her son's death. "If he has forgotten his mother-tongue then for me he is dead."

One of the most regrettable episodes in Rasul's life was when he was influenced by Party propaganda, that the great freedom fighter of Daghistan Imam Shamil was in fact a British and Turkish spy who sowed the seeds of hatred amongst the Soviet republics. Rasul in his youthful exuberance, perhaps trying to please the Party, although he denies it, wrote a very derogatory poem about Imam Shamil, condemning him as an enemy of the Soviet people.

His father, a very devout Muslim, felt deeply hurt and told him, "Rasul don't mess around with our Imam Shamil, if you do that you will not be at peace with yourself for the rest of your life." After some years he realized his mistake and regretted it so much that in 1961 when Soviet power was still at its peak, without fearing the wrath of the Communist Party he wrote an apology which is again a masterpiece.

He says in the beginning of the apology "Yes I became a shadow of those times whereas a true poet should never become a shadow, he should be a raging fire. I was like a raw unripe apple in those days. Now that I have matured I have realized what a fool I have been". Due to the shortage of space I cannot quote the whole poem, here are some selected lines;

And my father, few days before his death,

Sang in praise of this hero, Imam Shamil,

And it is a bitter truth that the whole world condemned him,

As an agent of the enemies. My father would have lived a few more days,

If this insult was not heaped upon Shamil,

Alas, it was my own hand, which attacked Shamil with swords of poetry, that sword of my ancestors, which always bathed in the blood of enemies,

I called it a traitors sword, I.

During the nights I hear the sound of his heavy boots,

When all the torches embrace darkness, his shadow appears in the window and addresses me, "I have never been wounded in the battle, but you have wounded me with the arrows of your poetry, This is the first wound which I have received from my own son, Your arrows have pierced my heart."

I am ashamed of myself for what I have done; I am ashamed from the shadow, which appears, in my window,

I am ashamed from my people. How can I ever apologize, I have to carry the burden of this guilt for rest of my life.

I am sorry my beloved land; don't shower on me the arrows of hate.

After all you are my mother, and a mother always forgives her son's crimes.

It was in 1996 during an international conference of writers that I had the opportunity of meeting Rasul Hamzatof, a pleasant and chubby fellow with dimming eyes which always filled with tears when Faiz sahib's name was mentioned. I presented him a copy of an Urdu version of Mera Daghistan and obtained his autograph just like a schoolboy fan. He requested me to translate into Urdu one of his poems, which I readily did. Last September, when I was in Qatar, I asked the Russian scholar Natalia Pregarina about Rasul's whereabouts. She told me that he is very ill these days. In Moscow you can see everywhere, posters with Rasul's photograph wishing him a speedy recovery. But that has not happened. According to an Uzbek source, Rasul died about two months back.

O, Woman

And if no one is in love with you

And you are forlorn and lonely,

Then be sure that somewhere on the high mountains,

Rasul Hamzatof is dead.

Spectacular Athenian results

THE good news is that I have selected myself as a member of the Pakistani contingent which will participate most honourably in the 2008 Olympics being held in Beijing. The bad news, however, is that I will keep the tradition and will not win any sort of medal other than some certificates of "Also ran" or "Also knocked out" etc.

If the Olympic gods ... I mean the Olympic committee ... hesitates to nominate me for the contingent I will present my excellent credentials which no one will be able to refute easily. For instance I will have the unique distinction of being the only participant in the history of Olympics who will compete for almost all the events single-handedly. I will guarantee that in athletics I will be the last man in every race and will reach the finishing line even if by that time all the people have gone home and the whole Olympic stadium is empty. After all, every morning I complete a five-kilometre walk in the local park and survive!

In hockey especially, I assure you I will go down with my team and in boxing I will request the referee to stop the fight in the first round; why wait for the second or third round for the same result? In swimming I will give a written pledge that I will not drown and come back home safe and sound. My dips in the village pond during childhood would help me achieve this distinction although in the Olympic pools there won't be any frogs or ducks to liven up the proceedings.

With these impeccable qualifications can anybody dare to exclude me from the future Olympic squad?

Although there is absolutely no chance of my rejection but let us suppose that the present president of POA, again a General, survives till 2008 and is highly jealous of my heavenly talents in the field of sports and blocks my way then I have an alternate action plan all chalked out. I will strive to become a Nazim of Gakkhar Mandi or Pattoki, depends upon my financial resources and my ability to switch my political allegiance. I can also become a minister of state at least because by 2008 the present number of more than sixty ministers will surely cross the hundred mark.

What sort of man am I if I cannot be one of the hundred ministers, and that too after playing my cards properly? I hope you are aware of the glorious fact that our minister for sports, along with some near and dear Nazims of his area, accompanied the Pakistani Olympic squad to Athens to have a little bit of fun and to encourage our listless athletes. I hope you can see through my plan, once a Nazim or a minister of some sort I am sure to attend the Beijing Olympics.

I must admit that I have always dreamed of becoming an Olympian and I also admit that I was always hopeless in all sports and related activities. For instance, no matter how hard I tried I could never hit a sparrow with my ghulail, the sparrows felt quite safe whenever I approached them with my rubber ghulail. Then I tried my hand at cricket and was declared a batta bowler or a chucker if you like, with the very first ball I tried to bowl.

I did not fare any better in batting, to tell you the truth. I never could see a ball coming towards me and always heard the crashing of wickets behind me. I tried sailing and could not manage the sails; my attempt at boating met the same fate, if I pushed and pushed the oars for one hour I found the boat stationary at the same spot and was in bed for the next few days with backache and blisters.

Although my initial training in swimming in the village pond gave me certain competence in this sport and mind you afterwards I have had the romantic honour of numerous dips in fabled Italian and Swiss lakes. But even then, as soon as I jumped into the water, I sank like a stone till such times that I could observe the underwater marine life. And of course when I surfaced I was saved by my friends or lifeguards.

I still marvel at the people who manage to stay afloat and do not drown. I hope the credentials which I have listed above will impress the then Pakistan Olympic Association and I will be invited to participate in Beijing Olympics, that is, if I fail to become one of the hundred ministers or one of the thousands of Nazims.

It was in the early 60s or the late 50s — I do not exactly remember when my Olympic dream almost came true. I was in England and the Olympics were being held in the eternal city Rome. Along with some hippy and non-hippy friends, a plan was chalked out to hitchhike through France and then onwards to Rome where we will sleep on the footpaths and earn millions of liras by shoe shining.

Those were the days when we were captivated by a song Three coins in a fountain relating to the Trevi Fountain of Rome and crooned by the thinnest American possible, Frank Sinatra. We reached Italy but on our way some of our lady co-travellers found better companions and left us high and dry! All roads led to Rome and were jam-packed. Still, it was well nigh impossible to hitch a lift. Finally we abandoned the Olympic project and cameback to England to watch the games on the tele.

I still remember that moment, vividly, when Ethiopia's Abebe Bikila entered the Olympic stadium, all alone and barefoot, after completing his Marathon, the whole world of Olympics stood up and clapped on this amazing performance. And although he had won the race, he did not stop and kept on running in the stadium. It was ages before the next athlete appeared in the stadium. It is said that Bikila was a royal guard in Emperor Haile Selassie's palace. He lived in a small village at a distance of thirty miles from Addis Ababa. Every morning he ran barefooted to his palace of duty and in the evening went back the same way. Someone calculated his timings and found out that this poor uneducated guard covered this distance equal to a marathon race daily and in record time. In Rome he refused to wear shoes and ran barefoot.

Upon his return to Ethiopia he was carried on a float with two African lions as his guards and taken to the royal palace where he was received by the emperor. If I am not wrong, he also won the next marathon in 1964. His life ended in a tragedy when he met a car accident and spent the rest of his life confined to a wheelchair.

As if the failure of the athletes at Athens was not enough, officials have come up with some hilarious and rather shameful excuses. The President of POA and a General in bargain stated "Athletes are not to be blamed for the Olympic failure, it is rather our supporting system that needs to be improved." So why don't you improve it General, while you are at it? You are the boss for heavens sake. If you knew that they were not going to make any headway then why did you send this hopeless lot to Athens?

The hockey federation people said "We are satisfied with the performance of the hockey team. They were caught on an off day in the match against Spain, going down 0-4 just per chance"! Then the boxing official chipped in by saying that we were pitched against the Cuban champions in the very first round so we lost.

As the saying goes, justifying a sin is worse than committing one.

Some wise guy came up with this figure from nowhere, saying that it costs $1.5 million to train an athlete to be able to make him win a gold medal and that the Cubans spend one-fourth of their national budget on sports.

I think the wise guy should contact and find out how many millions of dollars the Ethiopians, Kenyans and other African nations are spending on the training of their athletes who are leading the world in athletics these days.

I do, however, appreciate the inclusion of female athletes and the young swimmer in the squad, although beside their limited talent they were bogged down by the Pakistani dress code. It could have been worse if they were dressed in shuttlecock burqas to satisfy the religious and national sentiments.

Anyhow, the golden days are ahead. I will surely compete in the Beijing Olympics and restore the dignity of the nation by not drowning in the swimming pool.

A mystical experience

It was our first evening in Jeddah and we were about to step out for dinner when my one and only daughter-in-law said to her mother-in-law, who also happens to be my wife, "Aunty you can't go out in this attire. You have to wear an abbaya over it."

"But why?" my wife argued. "Don't you think my shalwar qameez and shawl is Islamic enough a dress?"

"Don't argue, my dear," I intervened. "It's compulsory around here to wear an abbaya over your dress. If you go out without it, you will surely be arrested by the police and even if your son is a diplomat, you will spend the rest of your life in a Saudi jail for sure."

This warning did the trick and a terrified Maimuna immediately wore a black abbaya over her dress. Now she looked like a black robed Dervish whose mental faculties were rather doubtful.

As soon as we stepped out of the house, Saljuk said, "Ammi do you have your passport in your hand-bag because if you don't, you can be arrested and deported!"

Maimuna erupted like a volcano, "I have worn this abbaya thing in which I look like an escaped mental patient, now I have to carry my passport? I am not a prisoner. I refuse to go out."

All of us had to beg her to comply with the local custom and she gave in grudgingly.

During the past one year, this was my second visit to Jeddah. And I was really amazed to see the changes in this once very close society, within a span of only a few months. Magazines and newspapers were littered with the once forbidden photographs of unveiled women, fashion models and film actresses. The police had decided not to be very pious and looked the other way when confronted with a female showing her abundant, streaked hair. Only the royal family was still out of bounds for the otherwise liberal Saudi press. So much so that even the police came under severe criticism for dragging a woman by her hair just because she was bareheaded.

There is a misconception in Pakistan that Saudi Arabia is a crimeless society. On the contrary there are murders, bank robberies, rapes and abductions, which are freely reported in press. I was almost a witness to a purse-snatching incident on Palestine Street.

During my stay, a controversy erupted about a recent issue of The National Geographic which carried a special report on Saudi Arabia. The Ministry of Information wanted it to be banned, but the liberal elements prevailed and it was allowed to go on sale.

The Cupid carries out his clandestine activities, despite being a persona non grata in the Kingdom. Saudi girls roam the streets of Jeddah in their latest four-wheelers, naturally with their drivers as they are still not allowed to drive, along the waterfront, or in the most fashionable street, Tahlia. There they would drop their mobile phone numbers in the vicinity of a boy whom they fancy so that he can pursue the matter later on. I had also observed this in Qatar, where certain enterprising young ladies, fully clad, will arrive in the parking lot of some superstore, instruct their Indian or Sri Lankan driver to wait patiently, and would meet the object of their desires, till their "shopping" was done.

While you are enjoying the delights of Jeddah, all the time you feel guilty. You are a fish which has been hooked and the line is being pulled and you desperately want to abandon Jeddah and head for the mother of all cities, Mecca. There you will find Him, who is truly pulling the strings and whose abode is in Khana Kaaba.

The very first sight of the universe that is Kaaba and thousands of white comets that rotate around it, the pilgrims, sent me in a reverie of unfathomable spiritual commotion and I became one of the comets performing the Umra.

Although during the Tawaf one should not look at the Kaaba, but I could not take my my eyes off it and I was rewarded with a sight which compelled me to smile. A black clad Iranian woman was holding an angel like child in her hands and was trying her best to persuade the baby to kiss the Kaaba with its rose petal lips. But the child refused to oblige and instead started playing with the cover of Kaaba, as if it was a plaything. Tiny hands were trying to clutch the black cover as a shriek of delight was let loose by the child. I am sure Allah, too, must have smiled on this little believer.

During Haj, despite all my best efforts, I could not kiss the Hajr-e-Aswad, the black stone, which has the honour of being kissed by my Prophet (Peace be upon him). I tried desperately but to no avail. It was not the rush of pilgrims only, rather the undisciplined pushing and jostling which threw me away everytime I approached it. At one time a young Pakistani recognized me and pulled me with his powerful arms through the crowd and towards the black stone. For the first time I could see the Hajr-e-Aswad. But I also noticed that there were some very old and feeble pilgrims who I had to push through to reach the goal. Here I gave up.

"Tarar Sahib, only a little more pushing would have done it. You have willingly given up a great opportunity," complained the panting young man.

"Well, I am a coward, I can bear the shoving of others, but I cannot push feeble old men and women. After all its just a stone as Hazrat Umar remarked, and its only sanctity is that our Prophet kissed it. So some other time."

During my travels I have come across many milestones that bore the name of cities towards which I was travelling. Reading the names of Paris, Cordoba, Granada, Rome, Damascus or Lahore always sent a strange sensation down my spine. But all these ordinary cities paled when for the first time I saw "Mecca Mukarama" and the name of "Madina Munawwra" on a milestone. Not just the first time, but everytime seeing these names mesmerised me. I cannot explain the magical impact of these names; they just float like dreamboats in your bloodstream.

Next day we were Madina Ke Musafir.

It was night and, Madina was truely Munawwar, as the brightest of stars had descended on earth to illuminate it. After travelling through modern highways and bridges, there emerged in front of our searching eyes the minarets of Masjid-e-Nabvi and in its cradle was the green dome of the Prophet's permanent abode. There has never been and never will be a structure which with its simplicity has the mysterious power of bestowing peace and love on all the billions who see it. Although Ustad Imam Din of Gujrat was a humorous poet not to be taken seriously, but in his uncouth innocence he came up with such a couplet that it became the envy of the greatest poets. The couplet, in rough translation, is as follows:

Where there is my Prophet's abode

That particular piece of land

Is in fact part of heavens.

As I was aware of the fact that Masjid-e-Nabvi closes at 11pm for the night, I repeatedly asked Seljuk in a state of nervousness "Do you think we will be in time to say our salaam to Hazur? Do you think ...".

We enterd the great courtyard at about 10.30 when the announcements for the closing of the great gates of the mosque echoed under the domes. We rushed towards "Bab-ul-Salam" as a sleepy gatekeeper was kind enough to look the other way and let us enter the mosque. Where during the day you cannot find enough room to place your forehead on the floor, even in the farthest corners of the mosque, at this time of night there were hardly a few dozen people and all in a frenzy to offer Nawafil on the spots where placing a Sajda is a dream for every Muslim. And that spot is the white carpet of Riaz-ul-Junnah which, as we Muslims believe it to be, a part of Paradise and will ascend to the heavens on the day of Judgment because it is exactly the same area where the original mosque existed.

The Pillar of Ayesha, Pillar of Ali, in front of Minbar-e-Rasul, and at the spot where our Prophet used to pray. I was trembling with excitement because this indeed was a very rare opportunity; the announcements of closure were being repeated in a soft but firm voice. The caretakers were requesting every individual to finish their prayers and leave the mosque. My forehead was at the spot where my Hazur use to stand, my forehead on his feet, tears rolling down wetting the carpet and I remained there till a keeper touched my shoulders to indicate that the parting hour had come.

Then I rushed towards the Roza-e-Rasul to say my salaam, and there again I was amazed and grateful that only a very few people were standing in front of the Jali. And then at that moment I considered myself to be the luckiest man on earth, because somehow or the other, it so happened that I was totally alone in front of the Jali beyond which I could see the green and red cover under which Prophet Mohammed (Peace be upon him) is resting. I stood there reciting Darud Sharif, talking to him and thanking him and I felt as if my whole body was illuminated with the golden rays of the moon of Madina.

All alone, standing in front of my Hazur, just him and me.

The fairies of Nanga Parbat

I haven't the foggiest whether you believed in fairies when you were a kid, but I admit I did. In those days of innocence Koh Kaf was a reality and there lived all sorts of fairies who frequently descended into our dreams, along with Madhobala and Ava Gardner. The next morning we avoided the eyes of our parents lest they find out what we had been up to in our dreams.

These fairies were of different varieties, shapes and colours, my favourite was the Sabz Pari who had the tendency of falling in love with anybody who crossed her path and this proved that I had a chance.

This fairy fantasy started with the bedtime stories of my grandmother who had a bag full of such tales. But then I grew up. I mean I attained the ripe old age of ten years and became self sufficient in fairy tales because I had learned to read and write. Now I was a very frequent visitor to the footpaths of Circular Road where I stood fascinated in the midday sun of Lahore's fierce summer browsing through the vast array of children's novels displayed on the road side.

These paperback novels had fascinating titles such as Koh Kaf Ki Malika, Kana Gin Aur Masoom Pari, Sabz Pari Ka Intiqam, Parion Ka Jazeera etc.

The cover jackets in gaudy colours depicted the dreamy fairies and the villainous Djins. Although the price of ten annas was beyond my pocket for a novel of two hundred pages. But I could manage to fleece my mother, besieging her that Master Din Mohammad would eat me alive if I did not buy a particular school book till tomorrow. I procured the desired fairy novel instead of a school book and retired immediately to Lawrence Garden, spending the whole afternoon under the Banyan tree near the mazar of Saint Turt Murad transporting myself to Koh Kaf and submerging myself in the breathless beauty of Sabz Pari.

I must have read hundreds of these novels in those days. Then I really grew up and came out of this trance of fairies because I realized that the fairies were not only residing on Koh Kaf only, they were walking pretty all around me in the city of Lahore, although slightly out of my reach. Time passed and with the passage of time the fairies dimmed and in place of fairy dreams came the nightmares of reality; family and making both ends meet. But the fairies did not admit defeat, confronting these obstacles and reappeared almost eighteen years ago in a passenger wagon which was taking us from Baltistan's capital, Skardu to the then comparatively unknown valley of Khaplu on the banks of river Shayuk.

My companions included Mati, Nizami and a British vagabond Chris who claimed to be a poet also.

In the Khaplu bound wagon an old Balti lady had a fairy problem.

The clerk of Skardu town committee told us that the old lady's youngest son had fallen in love with a local fairy and wanted to marry her but she had some reservations about this arrangement. We thought they were just trying to amuse us but when we laughed it off they were rather upset.

"It is a serious problem sir," the committee clerk frowned. "It happens all the time, you should know that Baltistan is called the Land of Salty Tea and Fairies."

"Well, what is the problem then," Nizami smiled. "Let the boy marry a fairy and enjoy himself. I personally would not refrain if I had the chance."

"Well sir, the problem is that the fairies do not attend to their household chores and would not go to the forest to collect wood for the winter evenings, they just produce children."

"That is fairy enough" Chris commented.

"How can one meet a fairy?" Mati adjusted his thick glasses, his beady eyes shining with excitement.

The committee clerk elaborated the process, "Sir first of all you have to dress nicely after taking a bath, then you should perfume yourself profusely, wait till the midnight hour and then head for the highest spot near your village."

Now the frequently married Nizami got really interested. "Tell me, can't the fairy come before midnight?"

"No sir, it must be very dark."

"That is risky, if it is very dark how do you know that it is a fairy in front of you and not a witch?"

"Nizami if you are there do you think a fairy would be foolish enough to appear, most likely a witch will confront you, clerk sahib please carry on with the fairy business and do not pay heed to Nizami's comments."

"Well sir, now you must wait, at times you wait there till the morning comes and the fairy does not appear which means that maybe she does not like you or your perfume."

"Nizami you are out of the fairy contest because you smell any way," Mati giggled.

"Look Mati, you know how many times I have married and that includes an English lady? What do you know about women, they fall head over heels for me, let a fairy come and take one look at me and her wings would start burning with passion."

I admonished both of them and told them to be quiet requesting the committee clerk to continue with the fairy tale. "And sir if you are lucky, first of all you will smell a very light scent wafting in the breeze, after that a strong wind will blow and then the fairy would appear, if she falls in love with you then you have to marry her otherwise she will ruin you."

Everybody, other than the local passengers, were very skeptical. "Have you ever seen a fairy yourself?"

"No, but in our village there are certain people whose wives are fairies. Other people can't see them, however, their children can be seen and they are very pretty. If you doubt my statement you can pay a visit to my village near Khaplu and I will show you the children of fairies."

"Yes he speaks the truth," the old woman nodded. "We have children of fairies in our village." Even a Maulvi Sahib who was travelling with us endorsed their statement. That evening while the Shayuk River was bathed in moonlight and we sat beside its waters as a very chilly night we were not too sure whether the committee clerk was far wrong, maybe the fairies did exist and we were simply unaware of the fact.

(To be continued)

The fairies of Nanga Parbat

IT was the same evening when Chris recited his poetry and in turn Mati translated one of Ghalib's couplet i.e. Dile Nadan Tujhe Hua Kia Hai, Aakhir Es Dard Ki Dawa Kia Hai into English. The translation went something like this;

O, stupid heart what has happened to you,

After all what is the medicine of this pain?

"You call him a great poet?" Chris asked after listening to this translation, we nodded.

"I think he is a stupid poet." We assured him that he does not come out well in translation, especially if Mati does it.

The ancient Dardistan, the present Diyamira district of Gilgit is also full of fairy tales and rightly so because it is called "The Land of Fairies". Underneath the ninth tallest mountain in the world Nanga Parbat, the killer mountain, stories of fairies and witches abound. The locals believe that Nanga Parbat is the abode of the queen of fairies who live in a vast palace of snow. There are giant frogs and snakes also made entirely of snow that guard the palace of this queen. Females living in the vicinity of Nanga Parbat refrain from wearing colourful dresses and shining ornaments because they believe that the fairy queen can be jealous and will cast a spell on them.

Once I asked Nazir Sabir, the famed mountaineer who had the honour of being the only Pakistani to reach the summit of Mount Everest, whether he believed in these tales and if ever during his mountaineering he encountered anything unusual.

"Tarar sahib it is true that up there in the highest snows you hear strange sounds and you feel that someone is around. But most probably it is due to the lack of oxygen that your brain starts hallucinating or it is the sound of a shifting glacier, although I admit that up there I felt a definite presence of my long lost friends who died on the mountains. But the

Pakistani North is such a mythical place that you cannot rule out any possibilities. Maybe there are fairies and maybe there are not."

Many years after the first introduction of fairies I was in the Lathobo Base camp of Nanga Parbat and during the evening I was jotting down some information about the area in my diary when my porter Sultan asked me, "Sahib tell me is it the fourteenth of moon tonight?"

"What if it is, Sultan?" I asked casually.

I saw a definite fear spreading on his rugged face, "The Japanese mountaineers who are buried nearby will descend from Nanga Parbat, visit their graves and go back to the summit."

Only the day before I had visited The Graveyard of Foreigners, situated underneath the snows of Nanga Parbat where two Austrians and three Japanese mountaineers are buried and there also Sultan had mentioned that he had seen the Japanese coming down from the mountains in the moonlit nights to visit their graves.

"Well Sultan, luckily it is the tenth of moon tonight so you need not fear the dead Japanese roaming around our tents."

"Maybe not the Japanese, but the fairies and witches may roam around sir." This was the young porter Bahadur Jamil.

"This is all your imagination Bahadur," I said although there was no conviction in my voice, only fear of the unknown. "No such thing exists."

Bahadur Jamil did not like my comment and sulked "Why don't you ask Nazim, he will tell you."

The other porter Nazim was slightly reluctant but he narrated anyway. "Tarar sahib it is about my grandfather. He was a very famous hunter and he had nine hunting dogs and he could kill a bear with their help. He used to live in Churat village near Tarshing and once he came to this Top Maidan area to hunt. He chased two Markhors and by the time he killed them it was too late to go back so he spent the night right here, where we are camping. He lit a huge fire to warm himself just as we have done and the Rui appeared."

"What appeared?"

"In our local language a witch or churail is called Rui, and this Rui appeared in the form of his wife. Only that my grandfather knew that she was not his wife because her feet were turned backwards. He asked her if she would like to eat meat and the Rui said, 'Yes, I love meat'. My grandfather roasted a leg of Markhor in the fire and then with this piping hot leg he beat the hell out of Rui, then grasping her hair he dragged her around Nanga Parbat till such time that the Rui apologized and agreed to marry him. My grandfather was a very clever man and he tied a knot in Rui's hair so that she could not escape. Then he placed those Markhors on Rui's back because a Rui can carry a load of five donkeys and then drove her to Churat."

Nazim was totally engrossed in the story and believe me at that moment underneath the snows of Nanga Parbat I started imagining Ruis all around me.

"So my grandfather married this Rui and after two years a daughter was born to them. When the daughter grew up one day both of them, mother and daughter, went outside the village to graze cattle. There the Rui requested the daughter to comb her hair and while trying to comb her hair she said, 'Mother there is a knot in your hair.'

'Untie it daughter' she said.

"As soon as the daughter untied the knot, she was transformed into a Rui from human being and then she flew away." "And what happened to the daughter?"

"She is my aunt sir," Nazim said proudly. "And another thing, before flying away the Rui said that my grandfather's tribe Kaiting will have very sharp tongues from now on."

"It is fact Tarar Sahib," Sultan added "The Kaiting do have very sharp tongues and Nazim is one of them."

I also agreed because how could they create such fantasies if they did not have sharp tongues! But the question is, do they create them or is it their genuine experience? Who is to know and who are we to judge?

If you believed in fairies when you were a kid and then felt ashamed of yourself after growing up, for believing this humbug, my advice to you is, never ever spend a night under the snows of Nanga Parbat otherwise you will start believing in fairies again as I did.

Will ye no, come back again

The rusty and creaking iron gate of 26-Westridge I, Rawalpindi is the last chapter of a heartbreaking tragedy, which closed forever after the death of its last young and impulsively intelligent occupant.

There lived once upon a time, a most famous and most loved humorist and fiction writer of the subcontinent; at times a General, a Rear Admiral but to his millions of admirers simply, Shafiqur Rehman along with his three tall and handsome sons, Atique, Khalique and Amin and his wife, one of the most stately and beautiful woman of her times.

Amongst them only Atiqur Rehman survives, presently serving with a mutli-national bank in London, may God grant him a long life. The rest of them are no more.

Aminur Rehman lost his vision due to a gunshot wound. Thereafter he lived all alone in that haunted house at Westridge. And then, one day, came the news that he too had died under mysterious circumstances. His death moved me deeply and the memories of Shafiqur Rehman, a person who despite the age difference allowed me to become a close friend overwhelmed me.

Like most of the youngsters of late-fifties Shafiqur Rehman's writings mesmerized me. His Neeli Jheel and Barsati were the stuff of our dreams. We lived with his memorable characters of Shaitan, Hakumat Apa, Maqsood Ghora etc. I wrote him a fan letter after visiting some of the places he had mentioned in Barsati and I was pleasantly surprised when my landlady in London handed me a blue envelope saying, "Mr. Chaudhry, I think you have a love letter. The lady has a beautiful handwriting I must say." It was from Shafique sahib, he always used blue stationery and his handwriting was so delicate.

That was the beginning of our "friendship" that lasted for more than forty-six years. Then I wrote my first travelogue in 1970 and sent him some of its chapters for his comments. He was very supportive and complimentary, and approved its title Nikley Tri Talash Main. I must admit that Barsati was the mother of my first travelogue.

Although we were in correspondence for many years, but somehow or the other, we never met in person. Then some literary organization arranged a launching ceremony of my Punjabi novel Pukheru in Rawalpindi. Shafique sahib and Col. Mohammad Khan of 'Bajang Aamad' fame, invited me for a cup of tea at the Pindi Club. Shafique sahib in a meticulous three-piece suit, was all smiles but with a touch of shyness. Whereas the Colonel, dressed in a blue-blazer was a picture of grace. Both of them were tall, handsome and full of colonial mannerism. Naturally I was thrilled to meet these greats who along with Mohammad Khalid Akhtar had influenced my writings vastly. And what a strange coincidence. This troika of great humorists and fiction writers were very intimate friends. Khalid sahib was a school fellow of Shafique sahib from Bahawalpur, where another great Ahmad Nadim Qasimi was also around.

When I used to visit him, he used to be exercising in his porch along with his elder son Khalique. Upstairs in a small room was his treasure chest and he would open it with the eagerness of a child and show me old manuscripts, photos of days gone-by, picture postcards and various mementos. He would excitedly point out his famous characters from the decaying photographs. He would go, this is Julie of Barsati, who placed a duck on my head during the convocation in Glasgow; this thin fellow is the inspiration of Shaitan and this is the Italian lady of Rome etc. At times, I would stay on for lunch and that was always a sumptuous affair because he was a connoisseur and loved food, always consuming a small homemade kunda of curd during lunch.

Then came 1981 and the black sword of death struck for the first time. Shafique sahib's smiling world went into mourning. His eldest son Khalique was found dead on a railway track.

I did not have the heart to attend his funeral, neither the courage to condole his death. What could you say to a father whose handsome young son dies a violent death? Instead, I wrote him a letter. He was a brave man; he came out of his shattered state and immediately wrote back.

"Mohibee, I am grateful for your extremely kind letter. My son, my dear son Khaliqur Rehman was in his twentieth year, preparing for his first annual examination of medical college. He was a very simple soul, saintly in habits. Perhaps it was due to his well-proportioned and strong body that he was nicknamed 'Joe'. Whenever my elder brother mentioned him in his letters, he always referred to him as 'Saintly Joe'.

"Last year he grew a moustache, which were of chestnut shade. He used to be my exercise companion before joining the medical college. We used to go for long walks. We would race each other in the stadium and swim together in the pool of Islamabad Club. He has gone.

"At times I remember that Scottish song which I had heard during the Second World War on the destroyers of the Royal Navy. When a ship steamed off from the port, the other stationary ship's band would play these lines—-

Will ye no, come back again?

Will ye no, come back again?

Better loved you canna be

Will ye no, come back again?

Shafiqur Rehman."

Later on, when I met him I did not ... I dared not mention the death of Khalique. And Shafique sahib kept on smiling as usual, although his smile and his face had shrunk, only once pointing to his family photograph in his room in which a young Shafique sahib and his beaming and beautiful wife were holding their first born. He said "This was the boy who has gone."

As far as I know Shafique sahib had only one close friend, Col. Mohammad Khan, besides Mohammad Khalid Akhtar who had shifted to Karachi. I was told that one particular evening of the week was entirely reserved for the Colonel. Shafique sahib would dress meticulously, well perfumed as he used to go on a date in the years gone by and would head for the Colonel's residence. They would have their pre-dinner refreshments and at times forgot about their dinner sharing jokes and tragedies and remembering the days when both of them were soldiers during WWII. Then Col. Mohammad Khan also died. Thereon, Shafique sahib seldom stepped out of the house.

His equally charming wife, as if the loss of a son was not enough, was terminally ill; she had trekked the Northern Areas in her youth and whenever she was admitted to a hospital, which was very frequent, she would request me to send her my latest trekking travelogue so that she could "dream again lying on a hospital bed".

Although I had absolutely no inkling that I was meeting Shafique sahib for the last time, as he was haggard but looked perfectly healthy, prior to my departure for China I presented myself and asked for some advice as regards China.

"During the War, I flew into China with a British pilot. Upon our arrival, we were served some sort of pulao that was rather delicious. Afterwards, we were told that it was Loomar Pulao — rice with fox meat. So, do avoid this Loomar Pulao," and he laughed heartily. That was the last laugh.

Shafique sahib joined his beloved son, the "Saintly Joe" soon afterwards. Mohammad Khalid Akhtar mourned our mutual friend and wrote to me, "Mustansar, every morning when I wake up I suddenly realize that my friend is no more, he is dead. And every night I dream that he is standing on the other bank a of thunderous river of no return, in a Khaki trouser and joggers. In the background there is a lush green hillock and a winding path is rising towards the top. The sky above is bathed with the colours of a rainbow. And Shafique is calling me, 'jump into this river Khalid and join me'." Khalid sahib also finally decided to jump in that river to reach his friend.

Soon afterwards Begum Shafique also died and only blind Aminur Rehman roamed in his world of darkness, all alone in the deserted house at 26 Westridge. A few weeks back, he sent me a copy of his stories Sehra Ka Safar and then telephoned me, "Uncle Tarar, I know abba loved you very much so you must guide me and tell me what you think of my book, I am in a hurry so please tell me soon."

He was in a hurry, to join his father, mother and elder brother. Atiqur Rehman came from London, buried his brother beside the three existing graves, locked the house at 26 Westridge and went back, perhaps for ever.

I remember Shafiqur Rehman like he remembered his Saintly Joe son.

Better loved you canna be

Will ye no, come back again.

I dreamt of Shah Gori

AND who is this enchanting Gori — Gori Gori O Banki Chhori, coming in my dreams? She is the most magnificent mountain in the world, Everest pales in front of her awesome splendour, an aloof diamond of snow hidden in the heart of the Karakoram. The Chinese call it Qogir, the Baltis, Chigori and the world at large, Mount Godwin Austin. And of course it is more commonly known as K2, the second highest mountain on this planet, Earth.

These are the days when the 50th anniversary of its conquest is being celebrated on media and in Baltistan, although I do not see the point of celebrating an event which polluted the eternal innocence of this king of mountains. The Italian mountaineer Mr Lino Lacedelli, who along with Achille Companoni (I am not responsible for the correct spellings of these gentlemen's names; I am sure they can't spell my name either) set foot on K2 is personally present in Skardu to take part in the celebrations.

It is almost thirteen years ago when Shah Gori and I were face to face for the first time in the icy wilderness of Concordia. The night before, it was absolutely freezing and I was sure that I had turned into a snowman and I will not be able to open my eyes that were full of crystals. There was a dim glow on the flaps of my tent, I slithered out of my icy sleeping bag like a lazy old python and peeped outside.

The frozen vastness of Concordia was still under the blanket of semi-darkness, some of the highest mountains in the world guarding it were only visible due to the glow of snow covering them from head to foot. But lo and behold, the left shoulder of the giant broad peak was glimmering with the very first rays of the sun that was rising from the Chinese side. My heart missed a beat, the rays indicated that the skies were clear today, if the view of Broad Peak was crystal clear then the great K2 will not be engulfed by the thick clouds like yesterday.

I hurriedly put on my thick down jacket and gloves and came out of my tent. The sky was cloudless, clear and deep blue, from here a small strip of K2 was visible and it was totally lit by the early rays. I held my breath like a hunter who spots a mythical golden bird in the jungles of fairy meadows, fearing that the slightest movement will warn him of a presence and he will fly away forever.

I retrieved my camera from my tent and trod softly on the debris of Boltoro like a cat-thief and reached the spot from where I hoped to see the K2 in full glory.

At the end of Godwin Austin glacier stood my Shah Gori, stamped on a dark blue sky like a white pyramid. I was breathless not due to the height of Concordia, but the view stunned me and I was afraid even to blink my eyes. Who knows when I open them again, K2 may not be there?

I, a fat old yak was actually leading a six member expedition called "Tarar's K2 Kahani". None of us was an experienced trekker and it was a journey of fear and misgivings which finally brought us in the lap of Concordia yesterday. We had survived the death drops over river Braldo and the gaping and waiting crevasses of Baltoro glacier.

The K2 track was devoid of any Pakistanis that year and we were the only local "Pagal Group". I remember meeting a female British trekker along with her guide who were coming back from Concordia and we were informed that it is snowing in Concordia and no one had cought a glimpse of K2 for the last many weeks. This particular female trekker, from her looks or body contours, did not indicate at all that she was a "she". I just guessed by her name that she is most likely a female. Anyway, she was surprised to meet us on her way back and asked, "It is amazing that I did not meet a single Pakistani trekker in these regions, how come you are here?"

The flirtatious, old man or old yak as I am, I said "As a matter of fact I came to see you, not the K2."

"Oh, really" the suspected lady smiled.

"I am telling you the truth and nothing but the truth."

"How come?"

"Well I read somewhere that if you journey towards the throne room of mountain gods, cross the river Braldo and on the other side there will be a sandy area full of blue bushes; if you wait a while you will come across the most beautiful girl in the world, and there you are. Now my mission is accomplished, I have seen the most beautiful girl in the world and from here I will go back."

"Not really", she blushed, establishing finally her female status and left.

"Tarar sahib", Shahid, one of my team members who had elevated himself to the post of deputy leader personally addressed me. "Have some fear of Allah, how could you lie so blatantly, she was not even ordinary."

"Look Shahid, I am sure she is aware of her ordinary looks but from now on whenever she will look at herself in a mirror she will say to herself, no the mirror is wrong. A crazy old man on my way back from K2 told me that I am beautiful and he said that he was telling the truth. My one compliment will make the rest of her life bearable, one should not hesitate to tell such innocent lies off and on."

Perhaps it was the magic of that single lie that the weather had cleared after many days and the majestic K2 was in front of me in full glory.

The man and the mountain, there is a spiritual relationship between these two. Prophet Ibrahim stood on a mountaintop watching the sunrise and considered for a moment that the sun is the creator of all things. Prophet Musa faced the burning bush on top of the Sinai and received the Ten Commandments, chiselled in Sinai stones. Hazrat Isa is known for his "Sermon on the mount" and above all our own, Prophet Mohammad (Peace be upon him) climbed the Jabl-e-Noor where in the cave of Hira he received the Command of Iqra.

I was standing at the edge of Baltoro flowing into one of the greatest ice masses in the world, Concordia.

Needless to say at this early hour it was bitterly cold and one felt naked, despite the heavy armour of mountain clothing. And standing amidst a world of eternal snow all alone and right in front of you, loomed the full might of the greatest ice pyramid in the world. It was an eerie experience.

The famous explorer, Younghusband wrote in his notes "It is amazing that such a great mountain was never named, perhaps despite its great height it cannot be seen from any human habitation, it is hidden in a far off mountain range and stands amongst such peaks that are no less equal to its beauty. The nearest village lies at the end of at least six days travel. A mountain which was higher than my wildest imaginations, I could see its full height because I was standing a few miles away from it."

Kurt Dumberger the famous mountaineer says "From certain angles the shape of K2 is like a perfect triangle, chiselled to perfection like a diamond. It will be apt to call it the Koh-i-Noor, mountain of light."

The Balti legends declare that K2 is the bridge between the world and skies. After the Italian pair, the first woman to reach its peak was the Pole, Wanda.

Wanda was a fascinating character. Whenever she descended from the mountains she was exhausted by the effort of climbing and the liaison officer accompanying her was exhausted with her. She died somewhere in the Himalayas; as the seaman's grave is the sea, a mountaineer's grave is the snow.

The very first Pakistani to summit K2 was Ashraf Aman from Hunza, a very dear friend and a very talkative dreamer. It is said that even if you fall into deep crevasses, Ashraf Aman will keep on narrating the fascinating tales of mountaineers and mountains along with the concept of Tibetan Buddhism, till the time that both of you freeze to death.

Once when I told him that I had reached the peak of Ratti Gali in 1955 with the Govt. College expedition and we were awarded the "Colour" for mountaineering, he jokingly touched my feet and said "Tarar sahib then you are my Ustad".

I asked Ashraf Aman the same old question, what were your emotions when you stood on top of the second highest mountain in the world?

(To be continued)

The survivor of Michni Post

A PICK-up, fully loaded with the local security forces i.e. Khasadars, sped through the maze of Khyber Pass escorting us to the Pak-Afghan border at Torkham. And with them, our car, engulfed in the dust raised by the speeding pick-up, tried its best to keep up with our escort. Their guns, instead of scanning the tribal hills speeding by, pointed at us, the possible victims of a possible abduction by the tribesmen.

The Khasadars are recruited from the tribes of Khyber and understandably are always trigger-happy. They have been trigger-happy for thousands of years, although before the invention of trigger they were sword-happy or something.

Whenever I looked in front of me, they were glaring at me with their guns ready to shoot. Naturally this gave me no comfort. Before venturing into this historical trip, I had objected meekly to a fully loaded escort. But my host Dr Jamil said solemnly "Tarar sahib these Khasadars are especially deputed by the Tehsildar of Khyber Agency for your safety and this is our way to honour a guest. Besides, in the tribal territories one can never be too careful. For a known person like you there is a reasonable chance of being abducted."

For the first time in my life I realized that I was important enough to be abducted and the realization inflated my ego considerably. However, much to my disappointment at the end of the day nothing of the sort happened, although at times I exhibited my presence openly. I grinned at the tribesmen so that they may recognize me and at least show a little bit of interest in abducting me. But no one bothered. What rotten luck!

"How much ransom would you be willing to pay if I am abducted?" I asked my wife who was accompanying me.

"Whatever they demand my love." I was vastly moved by her matrimonial commitment. "Only if they promise not to return you," she added. Who says true love is hard to come by these days.

Peshawar is one city that finds a special place near my heart, right next to Lahore. For me its charms include, leaving aside its haphazard traffic (dirt and guns are innumerable) its Kasera Bazaar near the gem of Mahabat Khan Mosque. I have spent many a delightful hours in its dingy and dark shops looking for antiques and Gandhara pieces.

The Shinwari Tikka, Lamb Karahi and all sorts of grilled meat at the famous Namak Mandi are stuff of the gourmet dream. Only the Pathan knows the art of cooking meat because besides religion he is a fanatic as far as love of eating meat is concerned. One can, and it is from personal experience that I say, consume more than a kilo of Shinwari Tikka followed by the magical herbal Qehwa without any after effects. And after only three hours, one is ready to consume more. However, the preference this time would be Chappal Kebabs and fish of Bakhshu.

The architectural amazement of Sethi Molalla's Havelis is unique in the subcontinent. Beside these charms Peshawar has produced a horde of actors who became a legend in their life time.

What with the dozens of Kapoors whose vast population even now dominates the Mumbai film world, it was the inimitable Prithivi Raj who started it all without ever giving a second thought to population planning.

The great Dilip Kumar and his talented brothers including Nasser Khan who was the hero of the first Pakistani film ever made. And there is the present heart throb Shahrukh Khan. Lets not forget the inimitable Gubbar Singh of Sholay? Amjad Khan's father Jaint, was also a unique film actor.

Another great from this area was Gul Hamid the most famous hero of Agha Hasher's stage plays. However, lets not forget our own TV great Mohammad Qavi Khan, Ajab Gul, Khayyam Sarhadi, son of Zia Sarhadi of Hum Log fame. Most of them are not Pathan in the strict sense of the word.

For instance Prithivi Raj Kapoor, although his haveli still exists in Peshawar where he produced most of the Kapoors, was basically a Punjabi from a small village near the present Faisalabad. Even today, their household clings to Punjabi and Hindko language. And the same goes for Dilip Kumar and brothers, and Shahrukh Khan, they are Hindko speaking.

It is this magic of the "Khans" from Peshawar, that in Bollywood, the new heroes from Tamil Nadu also add a "Khan" to their first name. A few years back a prominent Indian film producer came to Lahore to hunt for new scripts and when confronted with this question as to why every new comer in Bollywood prefers to be a "Khan" he explained:

"Whenever we produce a film with an entirely new cast the first question a distributor asks, 'Baba where are these new birds from?', and if we tell them that the new hero is a 'Khan' and the heroine is from Punjab, our film is sold right away because in Bollywood the charm of 'Khans' and the beauty of Punjab is legendary."

My apologies, I almost forgot to mention and what a great crime it would have been, the most unforgettable beauty unsurpassed so far; Madhubala was also a Peshawarite.

Peshawar has a very chilling dramatic sense of humour of its own. Some years back I was invited to preside at a literary function at Peshawar University. As soon as I was seated on the stage of Senate Hall, the student next to me, who was a functionary of the student union said, "Tarar Sahib you are sitting on a very historical stage." He was grinning cheek-to-cheek.

"On this very stage sat, on the very spot where you are seated, Mr Hayat Ahmad Sherpao when a bomb was placed underneath the stage that killed him." Although I tried to grin back for this great honour, but could not, and during the function all I did was to control my shaking legs.

Yesterday, while I was being placed on the stage of Khyber Medical College as a chief guest, the first question I asked the organizers, "I hope this stage of yours is not very historic?" Naturally the organizers were puzzled, just smiled back thinking in their heart of hearts that Mr Tarar has become a little foggy due to old age. Little did they know about history.

But today they were kind enough to take me into a historical Pass. The formidable Jamrud Fort neared. Built by the great Sikh General Hari Singh Nalwa in a record time of fifty-days as the legend says. However, we drove by and finally stopped at the foot of famous Michni Post.

On top of Michni there was a relief map of the surrounding area and Pak-Afghan border post, Torkham. In front of this detailed relief map was a comfortable seating area where normally head of states and visiting foreign delegations were seated while a young-man of the Khyber Rifles pointed out the major landmarks with the help of a baton. For a closer look, a mounted binocular was available. The young guide Mr Sami Afridi at first was slightly puzzled because we in no way looked like the dignitaries he was used to. Then he was kind enough to recognize me and smiled; with a sombre face he started the often repeated lecture.

"Sir, the Khyber Pass is one of the most historical passes in the world, on your way up you must have noticed a plaque declaring that during the first

Anglo-Afghan war the whole British Army was wiped out by the Afghans and only one surgeon survived to tell the tale. Michni was the post where this lone survivor arrived and collapsed", he looked at us triumphantly as if he had personally destroyed the British force, we looked reasonably impressed.

"Before the British, Alexander the Great descended through this Pass. Then came Babar, Taimur, Mehmud Ghaznavi, Abdali and Chengaiz Khan, this way." Although Alexander, according to my knowledge, did not cross-over from this point and I doubt if Chengaiz Khan personally led the Mongols into India, but we had to look impressed, so we did.

Then Mr Afridi pointed to an old Buddhist wall, a torture chamber used personally by Taimur. In the mountains beyond lay Tora Bora, the supposed hideout of Osama Bin Laden; the Ayub Chowki which was acquired in lieu of some other post in Chitral; the town of Torkham and the lecture ended and he invited questions.

"Young man, you have mentioned all the armies who came through this pass to invade India, but do you know that in the history of the subcontinent there was only one totally Indian army that went the other way i.e. crossed the Khyber and for once invaded Afghanistan?"

"No Sir!" he was again puzzled.

"It was the army of Maharaja Ranjit Singh which had a very strong Muslim element lead by General Hari Singh Nalwa, the founder of present Haripur town near Abbotabad, which turned the tide and crossed into Afghanistan and conquered it. For generations the Afghan mothers while putting their children to sleep whispered, 'go to sleep otherwise Nalwa would come', like the Punjabi mothers who frightened their young ones into sleep by saying, 'go to sleep, otherwise Abdali would come'.

"As a matter of fact when Maharaja Ranjit Singh was praised for capturing Afghanistan, he or Nalwa said, 'It is not difficult at all, along with swords, take a few bags of money and what the sword won't achieve, money will'. Our good friends the Americans tried the same method and succeeded."

"Sir we just narrate what we are told, if you write to the commandant perhaps he will add this bit of history also."

"I know he won't, what to talk of Ranjit Singh who was a Sikh, even the names of Chandar Gupt Maurya and Great Ashok are not included in the history of Khyber whose empires extended beyond Afghanistan into Central Asia, although they were Buddhists and well before the advent of Islam."

Well, all said and done, Michni Post was an experience and I thank the young Afridi and the lone survivor of the Anglo-Afghan War for that. If he had not survived there would have been no Michni around. My wife plucked a lovely creeper from the ground, we have replanted it in our home, hoping it will survive.

Roaming the heavenly Harlem

While humming the catchy tune of our very own Noorjehan, 'Kala shah kala, sadha kala hai dildar' we entered Harlem, a black island amidst the white supremacy of New York. We came upon a closed shutter of a store specializing in big, big undergarments for the big, big mamas of Harlem. Just like our garishly painted trucks the shutter depicted the skyline of New York with portraits of Nelson Mandela, Martin Luther King and Malcolm X emerging like black angels with a slogan "Let us share our dreams". Written across this was an announcement "Welcome to the heavenly Harlem".

A portly Negro reclining against the shutter was having his heavenly beer and when I directed my camera towards him, he glared.

"Abba, please don't be too touristy here. This is not New York, these people may react," Saljuk said as he also glared at me, wearing a bright blue T-shirt with matching jeans. At least in my eyes he was the most handsome boy in Harlem and Rabia, his wife, with her green eyes was most definitely the prettiest girl around. However, this pretty girl was least interested in the culture and traditions of Harlem. Her main interest were those numerous stores which offered marvellous sales prices unmatched in New York. I suppose due to my elderly presence they were refraining from holding hands.

Prior to my arrival in States, I was under the impression that the Asians and, in particular the Pakistanis, residing here will be sympathetically inclined towards the Afro-Americans. And they in turn will have a soft corner for them. Far from it — Afro-Americans generally abhor Asians because they readily accept all the menial jobs meekly which were normally the lot of the coloured population. And on top of this, these Asians are parroting "Yes sir, Yes sir" all the time, whereas the local African-American will just tell his employee to go to hell, or worse honour him with a four-letter word.

Even the educated Asians keep a safe distance from them. They have adopted almost the attitude of the whites that blacks are ignorant and aggressive and it is better not to socialize with them. These educated Asians have become mentally and physiologically "Brown Sahibs" of America because the whites also treat them just like they treat the blacks, and, in consequence, are wandering between these two extremes.

A Pakistani gas station owner told me "Tarar Sahib I never employ any black people because they are not hard working and very insolent. I am not here to fight for the rights of these people, I am here for business. Anyway, every now and then they take their share of profit at gun point. The Bangladeshies and Nepalese are good workers and they are always thankful because they are mostly illegal. The Sikhs are also OK if they are sober."

Whenever I spoke in favour of Afro-Americans, citing the historical injustice and times of slavery, the answer was: "You are a writer and it is fashionable for you to hold a soft corner for the cause of the downtrodden. But we assure you, if you stay here for a longer period you will understand our point of view and will become just like us."

Although I cannot deny such possibility, during my short stay it was my personal experience that the Afro-Americans were in no way any different from the rest of the crowd. However, their approach towards life is dominated by their tragic past and present uncertainty. We are at times shocked by their lifestyle and apparent insolence because our mindset is totally dominated by our "white" attitude, inherited from our colonial masters. To reach their inner soul you cannot adopt the same path which leads to the hearts of an average European or American. You cannot reach the top of K2 with the same method and technique which you adopted for Mount Everest.

Once upon a time Harlem was a "no go" area. Whosoever dared to stroll through it contributed towards the prosperity of locals, involuntarily of course. You could not go there with an empty wallet either, it meant that you did not trust them and they hated anybody who did not trust them, so they simply stabbed the disbeliever. However, the situation has entirely changed and one can roam around, shop or eat cheaply without any fear of being relieved of valuables or a friendly tickle by a sharp knife. The great footpath bazaar of Harlem is a fascinating spectacle — African herbs, pirated CDs, posters, old shoes, black literature and such home made scents which give you the finest headache this side of the Atlantic. Amongst the books you will find are those with the harrowing tales of slavery and white atrocities, Bibles and the Holy Quran. Some of these salesmen wearing long Islamic robes and caps, can be heard muttering, "Inshaallah" and "Mashaalah" continuously.

I saw a gentleman tampering with a parking meter trying to earn an honest living with the help of tools but nobody bothered. If somebody bothered, the gentleman in question could turn towards him to earn his honest living. Throbbing with eager customers were those parlours where your kinky hair were straightened, your head shaved in an abstract pattern and your nails could be turned into masterpieces of art. You could have a miniature Mona Lisa or naked Venus painted on your finger nails. The tattoo parlous were also doing roaring business, and you have a vast variety of options here too. Faces of black actors, athletes or models if preferred in nudes, landscapes, black slogans and animals. Real or imaginary.

You could come across former president Bill Clinton here who runs his social welfare organization from a Harlem office. Harlem is presently a vast open air museum of black culture and history, but its days are numbered. The prices of real estate here are phenomenal, old and crumbling houses are fetching huge prices as past classics, and the yellow devil is just lurking round the corner to engulf this last truly American outpost into the modernity of its city, New York.

Heavenly Harlem is almost safe these days, even then very few white faces appear on the black canvas of surging crowds. However, the safest way to "do" Harlem is from the open decks of double Decker tourist buses. The tourists gaze around with fear and wonder in their eyes while passing through this black museum.

All around me were the K2s and Everests of black humanity which seemed impregnable and you cannot reach them through usual routes. You have to devise new ways and paths to go near them and then, I assure you, their snow of aloofness and insolence will melt in no time with love and affection for you.

Black is beautiful

"Negroes for Sale: A bundle of young and sturdy Negro men, one of them good at brewing; two young wenches, one of them good at sewing and cleaning, highly recommended — for sale"

(New York Journal: June 23, 1768)

The same Negroes who were not called a group but a bundle, like they were just lifeless objects and once offered for sale, are in turn selling the white man in a different way, oozing with revenge of the days gone by. Because they are black, they are now blackmailing the whites.

In public transport, in buses or subway, they will occupy the whole seat spreading their sturdy bodies with an obvious insolence. A white person will rarely disturb their heavenly state of peace — he or she will rather stand for the rest of the journey. They, the Negroes, are polluting the race of their previous masters with a gay abandon and are paid for the services rendered by the grateful white females.

And those Negro ladies who were once only referred as wenches are a treat to watch. Most of them are large in girth and bulk, gobbling an enormous quantity of food to preserve their heavy weight beauty. But let me admit that some of those Negro girls are black Samris, well-versed in the art of body magic — they can turn you into a golden calf of ecstasy if you submit to their charms. They are stunningly beautiful and they walk like queens amongst the colourless white females. These Negro, or Afro-American, ladies will dress themselves according to their strange whims, caring two hoots for what white people think.

During a subway ride, there sat right in front of me a woman of certain charm and she was totally clad, covered and decorated with ornaments practically from head to foot. Arms covered with silver bangles, fingers, nose, ears and even toes laden with rings of all sizes. A huge jhoomer on her forehead dazzled the whole compartment of subway. I am sure there were other ornaments hidden from the naked eye. I felt that this was also a form of protest and defiance, as if saying: "You used to sell me as an object and now I am free to do what I want, free to wear whatever and wherever I chose to wear. Can you object to my hordes of ornaments which I am sure you detest?"

America's hallmark are Hollywood movies, junk food and music which have conquered the lands which could not be dominated otherwise. For instance, Mao called America a "paper tiger" and proved it to the hilt, but now the mausoleum which houses his mummified body glitters with the reflections of a nearby McDonald's neon lights. American movies are the rage all over the world, but it is the music which has captured the hearts and minds of the people all over the globe. Great music is always born from the pangs of sorrow and deep tragedy, the affluent society never hears the spiritual laments of Rumi's flute.

The American music is basically black music, a Negro musician once said, "As slaves our only expression of protest and sorrow was music, which came out from the nostrils of a trumpet or through the beat of a drum." In the vast cotton fields of the American south, from the crushed souls of slave labour emerged the heart rending laments of a musical form which is known as Blues.

At the end of the civil war, the ex-slaves gathered the musical instruments littered in the fields of war and started playing them. This was the beginning of "jazz" which mesmerized the whole world. America was known by the musical breath of those who were once offered for sale — Count Basie, Billie Holiday Duke Ellington, Dina Washington, Ella Fitzgerald, Eartha Kitt, Lionel Richie, Little Richards, Ray Charles, Whitney Houston, Nat "King" Cole, Harry Bellefonte and Sammy Davis Junior, to name a few.

I had the unique experience of listening to Duke Ellington's legendary orchestra when he came to Pakistan and performed at the open air theatre of Bagh-e-Jinnah, Lahore. Duke, attired in an elegant tuxedo, was overwhelmed by the response of Lahoris to his magical music. Perhaps the greatest exponent of jazz was the man with the golden trumpet, Luis Armstrong. Eyes popping out from the sockets, he blew the trumpet and could perform miracles of sorrows and happiness at will. Luis, like our Roshan Ara Begum, was not much to look at but when he started blowing his horn, he became the most beautiful human being on earth. His voice was husky and jarring when he sang tunes like When the Saints Go Marching in, and the same jarring voice was copied throughout the world by jazz singers because it was synonymous with jazz. Even now when I listen to his What a Beautiful World, the world becomes a better place to live.

Although Negroes dominated the domain of music, however, they were persona non gratis in Hollywood movies which were hundred per cent white with the exception of a black housemaid or butler, bowing all the time to their white masters. And then emerged Sidney Poitier, to my knowledge the first Negro leading man of Hollywood. He starred in Guess Who is Coming for Dinner with Spencer Tracy and Katharine Hepburn, and The Defiant Ones with Tony Curtis.

Today, one cannot even think of an American movie which does not star a black man, because they, with their vast talent and forceful personalities, forced the establishment to bow down to their talent. The list is endless, Denzel Washington, Morgan Freeman, Whoopi Goldberg, Halle Berry, Will Smith, Eddie Murphy, Jamei Foxx and Whitney Houston are the superstars of today. Only last year, Halle Berry was the first Negro actress to win the Best Actress Academy Award.

Although Martin Luther King, Mohammad Ali and Hajji Shahbaz Malcolm X fought for the restoration of Negro dignity, but it was the publication of a novel by Alex Haley, The Roots, and its main character, Kanta Kinte, which established that the blacks were not living in the trees like monkeys as the whites claimed but they were highly civilized people in their native Africa when they were abducted and brought to America to be sold as slaves. The ancestors of Kanta Kinte lived in a small village where they learned Quran by heart because they were Muslims and roaming scholars came to educate them.

The Nation of Islam movement had declared that all the last names of American Negroes were of their previous masters, hence they chose to be called "X" instead. Cassius Clay became Cassius X and then there was Malcom X. However, it was basically due to the impact of The Roots that the blacks started abandoning their American names and adopted Muslim names because most of them were Muslims when they were kidnapped by white slave traders.

Even the devout Christians opted for Muslin names. For instance, I met a friend of my son-in-law Bilal, in Orlando, a certain Mr John who was a Christian but his son was Malik and daughter was called Madiha, just to prove that they were highly civilized, free and Muslims once. But the most amazing and controversial personality in Negro history is Elijah Mohammad who preached his own brand of Islam and declared that the Negroes were much superior to the white races.

He was the founder of Nation of Islam. He and his followers mostly preached in jails to hardened criminals, murderers, rapists and drug smugglers and converted them to Islam. And these very hardened criminals became the most peaceful, law-abiding and pious citizens, abandoning alcohol, women and rest of the vices. Their women, who were "sisters", observed hijab.

Amongst these converts was a person who had committed every crime under the sky, a drunkard, rapist, drug peddler and a mugger. He became a disciple of Elijah, performed Haj and realized that Elijah's Islam was a distortion and rebelled against him. He was eventually murdered for his beliefs by Elijah's followers. Hajji Shahbaz Malcolm X was a philosopher to the core, and to my mind a dervish at heart. Today a street near Columbia University leading to the Negro world of Harlem is named after this amazing man. We were walking towards Harlem on the same street.

Black is our beloved

Today a street near Columbia University leading to Harlem is named after Malcom X. We were walking towards Harlem on the same street. "Welcome to heavenly Harlem" a banner declared.

The Dutch were the first land Mafia around here and they named the area "New Amsterdam", however, when another group of land-grabbers i.e. the British, arrived here they renamed it "New York" for obvious reasons. Harlem, which is a Dutch word, remained the same.

And what is Harlem?

Right in the middle of a sea of white culture it is a black island sprouting, bubbling and throbbing with life with its very own culture, dress code, accents and morality. The inhabitants do not stick to any particular dress code or colour — skin tight jeans, trousers almost falling from the hips displaying at times the great divide, knee-length oriental robes, shocking pink suits and at times just the undergarments. Their latest expressions and proverbs are immediately adopted by musicians, youths and copy cats of America throughout the world.

There is an amazing variety of faces and colours. For instance, a face so jet black that pitch darkness in comparison brightens, then a woman whose complexion is like golden teakwood and when she walks by you are mesmerized and want to follow her. There are light-skinned Negroes signifying that their past master's blood runs through their veins as slave girls were also legitimate in their owner's bed. Those who possess jet black complexion take pride in the fact that their blood has not been polluted.

The Negroes are cursed by God, was the favourite slogan once. If their entry into white churches was banned, it was according to the will of the God. In Michelangelo's city, Florence, there is the famous 'Door of Paradise' on display in a square. The door has six embossed panels depicting stories from the Bible and one of them is about Hazrat Noah and his sons. When my travel companion Wendy approached an elderly American for the details of the story, he explained it in the following words.

"After the great flood subsided, Noah set foot upon dry land and cultivated grapes to make wine. He was in his tent when his son Ham entered and saw the nakedness of his father and turned back. Then his son Sham took the precaution of spreading a sheet in front of his eyes and talked to his father through it. Because of what Ham saw, Noah put a curse on him till eternity, his fair colour turned into jet black and all these Negroes and dark people are the off-springs of Ham. Young lady, you should not be associating with this coloured man either."

Wendy, herself a thoroughbred American, in turn cursed the old man and then apologized to me, saying, "We still have sick people in our society."

For the Negroes of America, the message of Islam was a breath of fresh air in the suffocating racist society they faced. They found great appeal in the message that all human beings are equal in the eyes of Allah, no one is superior because of his race, cast or colour, the superiority is only in obedience to Allah. Naturally, Hazrat Bilal is the role model for them, a common Negro slave freed by Hazrat Abu Bakar, rises to such dignified heights that he becomes one of the closest companions of the prophet. After the conquest of Mecca, the Holy Prophet takes him into the sanctuary of Ka'aba, requests him to say the first Azan in Ka'aba.

Even the great Caliphs bowed before him out of respect, and would not speak till he chose to say something. When Hazrat Umer dismissed Khalid Bin Walid, commander-in-chief of the Muslim army, he requested Hazrat Bilal to deliver the dismissal order to Khalid who, at that moment, was about to conquer Damascus because he feared that Khalid may rebel and invade Madina instead. Hazrat Bilal, according to the orders of the Caliph, tied the hands of Khalid with his turban and in presence of the whole army pronounced his dismissal.

Then Hazrat Bilal said, "O, Khalid, these were the orders of the Caliph of the faithfuls and it was my duty as a Muslim to execute them. Now I will do what my heart desires." Hazrat Bilal untied his hands and wrapped the turban on his head and then prayed for him.

I have the honour of visiting the tomb of this beacon of light for the oppressed and blacks of the world in Damascus.

Dr Ali Shariety in his book Hajj states, "Amongst all humanity, a woman, amongst all women, a black slave woman whose name was Hajira, Hajj is basically paying tribute to her." And when you analyze this statement, you reach the conclusion that almost all the rituals of Hajj are directly related to our mother Hajra, wife of Hazrat Ibrahim and mother to his son Hazrat Ismail, who in turn was the forefather of our prophet (PBUH). Ummatul

Momnin Hazrat Maria Qibtia, who was the mother of Hazrat Ibrahim, the last son of the Holy Prophet (PBUH) was also dark skinned. The Holy Prophet instructed his followers that after his death when they will conquer the lands from where Hazrat Maria Qibtia came, they should treat those people kindly because they are his relatives.

In those days when these blacks were declared the children of Ham, a proud slogan emerged from this very Harlem — Black is beautiful. Black music, black faces, black culture — all that is black is beautiful.

I heard an old gentleman selling mineral water in Harlem and declaring it, "Black water". This slogan again was inspired by Alex Haley's The Roots. The Negroes who previously tried their utmost to be like the whites, wearing their dress, copying their mannerism and with the help of chemicals bleached their dark complexion, suddenly abandoned this attitude and became Afro-Americans. They adopted the ways and dresses of their ancestral Africa, the culture of Masai and Zulu tribes, wearing the same ornaments, doing their hair in pleats, wearing long robes and even carried the fly sticks of the African chiefs just to prove that they had a distinct culture of their own.

The tattoo craze which has gripped America has its roots in Harlem as this form of decorating the body was prevalent is Africa. Every second shop in Harlem is a tattoo parlour where this black art is practised. Get your body decorated with animals, flowers, cartoons, slogans, human and inhuman faces, anything which takes your fancy.

Almost 80 years ago this form of body art was very popular in our part of the world also. My father use to tell me that it was very fashionable in his childhood days and he, along with a friend, had their names tattooed on their arms when they visited a mela as kids. My father, when he blossomed into a tall and handsome youth, felt ashamed of this tattoo because according to him this art form was adopted by all tonga walas and drug addicts so he had it removed. But thanks to Harlem, once again tattoo is the "in" thing, especially the tattoo which is invisible works wonders. I had the occasion to meet a Pakistani lady who had a very funny elephant tattooed on her shoulder and was rather proud of it.

However, the credit of establishing that black is beautiful actually goes to our very own Noorjehan when she sang "Kala siyah kala, sadha kala hai dildar te gorian noon paran karo" which can roughly be translated as, "Black, jet black, my beloved is black and the whites can go to hell".

I am sure that in the near future when the Negroes of America become aware of this great song, they will declare it as their national anthem.

Who is on the right track?

It clearly goes to the credit of Jew ingenuity that they have resurrected all the men, women and children from the ashes of gas chambers and made them walk on the media, newspaper and Europe's guilty conscience as if they are still alive. These victims of the atrocities committed by the Nazis are the trump card which they used for the establishment of Israel, and are still using it for the continuous military and financial support of the West and America. Jewish film-makers and intellectuals were mainly responsible for keeping the holocaust tragedy alive and indeed it is a great achievement on their part.

However, in the meantime, the human tragedies which occurred in Palestine, Africa, Chechnya and in other parts of the globe were completely forgotten as they did not have genius film-makers, authors and historians who could record and imprint the atrocities their nations suffered.

Take the case of Spielberg, perhaps the most talented and innovative director in Hollywood, who would produce The Schindler's List but would conveniently forget as to what happened in Sabira, Shatila and Janin. Or how hundreds of ancient Palestinian towns and villages were bulldozed along with the centuries old orchards and the ancestral graveyards, their occupants either massacred or evicted forcibly. And then the new Israeli towns and settlements were built on this land which did not belong to them. Even the names of these ancient towns and villages were erased from the official maps along with their history. Instead, their Jewish past was dug up and a new history was created.

When an Israeli massacred dozens of Palestinians praying in the mosque of Abraham, he was dubbed as a madman and not as a terrorist, mind you. I assure Mr Spielberg that all these subjects are also excellent film material and I am sure that Mr Spielberg would assure me in return that let there be a Palestinian Spielberg to do the job.

Along with other holocaust victims, the Dutch girl Anne Frank is still alive. After the end of war, her father, who managed to save his life from the Nazis, returned to his house in Amsterdam where in a cellar he found some of the pages of Anne's diary. "We have no food left, I have not eaten anything for last two days and I am very hungry .... During the night I could hear the sound of German Boots who are searching for Jews, how am I different from other little girls that they want to kill me."

The diary of Anne Frank was published by her father and it became an instant hit throughout Europe and subsequently was translated into all the major languages of the world. During my visit to Amsterdam, I also visited the "Anne Frank House" which is a museum now, displaying some personal effects, family photographs, original pages of the diary and the translated versions. There is the "Anne Frank Foundation" which sees to it that her memory does not fade away. I also contributed a few guilders because for me she was not a Jewish girl, but just a girl who should not have died.

There was only one Anne Frank.

And there were dozens of Anne Franks who were shot while playing with dolls or bulldozed by Israelis and some of them maintained little diaries which were published in the Arab world. I had the occasion to read some of their extracts and they moved me to tears. After a while these diaries, just like the little girls who wrote them, went into oblivion only because their writers were not Jewish but Muslims and Christians.

One of them was a girl with golden hair, when in the middle of night the Israelis attacked their ancient village and started massacring the population and bulldozing their homes. she was so terrified that she just ran out of her home and kept on running. After a few months her moth-eaten body was discovered in a wheat field, only her golden hair remained and amongst them sprouted the golden corns of wheat shining in the sun. This Anne Frank had also written a diary describing the fear of oncoming Israelis and the way they had already murdered some of her relatives but this dairy also met the same fate.

Their one Anne Frank is remembered and is still living but dozens of our Anne Franks are not only dead but forgotten because we do not have the genius and planning of the Jews.

Although Jews are amongst my favourite nations because we have so much in common, but they have built a wall of hatred between us, the wall of Israel. However, the Pakistanis living in America are all praise for the local Jewish population, in their opinion only a small minority is adverse to Muslims, the rest of them are very liberal and feel closer to Muslims than the Christians. An average Pakistani will prefer to work for a Jewish boss who is very honest in his dealings and very helpful in times of distress.

A certain person by the name of Hussain Khan went to America almost 16 years ago. At one time he was working at the front desk of a hotel chain in New York. After about a year, his Jewish boss called him and said, "Hussain, I have been observing your conduct for a long time and I have found you hard working, honest and intelligent. You should not be spending your life on a front desk of a hotel. You deserve a much better mode of life. Son, if you want to progress in America you should first of all know the system in which you work."

The boss suggested some banking and finance courses which Hussain completed and now he is almost a millionaire as a consequence. He is trusted so much that he manages the affairs of a synagogue which his boss patronizes. The Jewish boss also appreciates his commitment to Islam and at times reminds him about his prayers, saying, "Hussain, go and pray".

Recently, when he built a new hotel of his chain, Hussain was given a proper share in it.

Another very interesting episode I would like to share with the readers. Hussain's elder brother, Fareed Khan who is a very devout Muslim, dresses in a long robe, a huge turban and naturally with a flowing beard. Soon after 9/11 his deportation was ordered because he had not informed the home department when he changed his last abode. Hussain immediately challenged this order in a court of law through a Chinese lawyer who was a close friend.

On the day of the hearing, Hussain received a call from the lawyer who said, "Hussain, start packing your brother's belongings, he is going to be deported in next half an hour."

"Has the judge already rejected the appeal?" Hussain's heart sank.

"It will be for sure, you know in what costume your brother has entered the courtroom? In a long robe, wearing a turban and carrying a prayer rug under his arm for heavens sake! And you know on top of it the judge is a Jew!"

The final verdict was such a surprise that nobody believed it. The judge had declared that he respects all those people who are committed to their faith and dress accordingly. So his appeal was accepted. The next day the Jewish judge sent the prayer rug which Fareed Khan had forgotten in the courtroom to his home with a Shalom.

Well there are both good and bad ones among the Jews, as there are in all other faiths.

The Jews and the Muslims

In my last column, King Solomon's Temple, I mistakenly referred to Herman the Jew as a "Hanud" whereas he was a "Yahud". The mistake occurred due to the frequent use of our favourite term "Hanud-o-Yahud" in Pakistan and I also got mixed up, although Nattha Singh and Prem Singh are one and the same thing, even then my apologies for the blunder.

Any way our fears that Herman was taking us downstairs to sacrifice us as rams on the altar of Solomon, were totally unfounded. Instead he treated us with some delicious brownies along with steaming hot coffee in a cellar which looked like a class room of sorts, perhaps a madrassah where Jewish fundamentalists were trained.

"Now this is my grand daughter, isn't she the prettiest thing in the world?" Herman showed us a framed photograph of a little girl who was so plain and ordinary that imagination had to be stretched to the limit to call her pretty, which I did, and then I produced my trump card, a photo of Noffel and showed it to Herman "Now this is my grandson."

"Well, he is almost as pretty as my granddaughter," he exclaimed.

This Herman the Jew must be stone blind I decided and did not pursue the matter further.

It is a strange phenomenon that Jews do not accept Christianity. And both Jews and Christians do not accept us, Muslims. But as the people of the book, not only do we accept them but it is part of our faith that Moses and Jesus were true prophets of Allah as we are the true followers of Din-i-Ibrahimi. So it is natural that in faith we Muslims are very close to Jews and there are a lot of similarities.

Jews greet each other with "Shalom" and we say "Salam" when we meet.

We consider the pig totally Haram and Jews also refrain from eating it.

We only eat Zabiha meat and Jews have their equivalent of kosher meat. Like us they fast. Their skull cap is similar to our Namazi Topi, and their dress code is very strict. On the streets of New York you will come across neatly dressed Jews, men in black suits and women in ankle length skirts and they never wear jeans or revealing dresses. We believe that a Muslim has no nationality; but Jews have proved it in the span of thousands of years and perhaps this is one of the reasons that they were persecuted throughout history as they did not abandon their faith and never committed themselves to any nationality. Jews actually suffered because of their conviction and remaining steadfast to their belief. They are very strict as far as personal hygiene is concerned. And they, like us, get circumcized.

In modern times as soon as the male child is born the needful is done immediately by a competent doctor; but in old days circumcision of a male child used to be a joyous event celebrated by the whole family. I wonder why have we abandoned this festive custom?

I still remember the day when I was hardly two years old when I felt that there was something special in the air. My mother was dressed as if she was going to a wedding and the women in the family were chirping and humming and extra ordinary love and kisses were being showered upon me. Even the servants wore new clothes and there were baskets full of Moti Choor Laddus wonderfully decorated. Little did I know what was in store for me. Then Ibrahim Nai, holding a small black bag, entered the house and my beaming father welcomed him like an old friend which he was. Needless to say that I was also dressed in a silk shirt, just the shirt mind you. I was garlanded heavily and then my father lovingly carried me to the roof of the house where two bricks were already placed in closed vicinity. I was made to sit on those bricks and I sat on them willingly because I was sure that we were going to play some new game. In the meantime Ibrahim Nai had opened his black bag and I don't recollect what fatal instrument he brought out of it. Then he sat right in front of me and suddenly looking upwards towards the sky he said, "Mustansar look a cheel is carrying a donkey."

I involuntarily looked up towards the sky and who would not look up if a cheel was carrying a donkey and at that particular moment the needful was performed and I was never the same again.

Jews and Muslims have been very close to each other not only through some common beliefs but have had a very strong relationship throughout history. They were included in the "Millat" by the Holy Prophet (PBUH) in the Islamic state of Medina. The most glorious chapter of the Muslim and Jewish co-operation is the common heritage of Undlus which lasted for almost 700 years. Some of the greatest philosophers, writers and Hakims of Muslim Spain were Jews, among them Ibne Maimun was the personal physician of the great Saladin. Maimun died in Cairo and according to his will his body was carried on the same path which was taken by Moses when he guided the Banu Israel out of Egypt. In Cairo, there is still a synagogue by the name of Maimun. Local Jews believe that someone with an incurable disease can be cured if he spends a night there. However, Alqafti states that Ibne Maimun embraced Islam before dying. In the old quarters of Almanzar and Ibne Rushd where in Arabs times Jewish population of Cordoba resided, I saw a memorial bust of this great Physician in front of his old house. Out of hundreds of prime ministers of Granada most were of Jewish faith, so much so that a Jewish historian claimed that the famous Alhamra was actually built by Jews — he could be partly right. When finally the Christian reconquest took place the wrath of the conquerors fell upon Jews heavily. They were massacred for their co-operation with Muslims and were deported along with Muslims. After the fall of Granada in 1492 the Sultan of Turkey welcomed them and rehabilitated them in Istanbul where to date descendants of those Undlasi Jews reside.

However, this historical relationship ended the day the state of Israel was established on the lands and bodies of the Palestinians. The day, according to western terminology, terrorism was born. I believe that Israel was the greatest injustice in the history of humanity and if there was no Israel this world would have been a comparatively peaceful place to live in. There would not have been any George Habbash, Laila Khalid or Hamas or 9/11 for that matter. I always get amazed that victims of the holocaust, which let's face it did take place — though its extent can be debated — the same people when in power descend upon Sabira, Shatila, Hanin and Ghaza and they are capable of committing such atrocities which even the Nazis would admire. I am also amazed that the Christian right in America fanatically supports Israel without realizing that a vast number of Palestinians are staunch Christians — Laila Khalid and George Habbash being two of them.

On American media a very aggressive campaign has been launched to rescue the poor Jews from their countries of birth and send them to Israel. "Fellow Americans, if you donate just $350 to the noble cause a homeless Jew can fly to Israel. If you give $700, a Jewish couple in distress can be helped to settle in Israel. And if you send $1400, a whole Jewish family can go to the promised land." Along with these appeals heart-wrenching scenes of Jews arriving in Israel, weeping by the wailing wall are flashed. Among these zealots is singer Pat Boone who in our heyday used to sing "Don't forbid me to kiss your lips". The Christian right believes that when all the Jews will be gathered in one place then once again Christ will descend from heavens and convert the whole world into Christians, including the gathered Jews. Jews don't mind this notion as long as the money is pouring in.

(To be concluded)

King Solomon's Temple

While strolling through the patchwork quilt of Greenwich Village, fascinated and captivated, we chanced upon a small synagogue and we knew that it was a synagogue because a Star of David was engraved on top of the entrance and an announcement was displayed on a board stating the following:

"Congregation Darech Amuno Sabbos Kithavo, Fri 6.20pm, Sat 9.30am & 8pm. NITZAVIM, Rabbi Yossie Rosenbaum."

Now please do not expect me to tell you what exactly it means, because I do not have a clue except that some Rabbi by the name of Yossie Robenbaum was to hold a congregation. And what luck that Rabbi was standing right in front of the main door in person, so we approached him. He was a beardless Rabbi wearing a black hat and was rather unimpressive. We introduced ourselves as Pakistani Muslims.

"Oh, you are from Pakistan" he shook our hands warmly and was so overjoyed that we suspected that he was some sort of Jewish tableeghi fellow who wanted to convert us, and then with sparkling eyes he asked, "You know Dr Qureshi?"

"No, we don't. Who is he?"

"My personal physician that is who. A gem of a person Dr Qureshi. How is it possible that if you are Pakistanis, you do not know Dr Qureshi? He is also from Pakistan, a very able doctor I tell you. You must know his sons...." and he started narrating the personal details of Dr Qureshi's sons, their profession, number of children they had and what they liked for dinner, etc.

After a long discourse, finally we convinced him that we really did not know this Dr Qureshi because we were new around New York and asked him whether he was Rabbi Yossie waiting for the faithful.

"No, no. I am just a caretaker of this synagogue. Basically, I am an IT engineer and my name is Herman. Are you sure you do not know Dr Qureshi?"

Now I knew how a communal riot between Jews and Muslims starts. It starts because of this Dr Qureshi, but we refrained from this course as we were definitely outnumbered by the powerful Jews of New York. You only start a communal riot when you are in a thumping majority, like we do back home.

"So Herman, you are the caretaker of this place and standing outside you are taking care of it."

"Well, I am standing outside the synagogue for three reasons. It is such a beautiful day, sunny and soothing. Perhaps the brightest day of the summer of New York so I am inhaling the calm beauty of it. The second reason is that I was preparing some chocolate brownies in my kitchen and forgot to add sugar in them. I felt so frustrated that I had come out to forget the tragedy. And the real reason why I am here is that my bathroom tap is leaking and I am waiting for the plumber who is coming to fix it. Do you know that in New York a plumber will simply touch your tap and charge you a hundred dollars for it?"

"No, we don't know because our taps are not leaking as yet."

"And pray to God that they never do, you will be bankrupt trying to have them fixed by a plumber. Isn't it agonizing to have a tap in your bathroom which is leaking continuously?"

He, this Herman was surely the most talkative Jew this side of Tel Aviv.

"Do you mind if I take a snap of your synagogue?"

"Oh, sure! Although you don't know Dr Qureshi."

When I pointed my digital camera towards the entrance of the synagogue, Herman immediately stepped aside. "Do not take my photo, just the synagogue."

In the meantime, Seljuk was peeping through the synagogue door curiously and Herman was good enough to invite us inside. It was a very simple place of worship, Victorian wooden stools, the copies of Torah placed on the shelf. It could hardly seat a few dozen faithful and at the end of the benches there was an altar covered with a red silky carpet.

"In the Temple of Solomon there used to be an altar of this shape where during worship two rams were sacrificed as an offering to the Lord Jehovah."

"Do you still sacrifice rams around here?"

"No." Herman smiled mischievously, "Rams are hard to find in New York and even if you find them they are very expensive, besides the law does not permit us to sacrifice."

"Can I take a few photographs around here?

"Why not."

I handed over the camera to Seljuk and placed myself near the King Solomon altar and tried to look solemn. "Herman why don't you join me?"

"I cannot be photographed today, it's Sabbath."

So Herman was a very fundamental Jew because on Sabbath day his community refrains from spending any money, does not light any fire even to cook the meals and do not like to be photographed.

Behind the altar stood two Greek pillars which were most probably a replica of those pillars on which stood the Temple of Solomon. On both sides of the pillars, typical Jewish candle stands were placed which are called "Manara". According to Herman, when the Romans devastated Jerusalem they looted King Solomon's temple and carried these Manaras to Rome. Even now one can see some sculptures in which the Roman soldiers are carrying these sacred Manaras.

Herman was a talkative Jew but I was sure he was not one of those "Hanuds" who were all the time hatching conspiracies against us innocent Muslims. Actually, we should be thankful to such conspiring Hanuds, because if they were not there who would we blame for all our failures and defeats? Recently, a campaign to allow Saudi woman to drive was also declared as a conspiracy of these scheming Hanuds.

After thanking Herman for his kindness, we were about to depart when he suddenly exclaimed "Do you know that I have become a grand dad. Have you seen my granddaughter?"

Now how could we have seen the granddaughter of a wandering Jew? I just smiled back and said politely, "Well no, but we would love to see her sometime."

"She is not around today but I have a very lovely photograph of her downstairs. Please come along." he did not wait for our consent and led us towards some dark and dingy stairs, probably leading to some underground abode. While going down those mysterious stairs a strange fear gripped me. Where is this Jew taking us and why. Right now nobody in New York knows that we are being led down to a cellar of a synagogue and God knows for what purpose.

Maybe, after all, he is a conspiring Jew and is planning to sacrifice us on the altar of King Solomon simply because rams are very expensive in New York. I was not all that worried about myself because I was a foggy old ram whos had lost some of his teeth and was not fit enough for a sacrifice. However, I was worried about the young ram beside me.

But Herman the Jew was definitely a good one because he offered us another cup of hot coffee and at least half a dozen more brownies. Finally, the much-awaited plumber appeared and we were vastly relieved. While parting, I thanked him profusely for his hospitality and said "Herman our faiths have a lot in common, only you are slightly off the track."

"Well only on the Day of Judgment, it will be decided as to who is on the right track and who is off track, you or us," he smiled amicably and went back to his synagogue.

Beggars of New York

NEW York subway is a throbbing and rattling city rushing through the veins of New York like a Wall Street bronze bull gone mad all of a sudden. This city vibrating underground is also blind and the occupants of its hurtling compartments are not made of flesh and blood but of cold and lifeless stone.

They are totally engrossed in their magazines, laptops, girlfriends and grocery lists — each and every one a statue displayed in the museum of human desires and greed. Only you are alive and watching with fascination this gallery of lifeless objects. However, as soon as the train slows down for the next stop some of these statues come to life and start moving towards the exit door.

If you step into any European country, within a few days' stay you become familiar with the language, faces, food, sense of humour, cultural traits and wine and women. For instance, if you are in Germany, you are aware that all around you is the continuity of an established way of life and history. There is Munich beer, sausages, Gunther Grass, Herman Hesse, Karl Marx, Hitler, Freud, Bach and black forest and you feel comfortable, but not so in America. In the compartments of subway all the sardines packed are of different species, different nationalities — Spanish, Asians, Africans — you name it and they are there. And, of course, with their different languages, food habits and body languages but where are the Americans? How very dull a subway ride would have been if on and off the beggars did not appear with their fascinating personalities.

In Pakistan, a beggar does not have to declare that he is beggar, you can spot him from a mile because his looks and attire are in accordance to the demands of his profession, he is dressed properly for the occasion, so to speak. But in the New York subway, a gentleman sitting right next to you formally dressed reading the eveninger will take off his spectacles, get up from his seat and will start begging. Just like in Pakistan, he will unfold some medical reports and prescriptions and will deliver a heart rending speech. "Ladies and gentlemen I am a self respecting citizen but a life threatening illness has forced me to appeal to your generosity and human kindness. My illness is such that I have to swallow dozens of very costly pills and capsules to keep myself alive. If I miss a day I am sure to be dead duck the very next morning. If you are in doubt, you can personally check my medical reports or just observe my face. Don't you see the shadow of death hovering over it? Would you let me die? You cannot be that heartless, letting a self-respecting man die by not going through your pockets, I will accept change willingly. The number of coins you donate to this noble cause will be equivalent to the number of minutes I will live." Naturally the dying gentleman has a crumpled hat or card box ready for the first note or coin coming out of a generous pocket. I do not remember a single subway journey which was without the appearance of these colourful and interesting characters. There were singers and musicians also who at times were of a very high calibre.

Another such personality had a very unique and philosophical approach, a long haired bespectacled young man carrying a load of books, invites the attention of the passengers and says: "I want to pose a question which will have far reaching effects on the society in which we live in. This society demands that each and every one should work for his living, earn his own bread and butter. Do you think this demand is justified? Why should everybody work, it is essential for the betterment of society that some people who posses a high degree of intellect should not work and just think. I am one of those persons, I do not want to work, I just want to sit down and contemplate the problems which human beings are facing. What is the direction of our society, which way is America heading? Is there a God and if there is why is He not doing enough. So this is your responsibility to support me, I know you have plenty of money and some of it is my right, so please come out with some dollars. I will accept anything, even food."

During this highly-charged lecture, he spots a Filipino girl munching a sandwich and approaches her: "Lady I don't think you are enjoying this sandwich very much. Why don't you give it to me."

The lady is taken aback and hands over the half-finished sandwich without comprehending as to what is happening. The long haired young man receives this voluntary gift with a bow and starts relishing the sandwich.

That "devil" of an actor and writer Kamal Ahmad Rizvi had the same intellectual ideas in his youth. When he was in Lahore he would occasionally invite me to his stylish abode, a house designed by incomparable Nayyar Ali Dada which was situated nearby. Kamal is during the sunlight hours very subdued and rather morose but as soon as the sun sets, he rises. During one of these very enjoyable evenings when he had risen and was full of golden rays, he recounted the days of his youth when he was trying his luck in the field of literature and was naturally penniless.

"You know Tarar how I survived? I used to enter Pak Tea House with a flourish and head straight to one of my friends sitting there. For instance Khalid Iqbal or Shakir Ali and would say 'It is your duty to support me because you are a friend and you have the money and I don't. Don't expect me to return it, just give to me because I am serving the cause of literature.' And they willingly obliged me."

Eventually Kamal had more money than he could count but, according to him, he never even thought of returning his loans as they were not a loan but a duty which the friends performed. During my stay in Montreal, I was roaming around in the old quarter of the city with a friend when a buxom young lady whose jeans were so low on her hips that some of the contours which are supposed to be hidden were rather prominent, approached us. "Do you have some change?" she asked and displayed an empty ice cream cup for the purpose. She was expensively dressed and rather pretty.

After a while, another neatly dressed girl with a poodle in her lap came along, "Would you buy my dog some food?" My friend informed me that these girls were not professional beggars but were doing it just for fun. I also observed two very smart girls squatting on the footpath smoking and laughing heartily, and they had a small cup placed in front of them and were asking for money from the passerbys. So the way their mice and our mice are different, their beggars and our beggars are also representatives of our cultures.

Another such character was probably Spanish or Italian. He was indeed an angry young man: "What do you know about life sitting pretty in your seats munching burgers, you cannot imagine what this life has done to me, the way I was mistreated by my friends and relatives — everybody deceived me. I am emotionally so upset that I cannot work and it is your solemn duty to provide for me," and when nobody paid any attention or money he almost shouted: "Don't you hear me, a human being in distress, is asking you to help him and you are busy reading your damn newspapers." While getting off the train at Times Square, he was almost abusing everybody loudly because he could not get a single dime from the passengers.

But the most dramatic and award winning entry was that of an Afro-American lady who was holding her head back and displaying her belly which most probably had some form in it which by the look of it could be born any moment. "Any SOB can see that I am pregnant, by whom, I do not know. If I ever find out who the bastard is, I will strangle him but in the meantime I do not have a health insurance so how and where am I going to have this innocent baby? In Central Park or on top of the Empire State Building, where? And after giving birth shall I, along with my innocent babe, drown us in river Hudson or where, you tell me. I do not know whose baby it is."

She approached an elderly gentleman, "Could be yours for all I know or yours or may be yours." She pointed an accusing finger at almost all the males travelling in the compartment but, regretfully, she did not accuse me although she was displaying her wares right in front of me. Believe me, I was deeply depressed, am I so worthless or innocent looking that I could not be bestowed with this dubious honour? My manly pride was hurt beyond redemption. Would you not feel the same way if you were in my place?

The village that is Greenwich

The pale rays of an autumn afternoon were like a painter's brush which was painting the footpaths, cars, iron railings and faces with subdued golden colour, turning them into some ancient Maya gold ornaments. The flowering creepers which clung to the abodes of poets, artists, intellectuals and gays were also turning golden, and their red and pink flowers followed suit changing to golden flames. These pale rays at times brightened a pretty face and while the sunshine was left behind, the face carried those illuminating rays with it.

The autumn leaves littered the footpaths, with a rustle of wind, moved like a brown lazy snake. This magical afternoon of miraculous pale rays had only descended upon a village situated right in the middle of Madness of New York called Greenwich, and we were wonder-struck with its amazing shades of light, its ancient houses, bars and art shops that seemed to be roaming around like children lost in a forest of creativity.

The dress sense of its inhabitants was unique and very artistic, unusual and subdued, nothing flashy or flamboyant. Even the showcases were entirely different from the Fifth Avenue's display of abundant wealth and gaudiness. Here in Greenwich village it was subtle taste which was displayed in colours matching with the autumn leaves and pale sun rays. Please do not smile when I state that even the dogs looked sober and well-mannered.

There was nothing in the colours, faces or dresses which hurt the eye. It was soothing and pleasant to look, just like its resident poets, writers, artists and gays because this category of humans is basically peaceful and does not believe in hurting anyone. They want to be left alone with their strange pursuits. I saw a hunchbacked old lady, who was dressed in a blue denim skirt and jacket wearing a large flowery hat. She could hardly walk but she had not given up on life and was fully enjoying it, so much so that her jacket on her hunched back was also beautifully decorated with a sunflower pattern. There are cozy coffeehouses, bars, bakeries and some strange shops which specialize in gay dresses and jackets. We chanced upon a showcase which was displaying specially designed sweaters for dogs with matching leather leashes.

The inhabitants of New York lovingly call this area "the village", and rightly so because in 1822 when the yellow fever epidemic raged in the city, some of the inhabitants shifted to a village on the outskirts where there was fresh air, farmhouses and streams. In recent history, this area became the refuge of gays and queers, and the police often raided their bars and meeting places as homosexuality had not become a fashion as yet. Now the queers are legally married and even church bishops declare their gay tendencies with pride. At least in this field we were far ahead of Europe and America, even now in some parts of our country it is fashionable for a well-to-do-person to dress his male companion expensively and parade with him during the evening walks with a musician playing romantic tunes, creating waves of jealousy in the onlookers as why they were not so fortunate to have such a beautiful male friend. Totally normal and acceptable I assure you. Our poetry, Urdu or Persian, is also very appreciative of male sexuality and most of our sufi poets chose to be in love with some Madhu Lal.

Greenwich village has dozens of very illustrious personalities to its credit as frequent visitors or as permanent residents, including actor Cary Grant, writer O'Henry who penned his 1902 work The Last Leaf here and I have a special love for this O'Henry, not because of his stories but due to a humorous reference by great Shafiqur Rehman who named him as "Abe O Henery".

The famous playwright Eugene O'Neil, along with John Reed, lived in Patchin Place whose eyewitness account of the Russian revolution The Ten Days which shook the World was filmed by Warren Beatty as Reds. The inimitable Mark Twain lived on the 10th Street, and in a bar named "Ninth Circle bar" playwright Edward Albee saw the question "Who is Afraid of Virginia Wolf" scrawled on a mirror which was the origin of his famous play of the same title. Edgar Allen Poe read his famous story The Raven for the first time in a literary moot just around the corner. For Irish tourists The White Horse Bar is a place of pilgrimage because their most loved poet Dillon Thomas drank himself to death here. So, in his memory, the Irish try to drink themselves to death and when they fail to do so, despite flooding their throats with drums of alcohol, they start singing his poetry with these flooded throats.

Seljuk and I were actually strolling through the patchwork quilt of Greenwich village, following the instructions of a tourist guide book and were loving it. It was easily the most captivating part of New York which touched my heart and if it, my heart, was a violin, surely I could hear the melody of The blue Danube vibrating through its strings.

During this enchanting walk I spotted an elegant shop of frames and art prints and my eyes focused on a large size print of Lautrec's Moulin Rouge which attracted me. Although I had obtained a number of reprints of famous paintings from Metropolitan, Moma and Guggenheim museum shops but this was the poster I was looking for. The shop owner, who looked like a Mongol, came towards us and then suddenly burst into a broad smile, "Wah Tarar sahib what a surprise! When did you come to New York?" he said in chaste Urdu.

"Well, I have been here for some time and when did you come?"

"About eighteen years ago. I am from Peshawar. We are of Uzbek stock but my elders settled in Peshawar centuries ago, I will go and fetch you a coke or something." He made no attempt to fetch anything so it was established that he had been in America for 18 years and his Peshawari hospitality had evaporated in the meantime.

"You have a splendid showroom here," the premises were rather spacious considering the rents in this area.

"Well Tarar sahib, I use to watch you on television when I was a kid and I have read some of your books also so you are a relative of sorts. I will let you into a secret, the premises is owned by an Italian gentleman who has a small office in the back, he comes here attends to his business quietly and leaves and nobody bothers him."

"Why should anybody bother him?"

"Well, sir, in New York if somebody wants to earn an honest buck, the police won't let him do it. Here I run the frame shop in front and he has his office in the back and he charges me nominal rent so both of us are happy. May be some ignorant people call them Italian Mafia, but Tarar sahib they are honest and God fearing people, ready to help the poor and needy, but look what ex-mayor Giuliani has done."

"The very energetic Mayor of New York at the time of 9/11? I hear he made Harlem a safe place and cleared the gangster crowd from Times Square area."

"Yes, the same mayor. He also crushed the Italian Mafia ruthlessly, and thereby paved the way for the brutal and heartless Russian Mafia which is a tragedy because the Italians had a strict moral code. They did not touch women and children, but the Russians, they stop at nothing."

The Uzbek Peshawari gentleman definitely had a soft corner for Italian Mafia but none for the ex-Mayor of New York.

As we came out of his shop without inquiring the price of the much-desired poster simply because we did not want to be involved with any kind of Mafia, Italian or Russian. He insisted that we must visit an Italian bar run by a Pakistani and frequented by Al-Pacino and Woody Allen. The owner was not there and neither were the celebrities mentioned, so we just said Hello to the buxom lady tending the bar and came out.

"Tarar sahib can you please give me your visiting card, my mother will be very pleased to see it. She was very fond of watching the cartoons in your morning show"

I hope the card really reached the old lady and will not be found by the New York police in the drawer of some Mafia boss. We were shortly to meet Herman, the Jew, outside Greenwich Village's only synagogue, who offered us some very tasty self-made brownies.

The bitter Rice

The images flashing on television screens are familiar. I wonder why such old footage of the Second World War is being shown again and again! Exodus: thousands of dark-haired people forced to leave their ancestral homes, children carrying small suitcases and dolls, old men with fear of death writ large on their wrinkled faces, women whose eyes refuse to dry, the rivers of tears make the landscape muddy, their homes collapsing under the impact of ruthless bombing, and then the burnt and charred bodies of hundreds of children — an act of ethnic cleansing.

I know my history. I am not dumb. Then why am I being shown these old images of the Second World War? My heart bleeds for these thousands of European Jews who are to be massacred or burnt in gas chambers, evicted from their ancestral homes, old men weeping, children starving. For heavens sake, why is the media showing the images of holocaust once again?

Wait a minute, though the scenes of misery and murder are the same and the faces of holocaust victims are no different, the backdrop seems to be very modern. The bloodied faces of dead children are pierced by shrapnel. And then I spot a car of the 2006 model in the footage. Besides, Jews were evicted from their homes, but their homes were not destroyed or burnt. All of this is very puzzling and disturbing; but as you are aware that I am a genius of sorts, and I have spent some time in Europe too, I solve the puzzle immediately.

To celebrate their famous battles or to commemorate some of the historical events of their past, some nations have the tradition of recreating those battles and events with the local population as main actors, so that their younger generation and the world at large should not forget their past glories or the tragedies of their history. The tradition of "passion play" in Germany is very well known where the crucifixion of Christ is enacted with the whole village taking part as actors. The person who plays Christ becomes famous overnight. Now this must be the explanation for this puzzle. As the majority of the Israelis are of European descent, they have brought along this tradition to the Promised Land. The most horrific part of their history is the holocaust, hence just to relive their past and remind the world of the atrocities committed by the Nazis, they are staging a "passion play". The Israelis have done a wonderful job. The play is well directed, each and every actor deserves an Oscar. Perhaps there are at least one million actors taking part in this drama. I suppose one million Oscars cannot be reproduced in such a short time, so a collective Oscar will do. If a woman weeps for her dead son, it seems in reality her son is dead and you weep with her. If a dead and burnt child is shown, you marvel at the makeup and the acting talent of the child who plays this role looking totally dead. The set which shows a city burnt and destroyed is a masterpiece as well — though it's a painting, you feel the heat.

I am also puzzled as to why the Israelis are not playing these roles themselves! Why did they have to hire Lebanese actors for the play? How could they spend the hard-earned money of their uncle Shylock for hiring one million actors? I suppose they wanted to watch this holocaust play as spectators and weep against the Wailing Wall. If you are an actor, you cannot show your real emotions; you cannot weep at will — imagine a dead child or a blown up old man weeping with a severed head. So they're forced to hire actors who're doing an excellent job. I hope they will keep this tradition alive and stage a replay next year; but again, wait a minute, the play is not ending as yet. May be it will continue till next year.

I am sorry but you have to wait another minute because I have committed a blunder. It is the age, you know. I have been watching television with the mute button on, hence the images are without any sound. I click the remote and the sounds of planes, falling bombs and cries of dying children fill the room. The statements of Israeli leaders are flying over the ruins of Lebanon like hungry vultures. "We are bombing civilians because all those homes are full of terrorists and if the children are killed that is not our fault. Every home is full of rockets, grenades and bombs which could kill innocent Israeli civilians. Can you imagine a home in Europe or America full of such weapons of mass destruction? If we do not destroy Hezbollah right now, tomorrow they will be sending rockets into Washington and London, so we are fighting for America and Europe." And the thankful Americans are applauding giving them enough time to destroy the whole of Lebanon.

Then there is madam Bitter Rice who could frighten the wits out of a horde of Draculas by just smiling at them. In my youth I had seen an Italian classic by the name of Bitter Rice, starring Anna Mogano. I never knew that I would someday see her in person, this Bitter Rice. Ask the whole of Middle East and they will testify that she is bitter, they have tasted her.

And then there is this mythical Muslim Umma. If a Muslim anywhere in the world is hurt, this Umma is supposed to feel the pain. The Saudis immediately condemned Hezbollah and Hamas branding them terrorists and almost justifying the Israeli invasion. In Washington, some Rabbis personally thanked the Saudi ambassador for his support for Israel. The Pakistanis also murmured something which nobody could hear and since then are sitting pretty in their uniforms. Even the masses are unmoved. They can destroy and burn their own cities for the glory of Islam, but it seems that right now Islam is not in danger, so they are sitting pretty. It appears that most of the world is totally in agreement with the great man of the last century, Sir Winston Churchill, who commented on the massacre of Arabs in Palestine that their killing is not an occasion to mourn because they are savages and mere camel-dung.

However, amongst all these vultures and the Muslim Umma there in Beirut is a man, a Pakistani man, who is in my humble opinion the greatest man of the century. In his torn black cap, militia shirt and a worn-out cotton bag slung over his old shoulders, trying to buy ambulances, food, medicine for the shattered humanity and at present heading towards the south of Lebanon to help the wounded and to bury the dead. I pray for the safety of Mr Abdul Sattar Edhi and his companions. He is more precious to me and the nation than all the leaders surrounding us, in or out of uniform.

Perhaps this is the first time in history that an element of fear can be detected in the gods of Israel. The rockets of Hezbollah are falling in the citadel of the Promised Land. Though the causalities are few, the psychological impact has shattered the Israelis. For them killing hundreds of Palestinians and now Lebanese children is a routine matter; but if an Israeli is hurt, they declare it holocaust.

The images of Lebanon and Beirut shown on television look very familiar, especially those of the port of Beirut. I know it like the back of my hand because in 1975 while my taxi was fired upon I escaped from a burning Beirut about to be plunged into a civil war from that very port.

The egg merchant and the moon

Almost a decade ago after traversing the largest ice mass in the world outside the Polar Regions, i.e. the Biafo Hesper glacier track, I along with my bewildered and snow bitten team members reached the first human settlement of Hesper village. During this 17-day trek through the wilderness of snow and mountain masses we had not encountered a single human being, hence we were rather overjoyed to be back in "civilization". But when we unfolded the latest newspaper, we were amazed to see that the headlines, editorials and issues were exactly the same which adorned our newspapers almost three weeks back.

Nothing, absolutely nothing, had changed. The world was whirling past us and we were still rooted to the same spot as far as politics, religion and issues were concerned.

I have recently returned from another wilderness adventure in Alaska where during an eleven thousand kilometer jeep ride which took more than 17 days to cover, I captured dozens of red foxes, rabbits, wild squirrels, one bull moose, numerous deers, wild horses, massive buffalos and a total of seven bears in my digital camera. I assure you when you encounter an animal in its original habitat, specially a cuddly black bear, it is simply magnificent, so much so that after seeing this bear beauty you don't want to set eyes upon another human being because they are rather ugly in comparison.

Anyway, when I returned from this bewildering experience and opened the first Pakistani newspaper, lo and behold! Nothing had changed in the past two months! We were still engulfed in the same old senseless controversies. While the world was whirling past us we were in the grip of moon madness and "in the line of fire", both non issues if we had an iota of grey matter. The self-elevated holy priests were hurling abuses at each other, calling the dissenting parties liars and declaring that the faithful who dared to celebrate Eid on Tuesday, refusing their verdict, were infidels. These infidels numbered in millions.

I saw a horde of these priests adorning the television screen with their beards and piety, jostling for a better camera position and then finally declaring that the moon had not been sighted due to hazy conditions. The nation was held hostage by these self-proclaimed holy men whose only job is to sow the seeds of disunity and, mind you, they do not perform this noble job for free. They get hefty sums, air tickets and five star accommodations just to gaze stupidly at the heavens.

Only yesterday the head priest demanded that if anybody dares to disagree with their verdict he should be punished by law. How these prophets of darkness long for the days of Ziaul Haq when imprisonments and lashes were the order of the day. One of the zealots gave the verdict that celebrating Eid on the same day throughout the country was against the Sunnah of the Holy Prophet. Pray where did he get this false information? Actually it suits the government in power to "feed" a few dozens of this religious royalty to keep their mouth shut. It is a bargain in fact.

On these auspicious occasions when we encounter them every year, I always miss Allama, the egg merchant. He was a big hunk of a man with a huge pot belly that was exhibited throughout the year because Allama adorned himself with just a dhoti, and if it was bitterly cold he will wear a cotton vest to oblige the populace. Being a Kashmiri, he was of fair complexion and his ears were so huge that if he wished he could flap them like a baby elephant's. Overall, he looked like a Japanese version of Buddha and could win any look-alike competition.

Allama was born in a remote Gujrat village by the name of Jokalian, which is also my ancestral reference and at the tender age of ten, abandoned home in search of a guru who could teach him astrology which was a passion with him. According to him, he finally reached a temple near Madras where a certain priest was known to possess the ancient knowledge of the universe. The hurdle was that only Hindus could benefit from his wisdom. But Allama by then possessed enough knowledge of Hinduism to pass for a devout Hindu boy. He studied this ancient science for years and became proficient in Hindi and Sanskrit in the meantime.

In time he opened a small khokha at the corner of Gowalmandi Chowk. At nine every morning, he received his supply of eggs packed in crates which he disposed off within the next 15 minutes to the whole sellers and then for the rest of the day he roamed around the area and chatted with friends, including my father. I loved to drag him into serious socio-religious discussions and at times asked some very provoking questions to irritate him.

"Allama sahib, do you think that God really exists or it is just a fabrication of the human mind?"

"Come here," he was standing near a vegetable seller munching a turnip and he gestured towards the North, "Can you see Gujranwala from here?"

"No, I can't," I said smilingly.

"But Gujranwala exists you know that so, why can't you see it?"

"Because of the structures, trees and towns which obstruct the view."

"All right, if nothing obstructs you and it is a plain from here to Gujranwala, then could you see it?"

"No, I would not be able to see it."

"Why."

"Because my vision cannot reach that far."

"So, like Gujranwala, God exists but your vision is limited."

Allama, even when he was a "Hindu", never missed a prayer and his study of Islam was amazing, but he was a sworn enemy of Mullahs, who in his opinion, were distorting the beauty of it.

It was the twenty ninth day of the Ramadan once and I asked him, "Allama sahib, kindly pray that the Eid moon is sighted this evening. The moon sighting ulema are to be on the top floor of the Habib Bank Plaza, let us see what they decide."

Allama blew his top. "Who are they to decide? They go against the Holy Scripture which says that the whole universe, sun and moon move according to a set plan by Allah. How dare they doubt it just for their halva?"

Then he let go a barrage of abuses for the moon sighters.

"Give me a piece of paper and a pen," he said. I immediately complied, he scribbled on it for few moments and gave it back to me. "I have written down the dates on which the moon of this Eid will be sighted for next thirty years."

I have consulted this piece of paper every Eid even after Allama's death and the moon was always there whether the ulemas could sight it or not. We need more of Allama, the egg merchant, than these shortsighted bigoted merchants of religion.

The Idiot Box

Guess who has produced the largest number of idiots in the world. Well it is the "Idiot Box" which we mistakenly call the television. It is in fact a machine which has the capability of turning a perfectly intelligent and normal human being into a perfect idiot if he keeps on gazing at it for a certain period of time. And believe me it is directly from the horse's mouth, and I am that horse because I have been associated with this box for almost 40 years now.

There was this high level meeting of the Ministry of Information where I was the only one with a low level, and the minister of information, a journalist-turned-spin-master, turned towards me and said, "Tarar sahib, how would you define as to what media is?"

"Sir, media means turning the masses into idiots."

The high and mighty of the information ministry present in the meeting smiled sarcastically to signify their displeasure at my definition and wondered as to why I was invited to this august gathering. Although the minister also smiled, but his smile was bathed in amusement, "Tarar sahib, we were expecting that you will come out with an in-depth and intellectual definition of the media."

"Well sir, if it is your desire then I will try to present such a definition, the media is in fact...." then I presented a thesis referring to culture, traditions, history and society, etc., and laced it heavily with references of Plato's Republic and Machiavelli's The Prince, and how these factors are ingrained in the minds of masses through media, making them better human beings, etc.

I noticed that this senseless discourse had the desired effect on the high and mighty and they were nodding their heads approvingly and before they came to the end of shaking business, I said, "However, if you sum up this definition, the conclusion will be, media means turning the masses into idiots."

I wonder why I was never invited to such a meeting again. Do you have any clue?

Not only in Pakistan but in most of the underdeveloped countries, the idiot-making box is at full swing. In the days when Z.A. Bhutto was sentenced to death, which was judicially managed by his God-fearing ex-army chief, I used to contribute the script for the morning show of Radio Pakistan Lahore. It was a normal practice to quote the Holy Quran and Ahadith for a pious beginning of that morning and for this purpose a selection of these Holy sayings was compiled by the radio library to facilitate the scriptwriter.

One day while consulting this compilation, I noticed that numerous quotations were crossed with a red marker, I was amazed. When I enquired from an insider, he said, "Well the President is receiving numerous appeals to pardon Bhutto, the press is also demanding that his death sentence should not be carried out hence all such quotations from the Holy Quran and Ahadith which refer to forgiveness and pardon are banned on the media."

So much for the God-fearing and Islam-loving President.

In the same era a dupatta policy was enforced when Mehtab Rashidi opted to abandon TV and refused to cover her head. There was this climax scene of a drama when the heroine decides to drown herself in the Ravi, as her head emerged from the water for the last time before going down forever, there was no dupatta covering it so the drama could not go on air. And then there was this comedy programme in which a character with surma-loaded eyes was playing the character of a match referee. As the promise-abiding President had dubbed himself as a mere referee in the political game, the makeup man and the producer of the comedy programme were fired.

Normally, suspicious-looking dubious characters in dramas were usually portrayed with an unkempt beard. The ministry considered it sacrilegious and banned the practice. From then onwards all the villains, thieves and even beggars in the dramas were meticulously shaved.

And who can forget those heart-rending and tragic days when we lost our Eastern wing and our army had surrendered and even then the media echoed the speech of Yahya Khan that the war would go on in the deserts, jungles and plains, etc. Most of us became idiots and doubted the authenticity of BBC and All India radio. How could our very own radio and TV stations lie to us?

I still remember the image of a certain gentleman on the inauguration of the Motorway who was crying hoarse on the screen comparing Nawaz

Sharif to Sher Shah Suri and a wee bit superior perhaps. And then I see the same face again shouting slogans and crying hoarse conducting a meeting in honour of the then recently-arrived Gen Musharraf. I would not mention his sentimental liaison with Bhutto and then immediately afterwards embracing the title of "Preacher of Islam" bestowed upon him by the man who had managed to hang Bhutto. Actually, the gentleman earned notoriety only because he was a media man, otherwise majority of our politicians are no better, actually worse. Because they think we are idiots and perhaps we are.

When Nawaz Sharif won the national election, naturally the media policy had to change immediately so a meeting was convened at PTV HQ by the authorities in which some prominent media personalities were invited, including the playwrights. A very favourite media person of Gen Ziaul Haq, after disappearing during the reign of Benazir, reappeared with full swing and swagger and gave us an instruction menu as to how and on what moral lines we should write the plays from now onwards.

One of the instructions was as follows and I quote: "No love making will be shown in the dramas". I, in my turn, stated humbly that in my entire career with TV as drama writer I have never ventured to show "love making". Then it was explained that by love making it is meant that no love scenes are allowed, especially if the couple is not married.

In those days the term Abbaji for father was abolished in dramas and the son could only address his father as Daddy or Walid Sahib.

As most people are aware, on the occasion of national elections the PTV arranges a mammoth election transmission to announce the results. At the end of one of the transmissions when Nawaz Sharif had won, a "seasoned" political analyst barged into the studio and shouted, "We have won, we have won", and shook hands with everybody.

Now a flash forward to the end of next election transmission in the same studio, and this time Benazir Bhutto has won and the very same gentleman enters the studio and shouts, "We have won, we have won".

We looked at him like idiots do and perhaps we were.

Beware, my dear birds

In Punjabi folklore there is a song which goes as follows:

"O parrot, dear to my heart parrot,

Refrain from going into that street,

The Jats of that street are villainous in their nature,

They will capture and strangle you for sure"

This song is not very complimentary to Jats, I being one of them as a Tarar, but these days it seems that all Pakistanis have become such villainous Jats who are the sworn enemies of all bird species. They kill them in thousands and feel no remorse about it. Their killing spree is specially aimed at the migratory birds that are foolish enough to leave their Russian winter of discontent and head for the warmer climes of Pakistan.

A recent news item informs us that two federal ministers shot no less than eight hundred partridges in their hunting madness in Sindh and got away with it because no one, absolutely no one, in the wild life department blinked an eye. And why should they? If they blinked an eye they would be kicked out of their jobs by the same two federal ministers whoever they are because their names were not mentioned in the news report.

I am intrigued as to how they disposed off all those eight hundred partridges. Maybe they personally ate one or two, sent some to their influential friends as season's greetings and threw the rest to their dogs. After all, their dogs do deserve a bite or two of a partridge now and then. What is the use of being a dog of perhaps a lota minister if you don't eat better than the masses of Pakistan?

In my novel Raakh when Mushahid returns home after a hunt in the lakes of Qadirabad Barrage, his wife Brigitte asks, "How was the hunt?"

"Four." "Four what?"

"Four partridges and three neelsar."

"But you are not happy."

"No, I am not happy."

"Why?"

"Because four partridges have nothing to do with happiness."

It seems that the honourable hunter ministers must have read the above lines and reached the conclusion that merely killing four partridges will not bring them happiness. So, to be on the safe side, they killed eight hundred of them. Now their happiness has something to do with eight hundred partridges.

On the other hand, it is heartening to learn that our prime minister has personally granted a license to kill the endangered houbara bustard to Gulf dignitaries who entirely depend upon this bird's meat for the amazing rejuvenation of their marital bliss.

Who says beggars can't be choosers? We chose to grant a license to kill. How can you rattle your begging bowl in front of the Gulf dignitaries if their tummies are not full of houbara's glowing miraculous meat? And who says that our PM is just a picture postcard and does not enjoy any executive powers? He has proved all the political pundits wrong by exercising the powers to kill the houbara bustards.

There are not very many countries in the world that have the honour of receiving such gift of nature, the migratory birds as their guests for the winters. They are treated with respect and their habitats are protected, and we in Pakistan kill our guests in thousands. Yes, morally it is a murder of a guest who is taking refuge in your house for the night from the bitter winter outside, thinking he is entirely safe and you stab him.

In her early days in Florida, my daughter Annie was amazed to see three tall and graceful herons strutting about in her backyard overlooking a golf course and some lakes. She was tempted to feed them some breadcrumbs which she promptly did. Now this habit of feeding the birds is an impulsive cultural trait in us Orientals. My wife will not waste a single crumb or a rice grain, she will religiously spread all the leftovers on the walls for the benefit of the sparrows. I personally know a gentleman who in the last 40 years has not missed a morning when he has not fed the birds residing in the thick foliage of Baghe Jinnah, Lahore.

Anyhow, poor Annie was not aware of the consequences of feeding birds in America. Somebody reported her unlawful activity to the concerned authorities and a gentleman came knocking on her door and warned her not to feed the birds as they will forget their natural instinct to search for food and will become dependent on her breadcrumbs. Annie was absolutely heartbroken but she had to abide by the law. However, it was not long before she was involved in the unlawful activity again. The very next day when the herons again landed in her backyard to enjoy the breadcrumbs feast and there was no sign of their host Annie, they started knocking on the window glass with their sharp beaks in a fit of extreme annoyance and then they practically started begging by making strange noises and cries.

What could Annie do, who was misty-eyed already? She took care not to go out in the backyard but fed them by remaining inside the house. Her little son Noffel, who called the herons "sparrows", also took part in this activity and at times fed himself with the bread and then reported to his mother that herons wanted more food.

The bald-headed eagle is the national symbol of America and it is almost sacrilegious to disturb its habitat. If a nest of these eagles is discovered, you cannot build or construct anything within a radius of half a kilometre. So much so that I saw a great loop on the otherwise dead straight highway to Miami simply because there was a nest of bald-headed eagles in the vicinity that had to be protected.

I saw hundreds of water fowls and partridges swimming lazily in the numerous lakes of Alaska and you could not even talk loudly if you go near them lest they are disturbed.

Thousands of years ago, on the banks of the mythical river Sarsvati there was a thick forest and in the centre of it there was a lake of dead birds. All those birds who wanted to die headed for that lake and fell on the rotting bones of their long dead comrades, breathing their last. That was a mythical lake, the imagination of a novelist. But we, in present-day Pakistan, have turned that myth into a reality. The birds do not come here to die but we make sure that they do not return to their ancestral abodes. We kill these guests with gay abandon.

If I could speak the bird lingo I would beg them not to come to Pakistan and fly to some friendly and humane lands. I would rephrase the ancient Punjabi song and say to them:

"O birds, near to my heart birds,

Refrain from going into that street,

The ministers and the stone-hearted of that street are villainous in their nature,

They will strangle and kill you for sure."

The hawk speaks

I sincerely hope that you will not consider my statement a sweeping one when I declare that we, the Muslims of the subcontinent are basically a "spur of the moment" people; suddenly we become enamoured with an impulse and then it becomes a matter of life and death for us.

Normally, we Pakistanis and Indians would like to cut each other's throats. And now, suddenly, the "Crush India" and "Crush Pakistan" slogans are gone and we are embracing each other like long lost brothers wailing about our common culture and values, another, yet another spur of the moment movement which I am afraid is not going to last for long, it is too good to be true.

Kindly do not consider me to be a hawk; far from it, I abhor wars and vendettas and throughout my literary career I have supported the cause of normal and friendly relations with India, exchange of writers and artists, books and magazines, educational and scientific knowledge, a trade which does not hurt our industrial growth and most important of all, abolition of visa restrictions. When I used to express these sentiments I was dubbed as a doubtful Pakistani. And now, the same quarters are on the rooftops, crying hoarse for friendship between the two nations. Couldn't we possibly for once adopt a sane and balanced approach; an approach, which withstands the test of time and does not fizzle out when the euphoria of the moment cools down?

The present India Pakistan friendship eruption is not the first time in the history. I remember that way back in 1953 or 54 some hockey contests were arranged on both sides of the border. Lahore received thousands and thousands of Indian visitors who instead of going to the hockey matches roamed in Anarkali and the Mall road, with misty eyes remembering the good old bygone days. The impulsive Lahoris opened their homes and hearts to these Indian brothers and sisters; the tongawalas refused to accept any money from the visitors taking them around the city giving them free rides, there were signs on some of the restaurants that the Indians can have free soft drinks and so on.

Likewise, thousands of Pakistanis stormed Jullundher and Amritsar, most of them went straight to the cinemas and spent their entire stay watching Indian movies like Hemant Kumar's musical hit Nagan; they came back almost half-blind. Then there was this shopping to be done, cotton cloth and winter suiting, because in those times the Pakistani textile industry had not taken off. People returned with huge turbans because unstitched cloth was not allowed into Pakistan. However, you cannot possibly stop a gentleman with a turban even if it measured forty yards! That was the first and perhaps the last time I wore a turban so huge that I almost broke my neck and crossed the border along with hundreds of other Pakistanis with similar turbans.

The Indians were no less hospitable, I remember a certain middle-class Hindu gentleman who upon my arrival on Amritsar railway station begged me to do the honour of staying in his humble abode. He almost snatched my suitcase from my hands. Needless to say that these brotherly feelings did not last long.

Another emotional drama was staged recently in the times of Nawaz Sharif when the then Indian Prime Minister Mr Vajpai visited Lahore. The PTV decided to telecast live the grand reception for Mr Vajpai on the Wagha Border as he arrived on a bus. I was entrusted the job of covering this event, live.

Prior to the transmission I was mobbed by the personnel of different agencies; foreign office, TV bigwigs advising me to use certain phrases while welcoming Mr Vajpai and to refrain from uttering certain other expressions. A certain gentleman from some uncertain agency handed me a list of expressions which were to be avoided completely and these included, 'friendly relations between India and Pakistan', 'pleasant relations', 'mutual understanding', 'striving for peace', 'historical bonds', 'cultural affinities', 'welcome on behalf of Pakistani nation', etc.

"If I am not going to use any of these phrases then what am I going to talk about for one hour?" I asked the certain gentleman humbly.

"Well this is the policy Mr Tarar and you are the compere you should know what to say."

"Then I will just say that dear viewers this dhoti clad gentleman you see on your screen is Mr Vajpai the Prime Minister of India; he has come to

Pakistan, I hope you like his dhoti, thank you and goodbye." The gentleman did not smile, he just glared at me and risking my TV career I glared back.

Then, to my good fortune, the Information Minister Mr Mushahid Hussain turned up and I narrated my woes to him and he was all smiles. "Tarar sahib, you can say what you want but try to project the vision of our PM as regards South Asia".

"Which vision?" I was dumb founded.

"In short", he laughed, "our baba should be on the top, and not their baba". And I understood entirely because he was referring to a joke of two amorous babas which propriety forbids me to relate. The transmission at Wagha went very smoothly and all went well that day.

Presently everybody is busy making hay while the sun of Pakistan-India friendship shines. And believe it or not, it is a big business bonanza also. Not very long ago a gentleman from some NGO strolled into the Model Town Park and offered a free trip to India to all and sundry, only a valid passport and visa fee was required. Most of the babas, retired long ago from service and active life, accepted this offer gleefully and in a week dozens of these oldies were dispatched to India. When they came back they hesitated to discuss this free ride to India. However, a baba was kind enough to narrate his experience. "Tarar sahib, on the given date we made ourselves available on Lahore Railway Station and we were amazed to see that there were more than five hundred 'Peace delegates' gathered there. Our passports, with visas duly stamped, were handed over to us and after a very tiring journey we reached Jullundher where we were lodged in a ramshackle school building that boasted a few toilets, without water. At meal times we were herded into a ground, where some charitable organization served us with dal roti. The next day, we were taken to a big peace rally where a local lady politician made a fiery speech in favour of India Pakistan friendship and we clapped heartily and that was the end of our visit to India."

"But Babaji, who paid all the expenses of your journey, your stay in that school and those sumptuous meals?" I asked.

"Well I am not sure, but there was a rumour that this lady politician wanted to boost her political career by holding a peace rally in which thousands of Pakistanis will participate voluntarily, so some NGO arranged these peace activists and charged the lady in question."

A few months back I had the opportunity to participate in the Saarc Writers' Conference in New Delhi and most of the Indian writers and intellectuals sincerely desired a normalization of relations between our countries. But writers and intellectuals can only dream and they do not have the political leverage to decide the fate of nations, the decision makers are the leaders who represent the masses and the masses on both sides have been fed on hatred for so long that there minds have been poisoned. This poison can only be extracted by constant efforts and not by impulsive behaviour. Let us purge our history and syllabus books of Hindu hatred. Let us know India better by including their history and geography in our school books. Let us refrain from using phrases like "Bharti Darinde" "Mukkar Baniya" or "Chalak Hindu" etc. During my sojourn in Syria, I found that bookshops were stacked with Israeli magazines and books. Amazed I asked a Syrian friend, "Israel is a sworn enemy of yours and you read their books and magazines!"

"If you know your enemy better, you fight better and if you want to be friends even then you should know him better by reading what he is writing," he replied philosophically.

So first of all, let it not be a spur of the moment thing and know India better and this cannot be a one-sided affair, India has to know us better also.

Do I sound like a hawk?

Tears of Shiva

A very secret and silent invasion has taken place on one of the most historic landscapes in Pakistan. And unfortunately very few people know about it because the history or the monuments of bygone days cannot protest, they cannot raise their voices and the invasion engulfs them silently.

The invasion is like the Israelis, creeping upon the Palestinians with bulldozers and guns with silencers, occupying their ancestral lands, although promising that they will be compensated according to the laws laid out by themselves and then on that occupied land, building their settlements, raising walls to keep away the locals, polluting fresh water streams, devastating ancient olive orchards, all in the name of progress.

In Pakistan, this invasion is made of pure cement, durable and everlasting turning the whole population of at least fifty villages into living fossils. The landscape I am referring to is the famous Salt Range, which will turn into a "cement range" if this invasion is not stopped or limited immediately. It will not be out of place if I describe some of the historical jewels scattered all over the Salt Range, presently under threat from the cement invasion.

The first and foremost is Katas or Katakshila Temple complex which dates back to the Buddhist era, situated at a distance of 2.2 kilometres from Chua Saidan Shah. Besides small Buddhist stupas, there is a temple complex initially built by the Buddhists and later on, by the Hindus who turned it into a place of worship according to their beliefs. Locally it is called "Satgrah". In the middle of this temple complex, there is an ancient pond, fed by the waters spouting from its bed; it has been claimed that the depth of this pond has never been fathomed.

According to Hindu mythology, Lord Shiva had seven wives and when one of them, his very favourite, died, he shed so many tears in her grief that his endless tears formed this pond. The pond is not merely a historic decoration; it is not only a source of fresh water to thousands of people but also irrigates orchards sprawling on tens of thousands acres of land.

After quenching the thirst of people and their land, this source which flows throughout the year, finally merges into the waters of the river Jhelum. It is believed that Al-Beruni stayed here and calculated the circumference of the earth from a hill nearby. It is indeed amazing as to how this man managed to calculate the circumference in those days with simple instruments, when in recent time the same was measured with the most sophisticated equipment. There was hardly a difference of a few thousand feet from Al-Beruni's findings.

Near Katas Raj there is a village Dhok Amir Khatun where during excavations under the supervision of Ahmad Hasan Dani, fossils of a mammal, dating back to ten million years, were found.

Kallar Kahar Lake, although not much of a lake, is known for the garden "Bagh-e-Safa" which was laid out by Mughal emperor Babar. The seat of Babar or Takht-e-Babri is also nearby, from where the emperor used to enjoy the panoramic view of the surroundings. Kallar Kahar is mentioned in Tuzke Babri also.

The third most important sight is "Gumdhala" or "Gandhala" which could be the corrupted version of Gandhara as its origin again is Buddhist. It is said that with the advent of Hinduism, the local Buddhist population chose to live on the adjoining hillocks where they were safe from the onslaught of invaders.

This is, in short, the historical perspective of this area. However, there are some ground realities to be considered also.

Almost 60 per cent of the area's people serve in the armed forces and work abroad, specially in Middle East and Saudi Arabia. Rest of the 40 per cent, mostly woman, children and the elderly, look after the cattle and work on their meagre agricultural land, sowing maize, barley and sesame. The land holdings are very small and the crops not only provide sustenance to people but the domestic animals as well. The whole area from Kallar Kahar up to Chua Saidan Shah is in the form of a corridor, and is called "Kahun" by the locals.

The people overall are content with their simple living and are never known to agitate for their legal rights, perhaps a Buddhist streak.

Now in this valley of serenity and content, at an elevation of 2470 feet from the sea level, rightly called a mini-Skardu, enters the dragon of six cement factories and a thermal power plant, fuming with pure carbon dioxide into the 100 per cent pure air of this valley, loved by Emperor Babar. In the madness of industrialization, nobody including the government, gave a hoot as to the havoc these cement factories are going to play on the environment, local population and the historical monuments.

These factories have gobbled up at least 80 per cent of the already poverty stricken farmer's land; they have been promised compensation naturally but it will be according to some 1962 rule or regulation which amounts to peanuts. As yet, the farmers haven't accepted any compensation. Those who protested, were declared terrorists, like the Palestinians.

To feed these factories the surrounding mountains will be blasted and decimated, the tremors affecting all the historical sights including the Katas complex. Besides the blasting, the chemical fumes discharged in the process will cause, according to the medical experts, cancer of the lungs, cell mutation and pollution of fresh water streams, though the factories claim that they have imported very modern plants to control the pollution. I remember the same argument was put forward when the Kala Shah Kaku chemical plants were being erected next to the G.T. Road and today you can smell the fumes when you are miles away from these factories. The famous Nullah Dek, a pure water stream, a heaven for the anglers when it used to teem with all kinds of fish, has turned into a chemical waste pond. In the next few years, the Salt Range is going to be a wasteland of polluted streams, abandoned villages and crumbling monuments.

According to Mr Zafar Malik, a local resident the area resembles an occupied land with boundaries at times jutting into homes and armed guards to keep away the "terrorists". Why for heavens sake were these factories not built away from the populated area, as from there onwards, there is no population for 150 kilometres; just the mountains and forest.

Normally when industries are setup in far-flung areas, the maximum number of locals are employed, a compensation of sorts for their dislocation. But till this date, the locals are shunned as natives and the working force in being "imported". Where are all those NGO's, with hefty purses bulging with dollars who cannot sleep during the nights, worrying themselves to death about the pollution hazards in Pakistan, organizing petite walks on the pavement of the capital, provided the weather is not too harsh for their makeup? Perhaps they are waiting for the Salt Range to turn into a wasteland so that some day an Eliot will create a poetical masterpiece.

The tears of Lord Shiva, formed a fresh water pond amidst the Katas complex but the tears of poverty-stricken farmers of Salt Range are not enough even to fill a cup of justice.

A stroll in heaven

DOWN below, way down below were the mirror waters of Lulusar reflecting those clouds that had discharged a heavy downpour this morning, almost jeopardizing our first day's trek. The three pack-horses lead by their keepers trotted laden with the expedition's luggage in front of us and we trotted the tiny patch, way above the waters of Lulusar.

We retraced our footsteps and were in Basil again which looked like a fairytale mountain-abode, what with the lush green slopes ornamented by the white gold snows and horses grazing straight out of Taimurnama.

We had a hurried cup of tea at the picturesque Basil Hotel and then left the beaten track and forayed into the mountains on our left side. Immediately a mountain torrent, fuming and foaming, blocked our progress. But thank goodness, there was a help-yourself-pulley i.e., jhula available on which we perched one by one and were pulled across by porters and Bashir.

The valley in which we entered was narrow with an icy stream gushing down to Basil. At one point we had to cross it with our boots on so that we may not hurt our feet with the sharp stones, with the result that for the rest of the day we trudged along with wet boots and dripping socks.

After a while the first glacier came into view which was not much of a glacier for us hardened sinners who had traversed the longest glacier chain in the world i.e., Biafo and Hesper. However, our new recruits, Zahid Butt and Qaiser were frightened beyond redemption. Now, here I have to make a confession. Whenever any of our friends or acquaintances showed the slightest interest in trekking, we assured them that the thing is a piece of cake, keeping them in dark about the perils of the journey. We enticed them by narrating the fairytales of unknown lakes and valleys, the magical vistas reached by merely strolling and whistling.

Needless to say that when the enchanted souls accompanied us starry eyed, these twinkling stars were suddenly extinguished by the very first sight of razor edged path clinging to a mountain or a glacier.

"Tarar Sahib, ye aap hamen kahan le aae ho? Sirji, if we slip while crossing this slippery glacier what would happen?"

"You won't slip."

"But what if we do?"

"In that case you will be in the river down below."

"But we can't swim Tarar Sahib."

"You wont have to, by the time you hit the waters you will most probably be dead."

"We abandon the expedition sir, we are going back to Basil."

"You are not doing anything of the sort," I would grin mischievously and then assure them that crossing this small glacier is really a piece of cake, although I personally held onto Bashir and some porters while crossing it, just an unnecessary precaution.

After crossing this glacier we rose to a height, which afforded a vast panorama of slopes rising and dipping and again rising. It was very tough going and soon we were panting, coughing and at times slipping. Now everybody was cursing me including, the old sinners.

"Tarar Sahib you told us that this year we are not going on a tough trek. It's merely a stroll in the green meadows."

"Bashir, Oi Bashir", Salman was totally worn out with fatigue and could not carry his heavy body anymore.

"Do you think we will reach Dudiput by this evening?"

"Nahin Sahib, not with this progress, we will camp as soon as we cross the last slope and descend into a valley in a place called DUKK.

"You mean a 'batakh' Bashir. There will be ducks around, maybe a Donald Duck?"

Salman was totally abstract.

"No sir, this dukk means a block, where a mountain river is blocked by a wall of stones, a small dam."

The dam dukk was an illusive duck and it took us another back-breaking three hours to reach it. The narrow valley suddenly blossomed in front of us and on the far horizon loomed some snow covered mountains under which we were told lay the shy waters of Dudiput Lake. But not tonight Josephine, wait till tomorrow.

The recruits upon entering Dukk were overjoyed and completely stunned, and when I told them that Dukk is not much to write home about they could not understand my apathy. Well I was some sort of a debauch of the mountains and could not be excited by a simple place like Dukk. Granted it was a green meadow by the river and the view from here had a certain charm, but it was ordinary compared with the places I had camped in the past or even last night by the Lulusar. However, I could understand their excitement as it was their first camping site ever at the end of a track.

The next morning after we had had our breakfast, that included limp parathas and sizzling desi eggs, we left Dukk and were almost immediately plunged into a valley of coloured miracles. All around us the slopes were engulfed in misty clouds. They were not littered with flowers but were made of pink flowers. There was no end to it. Mountains upon mountains were completely covered with these carpets of pink. Down below in a plain, quietly flowed a mercury stream on the banks of which grazed literally hundreds of horses. As we looked at them, these composed, and from this distance, still animals, all of a sudden panicked, due to some unknown reason and started galloping wildly. Amongst the chestnut brown horses I spotted a pure white stallion that stood out from the rest of them as though he was the sole galloper in this magical valley of pink flowers. He was straight out of a Saeed Akhtar or M.F. Hussein's painting.

Even the grumbling recruits forgave me upon entering this magic moment and Mian Farzand exclaimed "Wah Ji Wah, Subhanallah."

Many years ago, I saw a musical South Pacific in which the famed Italian actor Rossano Brazi sang Some Enchanting Evening. I assure my readers that this was some enchanting valley in which only the fortunate ones could enter. Then the white clouds over our heads became restless, and down came the rain, icy and sharp, and out came our lunda bazaar second-hand raincoats of various colours as they most probably belonged to some European ladies long dead and gone.

Soon the rain transformed into a minor hailstorm. The tiny snow balls in hundreds jumped in front of us like white frogs and soon enough we were treading on a carpet of snow. At that moment we were passing through a field of tiny white flowers and these tiny snowballs in thousands were falling in it and jumping like mad. This indeed was a mesmerizing sight, it seemed as if they were not the snowballs but tiny white flowers, leaving their stalks and jumping in the air madly.

And then there was Dudiput Lake.

Dudiput a place of Doodh i.e., milk, because of its vast grazing meadows where the animals had their fill and gave plenty of milk.

Enchanting Dudiput

AND then there was Dudiput lake. All of us gasped, we could not breathe. It wasn't only due to the breathtaking beauty of this elusive enchanting lake, but the real cause was the height on which it was located, 12600ft to be exact. We were slightly delirious at times taking self-smiling tours, grinning, completely happy with our life. When the initial euphoria subsided, we chose to pitch our tents right beside the lake. But our Buddha Bashir shook his head, "No sir. The ground by the lake is very damp. We will camp on the hillock overlooking the lake from where you can see the total view of the blue mass." Unwillingly, the bunch of us accepted his advice as he was the all-knowing-mighty guide.

So our tent city of red and blue domes rose on the hillock facing the full magnificence of Dudiput.

How would I compare Dudiput with Lulusar? Well lakes, no matter how small or insignificant they are, cannot be compared as they are like human beings, each with its own personality and form. Some lakes are very private and personal, like Lake Kromber situated in the shadows of the Pamir mountains and Wakhan corridor. One can have a lasting affair with such a shy lake, remembering its almost frozen waters in times of sorrow and stress and gaining strength from its memories. And then the snow lake signs its autograph with its icy fingers on your whole being so that you may never forget it.

And then the recently visited Lulusar, its vastness embraces you and fills you with its golden waters.

Dudiput was in a way a miniature of Lake Saifulmaluk, but much more private and personal. The glaciers ornamenting the green slopes; banks littered with flowers and certain aloofness which objects to the presence of strangers violating its serene sanctity. In short, Dudiput was a rare spectacle of snow, pink flowers, lush green slopes and crystal clear atmosphere. But as the evening descended amongst these heavenly watery heights there rose like a Loch Ness monster, spectre of bad news. Both of our recruits were stricken by the height, Zahid Butt was vomiting and running a very high fever whereas Qaiser had a splitting headache and had difficulty in breathing, they were not in very good shape to say the least.

"Tarar Sahib," the worried Bashir peeped into my tent "I am afraid Qaiser and Butt sahib have to be evacuated. Their lungs cannot stand this height and until and unless we take them down to Basil to lose height they are in grave danger, Salman is not feeling too well either."

This indeed was bad news, I was supposed to be the leader of the "discover the elusive lakes" expedition and was responsible for the safety of its members. So an emergency meeting was held in my tent and I decided that with half of our team gone it will be useless to carry on with the expedition. Hence, it is abandoned, all of us will go back to Basil tomorrow morning and with luck we will come back next year.

Butt and Qaiser, shivering in their tents, felt very guilty but I assured them that it was part of the game, it happens, when you don't mind your business and meddle with the mountain heights; it happens. But Khan Salim was impertinent enough to disagree with me, flashing his Bugs Bunny smile he said, "Tarar Sahib this is now or never, who knows next year comes or not. I suggest that we dispatch these sick fellows back to Basil on horses and I further suggest that from now onwards instead of walking we also hire some horses to complete the trek and horses are plentiful around here."

"Are they plentiful around here?" I asked Bashir

"This is a horse valley sir, you can raise a cavalry regiment here, plenty of horses"

So be it, the height stricken members will be evacuated tomorrow morning and we will be riders instead of walkers for the rest of our trek.

The pitch dark veil of the night fell suddenly and in its blind darkness glowed the kitchen tent, inside which our cook Hafiz Anwar cooked kofta curry and rice over the gas cylinder. There were only three of us in the kitchen tent that night to have dinner and now we felt guilty that we were abandoning our companions. Love of elusive lakes had made us into selfish animals.

Dudiput at night, a cold cold night, at the height of 12600ft glowed in the darkness like a huge overcharged firefly and its glow filtered through my tent. I could not sleep. I was also short of breath. Then the firefly of lake dimmed and the morning came as Homer described, with its bright fingers and the surrounding green slopes, mass of flowers and snow were a still reflection on the still waters. It was a breath taking sight as there was still some breath which could be taken. I stood on the banks of the lake and wondered as to which was real, fact or reflection.

And with the morning came the horses, plenty of them. Three for our dear departing friends and their luggage, back to Basil friends and four for us as Salman was feeling much better and he decided to drag along, along with three pack horses which made a respectable number of horses i.e.; seven in all along with their owners of course.

The dear ones departed with Byron's "parting is a sweet sorrow" departing.

Today we were supposed to climb and climb and cross the Saral Pass at a meagre height of 13600ft and descend into a valley guarded by high passes and in its lap was hidden a lake of unsurpassed beauty, the Siral lake.

But at present by the lake of Dudiput I had a minor problem. In all my sinful years I had ridden many a species but never a horse or a donkey for that matter, except a short ride in the Pamirs and when with the help of two porters I was placed upon a saddle I transformed into an astronaut, totally weightless, helpless and without any control over my aging limbs. Rest of the members had some sort of minor or major experience of riding a four legged beast and felt comparatively at ease.

So far so good but, perching on a still horse was one uncontrollable condition. But as soon as the horse moved the whole universe moved around me and I begged very loudly to be excused. But the die was cast and it was either do or die so I decided to die. When the horse started moving, in this moment of crisis suddenly all those cowboy movies of the past came to my rescue in which Gary Cooper or John Wayne handled this awful beast with careless ease. So I followed their example, I stretched myself backwards when the horse decided to take a sudden plunge and leaned forward almost kissing the neck of the beast when it climbed.

By the way, most of these animals carrying our sinful burden were not horses, but mares whom our male chauvinism declared them to be horses.

As soon as we parted with the flower strewn valley of Dudiput instead of us, our horses started panting because they were climbing towards an impossible height, which looked daunting, and totally beyond our meagre mountaineering skills. The formidable pass of Siral looked as though it was not on this earth but situated in the skies above. After crossing a minor glacier on which our horses slipped and at times shied back on all fours from where we had started. So we abandoned them and started climbing an unfriendly rocky height.

However, Salman persisted that he will manage his pony on the heights but the pony could not manage his weight and Salman fell and almost went down the ridge. But at this juncture our porters and Ghora Wallas proved to be the real heroes. They unloaded the pack horses, carried the luggage on their backs, up to the high pass, came tumbling back and then almost dragged their horses over boulders and rocks up to the pass again.

Finally we also managed to reach the Siral top at a height of 13600ft and below, down below in the midst of a green valley glistened the emerald of almost unknown Siral lake. The flower-strewn slopes descended into the aloof valley and then there was Siral.

A resplendent lake, indeed

SO down below the flower-strewn slopes and across the valley, hidden amongst glaciers lay the elusive Siral lake. Needless to say that we were captivated mesmerized and thrilled beyond description.

I am painfully aware of the fact that I am indulging in superlatives rather too frequently. But then what are superlatives for if they cannot be showered upon a lake like Siral? Just place yourself atop a 13600-feet-high pass and look at Siral down below and you will be after my blood because I have not used enough superlatives to describe the wonder that is Siral, glistening like a sapphire below, down below.

We relieved our poor horses of our weight of sins and stretched our limbs on a field of alpine flowers. We could call it a day here, camp for the night, placing our tents in such a way that the beauty of Siral may be framed in the openings of our tents. But we knew that the night at this height will be rather cruel hence the thought was brushed away. And anyway, we were now treading upon the ground, which was Azad Kashmir, we had parted from Kaghan.

"Salim", I inquired from my ghorawala "How long will it take us to reach the banks of Siral?"

"Not more than two hours saabji, all we have to do now is to go down."

And go down, I did. In fact, I almost went down and out because the flower strewn slopes were not gradually descending into Siral valley, but falling into it, almost vertically. And no matter how far back I stretched myself, I could not balance myself on the saddle of the horse who was also just falling down the slopes. Believe me I was almost standing on the stirrups.

Needless to say I forgot all about the beauty of Siral and concentrated on saving my dear life for future events. Finally I got off the horse in the same standing position and started to walk down. Soon all my aged joints started creaking and moaning and my knees, without taking the rest of the body in confidence, started the jerk dance, climaxing my collapsing on the slope.

The ghorawala had pity on me and told me to mount the beast once again as he had an action plan which would enable me to stay firmly in the saddle while going down. I mounted with his help and then the good fellow, instead of leading the horse downwards, started to zig-zag on the slope. It was time consuming but less hazardous, understandably all other members by now had reached the valley floor. While we were criss-crossing the slope like a dog that follows his own tail, suddenly a small gem of a lake appeared on our left, fabulously placed in the lap of some green mountains. Nobody knew its name, not even the all knowing Bashir Buddha: "It's just a lake sahib."

But it was not just a lake; it was an enchanting blue dream, which faded away.

Finally the ordeal came to an end and we reached the floor of the valley and this called for a much-needed rest. One of the ghorawalas, Aurengzeb went up to a stone hut, which was reputed to be a local five star facility, to procure some hot tea and we stretched ourselves amongst some foul smelling flowers on the banks of a mountain stream.

"Tarar Sahib," Bashir the Buddha was smiling, "Besides that stone hut there resides the first wife of a local MP with her children."

"And where does this honourable MP of AK Assembly reside himself?"

"With his second wife in Muzaffarabad who is only fifty-five years junior to him."

"Well Bashir you give me hope, please carry on."

"Sir there was this very sohni young mountain maid whose father was marrying her off to some obnoxious and ugly looking brute and the maid obviously had some objections. So according to the local custom she presented herself in front of this humble MP in search of justice and implored him to save her. So he saved her by marrying her."

"She was willing to marry this old man of the mountains?"

"The MP told her that if she does not want to marry anybody in particular he can arrange the same in his own family. The sohni girl was sure that the old man intended to marry her off with his grandson so she agreed readily. Only when the bridegroom appeared on her door step with the barat the girl realized what was in store for her, a cold storage. But by then it was too late"

"Some people have all the luck even if they live in Siral valley," I sighed.

We had our cup of tea and felt sympathy for the sohni girl and a pang of jealousy for the old man and then resumed our journey. We, or rather our horses climbed a steep slope and down below was another small and silent lake, another climb and suddenly the waters of Siral lake hit us like a bullet; we almost died. Famed novelist Garcia Marquez said, "Every man is a non-man, till such time that a woman enters his life and makes him a man, if he is lucky that is".

Siral was such a woman. Aloof, protected by high mountain passes, almost unseen as I had never even seen a photograph of it previously, and stunningly beautiful. The blue and very still waters were decorated with some miniature icebergs one of which swam slowly like a huge white swan. Describing the Siral lake is a futile effort, even the superlatives abandoned me. I had squandered my word power, if there was any, and now felt like a beggar looking at this marvel of nature. If there are lakes in paradise, this is the role model, the serene Siral.

Ballet in the mountains

The Siral Lake surrounded us, dumbfounded us with its awesome out-of-this-world captivating beauty. We were indeed captives as the lake is guarded with high passes all around. We could not take our eyes off the mini icebergs floating in its magical blue waters. The rays of the setting sun paled and in their footsteps, came stealthily the evening to engulf us in its cold cold lap. The lake was not without habitation, there on the left slope almost descending into its waters was a nomad encampment. Some chestnut horses grazed by the lake without raising their necks to see that there were other visitors around.

As per my demand, my tent was erected right beside the waters of the lake at such an angle that I could sit inside the tent cross legged and watch the mini-iceberg floating like a royal swan. But then appeared "Groucho Marx", with his drooping moustaches in front of me and whistled.

The Groucho Marx was in fact a marmot that was perhaps the lone inhabitant of this lake and my tent was placed right in front of his den. Naturally he did not like this intrusion and came out of his den and stood on his two legs watching me and showing his displeasure by whistling. By the way I hope you know what a marmot is, if you don't then you have really not lived.

A marmot is one of the most adorable cuddly creatures you have ever set your eyes upon, generally found on higher grounds in our northern areas, Deosai plains, Khunjrab Pass and the valleys of Nanga Parbat are his favourite abodes. The marmot has all the cuddly charms of a miniature bear, swiftness of a rabbit and cunning of a human being. It will stand on his two legs, watch you pass by and then whistle mischievously behind your back. This "Groucho" the marmot was a senior citizen with drooping moustaches and at times practically winked and whistled at me. When I came out of my tent to have a closer look and introduce myself, he immediately disappeared into his below-surface den.

At the height that we were, above the tree line, there was no wood to be found. But our porters had very wisely collected some dry branches and twigs during the trek. Soon it was night, a bonfire was lit and we had our meal beside the fire. And all this time, little "Groucho" kept an eye on our activities, peeping from his den occasionally and then disappearing.

The night of Siral was an experience of a lifetime. The moon was almost full and the white icebergs floating on the waters almost became alive. Many years ago I had witnessed the famed opera The Swan Lake, on the stage of Bolshoi Theatre Moscow. The nimble footed ballerinas dressed in white floated like swans with grace and unparalleled beauty. In that moonlit night, sitting in my tent, wrapped up in my sleeping bag I watched the Siral Lake opera being enacted on the blue waters where the ballerinas were the little icebergs floating and dancing like royal swans. However, I was not the only spectator, "Groucho" the marmot also stood on his two legs and watched this opera, whistling at times to show his appreciation. During the night muffled sounds of glaciers falling into the waters of Siral Lake travelled deep into my sleepy senses.

I was lost in the dark valley of temporary death i.e. sleep, when I heard somebody calling my name repeatedly, I tried to open my eyes drowsily and there peeping into my tent was "Groucho" the marmot smiling with a trimmed moustache and plenty of oil applied to his balding head.

"Tarar Sahib," Groucho was brimming with happiness, "What will you like with your paratha, fried eggs or jam?"

So this morning's breakfast was on good old "Groucho Marx"? I hope he is a good cook and if he is I will send Hafiz Anwar packing and for rest of the trip, we'll employ "Groucho" as a cook. This will be the stuff of records, the first ever-trekking party to employ a marmot as expedition's cook.

"Tarar sahib", he again said, "Why don't you say something, eggs or jam?" And at that moment, when I regained my senses, I realized that it was not the head of Groucho that was peeping into my tent. Rather, it was Bashir. The fault was not entirely mine, there were certain resemblances between these two, specially the moustaches.

"So Bashir what is the action plan today?", I inquired after breakfast. However, whenever I looked at Bashir's face I felt guilty because out of it, always popped up, "Groucho".

"Well sir, we will travel on the slopes and go on the other side of the lake, then climb up to the Nuri Nar pass and descend on the other side and camp."

"Camp beside which lake Bashir?"

"Not tonight Tarar Sahib." He said in the same style as Napoleon had uttered, "Not tonight Josephine."

"After Lulusar, Dudiput and Siral we will be lake-less tonight. But after that, we will Insha-Allah camp beside your dream lake, Ratti Gali Lake."

"Bashir, can't you promise me this lake without saying Insha-Allah?"

Naturally he was shocked, "Why without it sir?"

"Well Bashir, it is my unfortunate experience that whenever we say Insha-Allah, we mean 'maybe'".

Then I told him about a certain German tourist who in my presence wanted to hire a jeep from Gilgit to Rupal, and after paying the jeep owner in advance he demanded, "I want my Jeep in my hotel tomorrow morning at 6.30." And the owner just said, "Insha-Allah", upon which the German demanded his money back and said, "I want my jeep at 6.30 in the morning and you say maybe and maybe not?" This he was stating from his experience in Pakistan.

"Sir, I will again say Insha-Allah", Bashir smiled broadly and very narrowly missed being "Groucho" who by the way was sitting on top of his den basking in the morning sun and watching us curiously.

Soon our ponies, horses, mares or whatever you may call them, were trotting on the high and precarious pathway above the lake on an almost vertical slope. This indeed was a bird's eye view, but the bird, which was me, did not want to view and most of the times kept his eyes shut. However, after reaching the other side of the lake I looked back and from here the view again was fabulous. There at the bottom of the slopes lay a cup of green wine, which had intoxicated me with its charm and icy beauty and on the edges of this cup lived my good friend "Groucho Marx". I missed him.

The dream lake

SO today was the Day of Judgment. The dream lakes, which I had seen in the early days of my youth, which had haunted me throughout my life. Today I will find out whether they really exist or was it just a fantasy.

Instead of the initial half a dozen trekkers, now with the departure of Salman, there remained only a triangle of Khan Salim, Mian Farzand and myself. Our horses by now had got used to our body weights and trotted merrily on a grassy slope rising toward another pass called Dawarian. However, before the final climb, there suddenly appeared an area larger than a football field, which was so completely covered with wild yellow flowers that even our horses hesitated to step into them, lest they trampled that carpet of yellow.

"Subhanallah!" Mian Sahib exclaimed.

Yes, there was no other expression of praise that could justify our feeling of amazement. Indeed, Allah is beautiful and likes beauty hence creates beauty as a heavenly gift for those who have wander lust in their eyes. I am sure, if at that moment somebody had looked into our eyes, he would have seen beside amazement, a mass of yellow flowers smiling.

The final assault on Dawarian pass did not present any unsurpassable difficulties, as perhaps we were still wandering amongst the yellow flowers and drunk with their beauty did not realize any danger, if there was any.

Finally we were there and down below in a valley of greens, a small lake glistened in the midday sun.

"Tarar sahib in front of you is the Ratti Gali area and there is your dream lake", informed the exuberant Bashir.

My heart sank; it was not much of a lake, just a mass of water surrounded by some greenery. So I had fabricated, manufactured in my nostalgic mind the image of a lake that did not exist, this was the end of a dream. And at that very moment, when out of depression I could have jumped from my horse into the nearby ravine Bashir added, "This is the first lake sir, the other one is still hidden behind those looming glaciers. It will come into view shortly." Then it flashed through my mind, that standing on top of the Ratti Gali peak it was the second lake, situated at a considerable height amongst the mass of blue mountains and glaciers. There was hope.

We did not exactly descend into the valley below, rather travelled at par with the opposite mountains on a green slope. Suddenly we found ourselves on a precarious slope, falling almost vertically into a deep ravine on our left side. There was a well trodden goat track. But what was amazing was that our horses managed to balance themselves, placing their hooves on the right track.

Previously I had enjoyed the ride, at times glancing at the first lake or making fun of Khan Salim's horse, who, at times, suddenly decided to abandon the path and head straight for the valley. And when Salim tried to bring him back to the path, the wayward animal would go round and round in circles, like a dog chasing his own tail. But now, I was so terrified that I just looked straight ahead and prayed.

At one time just per chance, I looked at Salim's horse, and lo and behold, the beast would, at times, when there was no place to put his hooves, would dangle one of his legs in the air for a while and then trod on. Now this circus act on an almost vertical cliff terrified me, because if Salim's horse was doing this trick, surely my mount was also indulging in the same pastime.

And just then, emerged out of the blue mountains, lush green slopes, and in the lap of white snow, a lake on the dark blue magical waters of which floated big chunks of glaciers like huge white swans.

"I was right, I was right," I started shouting like a mad old man, which I was, because what I had seen almost forty-seven years ago as a young man was not the product of my nostalgic romantic emotions, but a reality, a fact. In fact, it was even more beautiful than what I had been dreaming. When you want to pay the highest tribute possible to a painter or an actor, you say he is the painter's painter or actor's actor, so I will say, with all my honesty, that this Ratti Gali or Dawarian Lake is a lake's Lake. My companions also were too dumb founded to speak; they just smiled and smiled.

Unfortunately our tight schedule did not permit us to abandon our path and head for the glorious miracle of blue waters so without taking our eyes off that dream which was a reality we headed for the summit of Ratti Gali peak. Again, after forty-seven years I was standing on top of that red mountain which was the first height I ever scaled. The only difference was that in those days, I had trekked and reached it from the other side.

While we glanced at the Ratti Gali lake for the last time, there was one satisfaction in not reaching its shores and spending a night there; we will come again. Let there be a few unfulfilled desires to cherish and hope.

While descending on the Ratti Gali glacier we abandoned our horses for a while and chose to tread on our own feet because Ghorawala Salim had informed us gleefully that coming down from the summit, the last time, one of their horses fell into the ravine and the gora-loog had kindly paid them a huge sum in compensation. We chose to walk because we could not afford to pay for a dead horse. They never told us what happened to the rider, and if he was dead, then who paid for him.

The valley broadened and gujjar encampments appeared on the slopes. As the dogs barked, we camped by Nuri Nar Nullah beside a glacier, sitting outside our erected tents we saw Ratti Gali peak in the last rays of sunset turning into pure gold.

By tomorrow evening we will be back in Burawai, back to normality, back to "civilization", chained in respectability, taking-off our trekking attire to become normal and gentlemen, back to my writing desk and TV studios for another year. Soon the glow on Ratti Gali peak dimmed and darkness engulfed it but there was a glimmer of hope in our entire being, we will someday return, cross Ratti Gali and reach the Dawarian lake and spend a night there. Maybe those floating icebergs were not icebergs at all but real swans? We will return someday and find out.

The Day of Judgment

As I looked back to preserve the serene image of Siral, my awestruck eyes captured it for those rainy days in the future when once again I will be chained to my day-to-day prosaic and dull schedule, and these days will become distant dreams. I missed my friend Groucho the marmot.

Ahead of us towered another formidable pass which according to Bashir the Buddha was Noori Nar Pass, reaching the top of which did not present any unsurpassable problems. An entire range of strange mountains appeared before us and down below were the glaciers and small glacial lakes, beyond which we could see the winding ribbon of a new Kuccha road linking Sharda with Jalkhad.

It was almost evening when we came down to Nuri Nar Nullah, crossed it and then again climbed up to the road above. Beside the road was a welcome shack, locally branded as a hotel where we rested for a while. In the meantime, a fully loaded passenger wagon halted in front of us. Salman, who according to him was not feeling too well and had had enough of lakes and passes, was packed into it and dispatched back to Naran.

Naturally his departure saddened us as out of six original team members only three remained. In the meantime a military convoy halted in front of the hotel, out hopped a dashing major and sat right in front of me ordering tea for himself and rest of the crew. He looked at me absent mindedly and then suddenly his expression changed, "You can't be Tarar Sahib?"

"I am afraid I am."

"What the —, what are you doing in this godforsaken place?"

"I have not the foggiest idea myself."

"Isn't it strange that only this morning you were the topic of discussion in our mess and a young officer of mine declared that this Tarar fellow just makes up all those travel tales, and in fact never steps out of his study."

"Well, it seems that the Pakistan Army is very well informed," I laughed heartily, as this accusation was nothing new to me.

In the meantime the dashing major went up to his truck and when he returned a young officer was accompanying him almost wrecking himself to walk erect in the company of a senior officer who ordered him to sit and have a cup of tea.

"Well young man, what were you declaring this morning in the mess about this Tarar fellow?"

The young man could not fathom as to why here in the middle of nowhere his senior officer had brought up this subject but an order was an order so with a respectful cough he obeyed.

"Sir, I feel that he has not been to all those places he claims he has been."

"Well why don't you look very closely and find out who this shabby looking fellow is, sitting right in front of you."

The young officer looked as closely as he could almost touching his nose to mine and then went into a state of shock, stood up, did not know whether to slap me or salute me for being there. He then shook hands with me.

"Sorry sir, I did not mean it."

"Please do sit down young man, it happens all the time. I don't blame you; at times I do get carried away from facts and wander into fantasies."

High above the Jalkhad road we camped near a stream and Bashir was right; this was our first lake-less night. No more the golden waters of Lulusar, Dudiput or Siral.

While Hafiz Anwar prepared the evening meal underneath a rock shelter, a very stern looking character adorning a nondescript uniform appeared from nowhere.

"Who are you people? Are you after the medicinal plants or butterflies?"

"Kindly introduce yourself," I requested.

"I am a forest guard," he said.

"But there are no forests around here, there isn't a single tree as far as we can see." "Even then I am the forest guard."

I offered him a cup of tea along with some biscuits and immediately he became a very humble and friendly person, "Sir, you are right. There are no forests around here but if we have a forest officer here then there should be forest guard to look after him, the big sahib is expected tonight and I will look after him."

"What about these medicinal plants and butterflies you were talking about?"

"Well sir, I have been told that there are some very rare medicinal plants in this area and my job is to protect them."

"Can you point out any plants around here?"

"No sir, I have no idea but I protect them all the same."

So this gentleman was guarding a forest, which did not exist and protecting rare plants, which he did not recognize.

"What about the butterflies?"

"Well sir, they are there. On top of that mountain across the Jalkhad road and there is a team of foreigners residing there to collect these butterflies and I protect them also."

"Butterflies?"

"No sir, the gora loog. You know these days a lot of Jihad is going on and some bad people come from over the mountain and try to kill the gora loog, so I protect them. The gora loog are also mad people, collecting butterflies for the last one month."

Soon enough, this dutiful forest guard departed to guard the forest and to protect a bunch of mad goras.

The night was uneventful except for those two dogs that kept on howling from a nearby Gujjar encampment, disliking our presence in their domain.

Next morning, although I knew exactly where we were heading I asked Bashir, to satisfy his guide instinct, as to where do we go from here.

"Across the Dawarian pass into Ratti Gali area and your lakes will be there."

The dream lakes, which I saw in the early days of youth, which had haunted me throughout my life, do they really exist or it, was just a fantasy?

Today was the Day of Judgment.

The journey continues

Finally, a huge trailer screeched past me and halted. I could not believe that it had actually stopped for me, and I stood rooted to the ground

THE first year of textile studies drew to an end and I planned to spend my summer vacations in Switzerland, simply because there were mountains there. In the meantime, an English classfellow of mine, Johnny, who was a regular vagabond, suggested that travelling by hitchhiking would be more fun.

"Now what in the name of heavens is this hitchhiking, Johnny?"

Johnny replied, "It's simple, take any public transport to the outskirts of the city and stand by the road showing your thumb to the driver, and with a little bit of luck you will get a lift for, wherever you intend to reach."

"For free?" it was then a totally novel idea.

"Absolutely, only you have to amuse the driver during the travel, by telling him jokes and things"

"Any Jokes?"

"No, only dirty jokes."

"It's that simple?"

"Not really but the taste of the pudding is in eating it."

So I decided to taste the pudding of hitchhiking during my forthcoming travel to Switzerland. But first, I wanted to practise this method on home ground, in England. I was on a shopping spree, rucksack, walking shoes, tent, sleeping bag, Swiss knife etc. Wordsworth's poem Daffodils, still danced in my mind as taught and explained by great Safdar Mir Zeno to the general public. So I decided to visit the native village of this poet of nature, on the banks of Lake Windermere, in the fabled Lake District.

But immediately there was an obstacle in the shape of a distant relative of mine, Chacha Azmat. In his run down house I was lodged in those days, along with a few dozen Pakistani labourers. This Chacha, who looked after me like a proper Pakistani Chacha, stern but kind, went into a state of shock when I revealed my plans of reaching Lake District by means of hitchhiking.

"You mean to say you will just stand there like a bloody beggar and beg for lifts?"

"That is the general idea."

"I won't let it happen, over my dead body."

"But why Chachaji?"

"Aren't you a Jat anymore son?"

"I am pure and authentic as good or bad as they come, a Jat."

"But Jats don't do this sort of thing, begging from people only Kummi Kamin stoop so low."

"Well I stoop to conquer Chacha and I don't believe in your caste system. I am going to do it Jat or no Jat."

"I will report it your father Choudhry Sahib and tell him that your Crown Prince is begging on the streets," he threatened.

"I am sure he will be very pleased, I know my father."

Then Chacha Azmat offered me a bundle of pound notes.

"If you are short of money here, go buy yourself a train or bus ticket to wherever this Worthless or is it Wordsworth place is ..."

"It's not the money Chacha its the spirit, the freedom, let me explain..."

Finally he gave up and with a heavy heart dumped my rucksack in his Morris Minor and took me outside Manchester on the road leading to Leads and onward, to the Lake District. When I stationed myself and raised my thumb, he again pleaded with me and offered to take me personally in his Morris Minor to the Lake District to save the honour of Jats in general. I felt guilty when I refused again as he was doing all this out of sheer love for me. He shook my hand, embraced me then went across the road because he was convinced that by the end of day I will still be standing there without any success and he will take me home. I raised my thumb and kept it in that state for the next hour.

Finally a huge trailer screeched past me and halted. I could not believe that it had stopped for me. I stood rooted to the ground when a burly

Scottish looking driver looked from the window of the trailer and shouted "Hey Laddie, you wan a **** lift or not?"

I was on my way to the Lake District and the last thing I saw in the back-view mirror of the speeding trailer was Chacha Azmat's face, smiling and waving.

In search of daffodils

AS SOON as we were out of Rochester I remembered the good advice of my English friend Johnny that you have to be friendly with the driver who gives you a free ride, amuse him and tell him dirty jokes.

"Sir, would you like to hear a dirty joke?"

My benefactor was not exactly shocked but he was slightly shaken.

"Lad, I thought you were a gentleman."

"I think I am sir, so far ... but the joke is very funny."

"Fire away lad, but it better be very dirty."

"Well there was this Sardarji riding a motor bike with his sister on the back-seat when another Sardarji, a friend of this Sardarji saw them and shouted gleefully, oi riding with your beloved you bastard? And this Sardarji shouted back, oi she can be your beloved but she is my sister."

Although in the pit of my stomach I felt that the Punjabi joke had lost some of its meaning in English due to my faulty translation, but even then I expected hearty laughter which never ensued.

The driver sat glum and waiting "Then what lad?"

"That's it Sir, don't you think its hilarious?"

"You better not tell me anymore jokes, dirty or otherwise, if you want your ride to continue", he almost threatened me.

Well, strange man, no sense of humour, I thought and kept my mouth shut till the end of the ride.

Suddenly he halted the trailer, "This is as far as you go lad and don't tell such silly jokes to the next driver who gives you a lift. And by the way, why can't your sister be your friend's beloved? What's so funny about it?"

I then realized that I was in a different cultural environment where standards of humour and morality were totally different from where I come from.

My next ride was with an old man whose age and body condition was at par with the rickety car he was trying to drive and it was not the milk of human kindness which had prompted him to give me a lift, his motive was entirely different. The car would cough and shiver after every mile or so and stop. "Come on young man give us a push" he would say and I kept on pushing his World War II vintage car and finally decided to call it a day. "Thank you for the ride sir I am sure you have saved a lot of petrol meanwhile."

"You are welcome young man but give us a push before you go, hurry up."

My very next ride was on a different mode of transport, a two wheeler, a Triumph Tiger Cub motorcycle. While I was being pulled by the weight of my rucksack, trying to keep my balance I felt like the sister of Sardarji of dirty joke fame.

To cut the matter short, after camping in a field outside the city of Lancaster for the night, I finally arrived at the bank of Lake District's first lake, Windermere, at noon.

The first sight of the Lake did not stir a single chord of excitement. It left me cold, it was no better than the duck pond where I had camped last night, it was bigger and longer if that was any satisfaction. A mass of grey waters surrounded by unimpressive hillocks. I was expecting an English sister of Ratti Gali's dreamy lakes and this was no lake at all in comparison. The famed crooner Frank Sinatra's song floated in my mind Whose that lady? That's no lady that's my wife ... so that's no lake just a mass of grey waters. However, this was my initial reaction which changed considerably in the days to come.

As there was hardly any traffic in these parts I took a bus and reached a small town Ambleside, where, upon inquiring, I was told that there was no camping site. Hence I decided to spend the night in a youth hostel by the lakeside. That evening after having dinner the hostel warden requested all the guests to wash the dishes and then we had a small party on the banks of the lake which cheered me up a little and the lake looked less gloomy.

Next day, acting upon the advice of the amiable warden I decided to walk up to the town of Grasmere which was situated right at the end of the lake. I was glad I took the advice of the warden as it turned out to be a fabulous experience, everything was lush green around me and I felt as I was walking in a cool green tunnel of tall trees and bushes. I felt free and happy for the first time.

"Hey, hey Mister," an old lady in a dashing blond wig emerged from a picturesque cottage. When I approached her she said "Do you only sell woollen stockings or do you have some nice underwear for young girls like me?"

"Underwear?" I blushed.

"Aren't you one of those Pakistanis who sell stockings and things door-to-door?"

"I am a Pakistani but not one of those Pakistanis, madam. I happen to be a tourist."

"Oh sorry," she said sheepishly, apologized profusely and disappeared. If the old lady had mistook me for a travelling salesman she couldn't be blamed as in those days this door-to-door trade was very popular with the Pakistanis. It was called "door bashing" i.e. keep on beating the door of a house till such time that the lady of the house opens it, you put your left foot forward so she cannot close it and then finally just to get rid of you she buys a pair of stockings or a pullover.

At the end of the day when I was dog tired I had the first glimpse of Grasmere, a picturesque village to be sure and the last waters of Windermere glistening in the last rays of the setting sun.

"Excuse me sir," I addressed the first local who came my way and the gentleman was found to be properly intoxicated, reeling and singing "Where is the camping site?"

"What, a sight or site did you say. Well let me think," and he went into his thoughts so deep that it was a waste of time to wait for his coming out. So I went into a local store for information and I was told that the camping site is located on the other side of the lake and I had to walk another three miles or so to reach it.

When finally I arrived at my desired destination, it was dismal and muddy with three or four tents fluttering in the cold wind. During the night it rained and I was totally drenched. My brand new English tent was no match for the English rain.

Next morning I walked back to Grasmere whose Taj Mahal is the Dove Cottage where Wordsworth spent most of his life. There is the local church, very ordinary looking structure and here lies in the graveyard Wordsworth and some members of his family.

In the afternoon with the help of a local guide I visited the spot where supposedly the poet of nature created his classic "daffodils". I was rather disappointed as there was nothing to look at, there wasn't a single daffodil or any other minor flower to speak of, a muddy bank, wild grass and some ordinary bushes.

Many summers afterwards when life had taught me some harsh lessons I realized how very wrong I was, that "spots" do not matter, it is the inner feeling at that very moment which creates those daffodils even if they are not there. It is all within you and the "spot" is just an excuse to bring out your hidden treasures. I am sure there must have been some daffodils in those times and a poet's imagination multiplied them into hundreds swaying in the wind.

Grasmere in those days, almost fifty years ago, was still in deep slumber lost in those times when Wordsworth after vagabonding in the woods and banks of Lake Windermere returned to his dove cottage, humming softly his love of nature his latest poem, as I hum today in my approaching old age the fond memories of those days I spent in Grasmere.

The road to Paris

"Have you seen the good old oak tree dear?" I clenched my teeth and wanted to hit the person who had asked me the question. But this time it was an old lady with a very funny hat perched on her grey hair, smiling.

"Yes ma'am I have, its right behind me, lovely oak tree."

She was not the only one who took pride in this old oak. For the last four hours I was standing still outride Canterbury waiting for a lift which had not materialized and in these four hours at least four dozen passervs by had asked the same question. By now I was fed up with this ordinary looking tree that I wanted to uproot and manufacture matchsticks out of.

Armed with my newly acquired hitch hiking experience in the Lake District, now I was on my way to Europe, continent to be exact. I had planned to reach Dover by lunch time, take a ferry across English Channel for Calais and then onwards to gay Paris. But as luck would have it I was stuck up here with an old oak and the passing motorists had been completely ignoring my raised thumb for the last four hours.

To my bad luck a school boy came along glanced at my rucksack lying on the pavement and said, "Mister, I wonder if you have seen our oak tree?"

"Buzz off little boy or I will wring your neck."

The little boy took to his heels immediately.

This spot is unlucky, I thought, now one of us has to move, me or the oak tree. The oak tree had been here for the last two hundred years and would face certain uprooting problems and I had been here for the last four hours. So I decided to move instead, again a matter of common sense.

As soon as I lifted my rucksack to move, a tiny Morris Minor appeared from nowhere and screeched to a halt. It was packed like sardines. The driver sardine was in fact a well groomed gentleman with a goatee.

"Going somewhere mate?"

"Dover", I said, but where would they accommodate me? "Hop in", he said "We are not going the whole way but hop in, till we turn left for Seashell Island."

So I hopped in, a brown sardine amongst three female sardines of various sizes and hair colours; a red head, a blonde and a brunette. Never in my life had I been packed amongst such lovely sardines. "What you do for living mate?" the goatee sardine inquired.

"I am a student and you?"

"I am the finest hairstylist in London town and these three are my assistants and we are going to Seashell Island for the weekend."

So they are the English NAAIS. This explained their flamboyant hairdos and colour. They were a very friendly bunch of Naais to be sure, typical cockneys whose strange accent at times surpassed my little knowledge of English. Soon we were chatting away like old cronies, however, their departure point also came soon enough and the car stopped.

"Well this is as far as you go, we have to turn left from here. By the way its getting dark and you won't be able to catch the night ferry to France so why don't you come along with us? We have a log cabin by the sea, plenty of room there for you to sleep." The offer was attractive, a log cabin by the sea and pretty sardines in the bargain. But I hesitated "I don't want to bother you, I am grateful for the offer to be sure and besides you don't really know me enough."

"I know you well enough mate, a barber can judge a person in ten minutes, the time he takes in cutting his hair. But suit yourself." Then the blonde sardine started chirping: "Oh come on be a sport, we are short of boys around here and what would you be doing in a place like France? Oh, horrible people, they eat frogs and speak French you know. Oh, come on we will have fun." So I came along and fun we did have. The Seashell Island was, indeed a sea of shells. Instead of sand, its coast was a mass of shells which creaked and were creaked under the tyres of the car. It seemed as if we were crushing thousands of crystal pieces and it left me guilty.

The log cabin was the only structure for miles around.

My hosts, all four of them were dripping with the milk of human kindness, especially the females, naturally. They were the finest human species to be found anywhere.

As night fell the roar of the waves increased manifold and it so happened that there was a full moon. While walking towards the sea for a night swim, the shells cracked under our bare feet, and the moonlight factor was responsible for the rage of the waves. So that was a night of the sound of the sea, sea shells, a full moon and three lovely sardines swimming and splashing in the water like mermaids. During the night although cozy and comfortable in my sleeping bag I could not sleep due to the noise of the raging sea and cold winds lashing at our log cabin.

The blonde sardine was so right when she said that they were already short of boys. I stayed on with this bunch of carefree and loving souls for the weekend. Then they were on their way back to London. But before that, they went out of their way and took me to Dover. Bidding farewell, all of them hugged me and kissed me profusely, much to the envy of those watching. The night ferry took me across the English Channel, into the city of Calais from where in a jiffy a huge black limousine picked me up. It was black and huge because it belonged to a funeral company and the driver in a black suit was in fact an undertaker who was carrying a dead body of an English gentleman, who for reasons of his own, wished to be buried in a Paris graveyard.

That still-gentleman was resting in peace right behind me in a black mahogany coffin. What a way to go, for the gentleman and for me, to Paris. I took comfort in the thought that at last I don't have to amuse this gentleman by telling dirty jokes to justify my free ride.

These were the times when the whole of France was chanting "VIVA DE GAULLE", begging the reclusive General to take over the Presidency.

When all three of us, the undertaker, the dead gentleman and myself entered Paris my ears were throbbing with the song, a tune related to gay Paris...

I love Paris in the springtime,

I love Paris and how I love Paris...

and then the sad and lovely Under the Bridges of Seine.

Although my aesthetic sense will be considered rather doubtful, but I will take the risk and state that I did not love Paris at all, springtime or no springtime. It was hot, unfriendly and overcrowded with tourists.

I asked a passerby "Sir can you guide me to the Louvre Museum, I am lost." And he replied with a grin, "I am also lost buddy, how about that? I am an American, where are you from?"

"Pakistan."

"Somewhere in Afghanistan or Africa?"

Americans have always been the most ignorant but friendliest people on earth. The food was expensive and I had to fill my teenage belly with French bread and milk. The girls were petite to be sure but they were not interested in a boy. They prefered older men. I did all the rites like a faithful tourist. Mona Lisa, Venus de Milo, Cathedral of the Hunchback Notredame, Flea Market, Napoleon's Tomb, Moulin Rouge, Eiffel Tower etc. And then abandoned this so called gay Paris, for the green valleys and snow clad mountains of Switzerland.

Although a time came when this drab and unfriendly city became my Piyar Ka Pehla Shahar (the first city of my love). But that was ten years later when Paris engulfed with its magical charm and I almost became a Parisian myself. But now I was on a fast train to Switzerland, abandoning hitch hiking because I did not have the stomach to travel with another dead body.

Far, far from the madding crowd

SWITZERLAND of 1958 was a place that was out of this world; my world of poverty, ignorance and dirt, to be exact. Not only was it different from my Third World, but England and France were no match either. It was so very very clean, fresh and neat. Even the air was so pure and fresh that like a bell it jingled and like a new coin straight out of the mint it was pure and musical. So much so that when I breathed, I felt guilty.

Geneva sprawled along Lake Lemon and Lake Geneva. It was a city that proved fatal for an innocent teenager like me. The camping site was situated on a green hill overlooking the city and a great expanse of blue water. On one side flowed the river Rhone. The most fascinating spot of this camping site was a small cafe from where you could see the famous Geneva Jet sending gallons of water thousands of feet high. I was swept away, mesmerized indeed and when I heard my favourite song Darling Don't Forbid Me by Pat Boone being played on the jukebox of this cafe, the fatality was complete. Although there were other matters in store for me which proved more fatal.

Presently I decided that I was going to stay put, spend my whole summer vacation here. After all what could be better than this paradise? However, now I realize that, paradise was in my young blood and inexperience, otherwise Geneva, although a fantastic city, was not the end of the world.

As soon as I erected my little tent on the greenest of green grass on that hill, had my first cup of coffee in the cafe and put coin after coin in the jukebox to hear my favourite song, I noticed a very shabby looking tent peeping from the bushes. In front of it sat a very dashing white haired gentleman with only shorts on. In front of him lay a self manufactured table which was covered with old newspapers upon which lay a glass of sparkling red wine. First he spoke to me in French and when I shrugged my shoulders he said haltingly, "Are you Indian young man?"

I was vastly hurt and said, "No sir, I am from Pakistan, Indians are never that handsome."

He did not mind my foolish ego a bit and stretched his hand, "We can be friends, my name is Pierre." When the pleasantries were over I asked him "Sir, where are you from?"

"Switzerland", he said.

"And which city?"

"Geneva."

"And you are camping in your own city? What is your profession?"

"I am a vagabond!"

Basically I wanted to reply in Urdu that Khoob Guzre Gi Jo Mil Baithen Ge Diwane Do, but I could not translate it. And besides, this Diwana was at least fifty years senior to me. So I said, "It's my pleasure to meet one of the kind."

Pierre, that evening, cooked some sausages and french-fries which he insisted that I share with him. Although he insisted that I share his wine too but till then I had not touched the cup that cheers.

Next day I descended from my heavenly abode and explored the city of Geneva. I noticed that the Swiss are so vastly enamoured of their flag that they hoist it, hang it everywhere, even in lavatories. Later I decided to refresh myself under the Geneva Jet in the cool, for me freezing, waters of Lake Geneva. In fact I am not a swimmer in the real sense of the word, basically a splasher i.e. if I am pushed into the deep waters, I go down and down and then finally when I emerge on the surface, I splash frantically to save my dear life. During one of these splashes underneath the Geneva Jet fountain, in the deep waters of Lake Lemon, I saw emerging from the waters a blonde head. She was Ruth, a German girl who in time to come would prove to be "Ruthless".

Ruth was here in Geneva to learn French part-time and, full-time, she was a waitress serving in one of the most expensive restaurants by the Lake. Needless to say that in coming days I enjoyed many free of cost meals in that posh and expensive restaurant courtesy Ruth, the Ruthless.

Eventually, in life I achieved the dubious honour of obtaining a certificate in ballroom dancing, from the prestigious, Victor Silvester School of Dancing, learning the intricate Tango, Quickstep and Waltz, besides the notorious Cha Cha Cha. However, at the time, I was ignorant at that time of reference of any dance form. And it was Ruth who was my teacher. In the midst of the night, when I was walking her home from my camping spot, in the darkness of a thick forest, from the depth floated a melody. In the hush of the night there was music. Ruth said "Lets dance."

And I said apologetically, "I can't".

"It's simple," and she put her arms around my waist "you just count one two three and swirl...it's simple."

I was a dumb headed novice but who wouldn't become a bright head if it was a Geneva night and there was a willing teacher?

Prior to this lesson, we had sat in the camping cafe and Pat Boone kept on crooning Darling Don't Forbid Me. A morning came when I saw a sight which was beyond my comprehension. That self-proclaimed vagabond, Pierre, was emerging from a chauffeur driven car in a three-piece suit, very respectable. Then he went into his very shabby tent and when he emerged, he was in his shorts, and sat in the sunshine of Geneva and looked at my disbelieving face.

"Pakistani, I am unfortunately one of the most famous dental surgeons in Geneva but when I get fedup with my luxurious life, I escape and come here, don't disclose my secret."

And when I introduced Ruth to him he was delighted, "If I were any younger I would have challenged you to a duel to win her over."

Those who are experts in hitch-hiking consider Germany the best place to raise a thumb and Switzerland the worst due to a law according to which you are not paid any insurance in case of an accident if a hitch-hiker is on board. So from Geneva I decided to walk along the shore of the lake upto Laussane. Years onward, on the slopes of Vichy, Charles Chaplin was to be buried and then stolen.

A few days of a short lift here and there, and walking I reached the magical city of Montriex at the end of Lake Geneva. Here although the camping was right beside the lake, but the charm of Pierre and the beauty of Ruth were lacking. The mediaeval castle of Chillon on the edge of the lake was the main tourist attraction. It is the castle of Byron's poem Prisoner of Chillon and the guide dutifully shows the dungeon in which the now famous prisoner rotted. But the star attraction of the place was Byron's autograph, engraved into a stonewall and to safeguard it a thick glass sheet covered it and rightly so. Because all the female visitors felt duty bound to kiss it with such passion that every now and then the layers of lipsticks of all shades had to be wiped clean. Byron must be a very happy man even now, in his grave or wherever he is.

From Montriex one could easily see the shores of France across the lake and one afternoon I hired a rowing boat with the intention of going across, having a cup of coffee in France and returning to Montriex. It looked very near but it was deceptive. I rowed and rowed but France never came any closer and finally when the evening approached and I decided to turn back, I was shocked to see that although Montriex was there somewhere, I couldn't locate the spot from where I had started my journey. When darkness fell, even Montriex and the villages around it got all mixed up. The mountain was a mass of lights and I was completely lost. Fortunately for such emergencies the boat was equipped with a lantern which I lit and hoisted it on a pole and then using my vocal chords fully, I started shouting for help.

Finally I was rescued by a police boat. It was almost midnight when I crept into my tent hungry and shivering but grateful that I had avoided the watery grave of Lake Geneva. Did I learn my lesson? Alas it is not so. I remained foolish and impulsive for the rest of my life, always itching to go across to see the other side of a lake, or a mountain. And in this life of mine, let's see what is in store for me on the other side.

Tourism tamasha

Once upon a time a full-fledged prime minister of Pakistan visited the Northern Areas to hear out the grievances of the populace. Wherever he went the locals complained about a certain glacier which was forcibly occupied by the Indians, thus dividing their families.

The PM was at a loss as to what these people were complaining about, so he asked his assistants to clarify the matter. He was told that they wanted their glacier back. The PM smiled knowingly and said, "Oh this matter of Gulsher missing has been brought to my notice repeatedly and I assure that the government is giving this matter top most priority. We will bring back this Gulsher Khan wherever he is. Don't you worry about it."

Khawja Mehrdad, who served as the principal of Government College Skardu, once participated in a high-level meeting in Islamabad chaired by the then federal minister for education. Khawja sahib complained about the lack of education facilities and funds in Skardu. The education minister haughtily replied, "Well the government is fully aware that in Baluchistan there is a lack of educational facilities and we have chalked out a master plan for the uplift of education in that area. Don't you worry about it."

"But sir, I am talking about Skardu," Khawja sahib said sheepishly.

"Well," the all-knowing minister looked at him with contempt, "This Skardu is in Baluchistan, isn't it?"

Khawja sahib dare not correct him as he did not want to lose his job.

The situation has not changed drastically since then. Our education minister recently mourned about the declining standards of education and to prove his point made fun of our cricket captain Inzamamul Haq's poor English. I had then humbly suggested that in future our cricket team should be selected from the waiters of five star hotels as they speak excellent English. Because this suggestion was ignored, our cricket team lost the first Test against South Africa.

But it was our prime minister who at bowled a real beauty by giving the target of one million tourists for the preset year to the tourist ministry and all concerned are parroting that this target will be met. I am sure this can be easily achieved by the agencies that can abduct a million tourists from all over the world and bring them to Pakistan, forcibly if necessary, and they can be listed as "missing persons".

If this is not feasible, I have another suggestion. All the city and district nazims should be ordered to collect as many people as possible, pack them in hijacked buses and wagons and take them to the next city as tourists. The Karachiwalas should be dispatched to Quetta and Quettawalas can be sent to Lahore. As a matter of fact, whole villages of the feudal areas could be transported to Dadu or Skardu, and this will be called family tourism. And I am sure the target of one million will be easily achieved. For the nazims and district authorities it should not be much of a problem as they have shown their competence in the past by providing these unwilling masses for the public meetings of the ruling parties.

As a chronic tourist I am overjoyed that year 2007 has been declared as a year of tourism. But how are you going to go about it? Holding senseless seminars, tourist melas, pathetic jeep safaris, camel races, Gandhara week and so on and so forth, repeating for the umpteenth time the same old cliché that Pakistan is the cradle of ancient civilizations? We have deserts, coastlines, mountains, hospitable populace, and if you want to see a madrassa, a visit can easily be arranged with a dozen guards to protect you and you can keep those guards for the rest of the visit if you care about your dear life.

There was this meeting some time in the past for the promotion of tourism where the officials were parroting the above-mentioned cliches and were sure that every potential tourist in the world is dying to visit Pakistan.

However, my point of view was rather radical: "Gentlemen, if I were an American or European with a pocket full of dollars, I would be an idiot if I headed for Pakistan. There are better beaches in Goa and Sri Lanka where bikinis will not cause a riot, deserts are much larger and scenic in Afghanistan and Iran. Nepal also has the highest mountain in the world and you cannot beat India for this cradle of civilization crap, so how are you going to entice the potential tourist? I maintain that Pakistan has a potential for the domestic tourism, please forget the gora and concentrate on the local kalas."

The initial attraction for any white tourist is a law-abiding country where he can roam about freely and safely. Here our police chiefs, advocate generals and even the president is not safe. A gora, even if he is not an American roaming around, is ideal for kidnapping. Even the Chinese friends are not spared. Has anybody seen a white tourist having fun in Peshawar or Miramshaha recently? So much for the law and order situation!

The other factor is the attitude of locals towards tourists. It is, I am afraid, utterly hostile with the exception of Hunza and Baltistan. We have not developed a culture of tolerance towards foreigners and, mind you, before the Russian invasion even the Afghans were very liberal in this respect. Indians are masters of this craft and even Iran is much more tolerant than us Pakistanis.

The other day I had the misfortune of watching a PTV discussion programme regarding this so-called tourism year and it was pathetic. One of the participants, Mr Iqbal from Skardu, raised some very relevant objections regarding the government's policy and the minister for tourism, lording over the discussion not like a lord but lady because she is a lady, got furious and said, "Don't malign Pakistan."

As if the politicians had left any maligning for poor Mr Iqbal! When he raised another point that tourists crossing from China into Pakistan had to travel all the way to Islamabad to procure a climbing permit and then go back from where they started and that can't these permits be issued in Gilgit or Skardu?

The lady said with a broad smile, "The prime minister is considering the proposal."

Now I know why our prime minister is so busy, he is considering a proposal that instead of Islamabad the climbing permit should be made available in Gilgit or Skardu. Tough decision to make I am sure. I personally know that Mr Iqbal, who is perhaps a member of Northern Areas council, has done much more for the promotion of tourism than the whole ministry, including the minister. However, at the end of programme the minister was very sweet and told the viewers, "These tourism matters were not addressed for the last one hundred years and it seems that we have opened a Pandora's box. So be patient, give us time to implement our planned policies."

I could be wrong but as far as my guess goes, Pakistan was created only about 60 years back. Where did these hundred years come from?

I wish the establishment a very happy tourist year and congratulate them for spending millions of rupees for attracting exactly one million tourists to Pakistan – no more, no less. By the end of this year if I discover a single white tourist freely roaming about in the streets of Pakistan, I will, if I am alive by then, personally go to Islamabad to shake the hand of the minister, if she is still the minister.

Cutting a lonely furrow

LAST week I visited an ailing friend who had recently returned from Canada, after having served four and a half years in solitary confinement!

My friendship with Talmiz Huqqani dates back many years. It was he who one fine morning in 1969 grabbed me and took me to the editor of Sayyara Digest, Maqbool Jehangir, and told him that 'in front of you stands a young man who has written a marvellous travelogue which nobody is willing to publish'. "Will you publish it?" asked Talmiz. Maqbool Jehangir the famous author of dozens of books on shikaryat (hunting) without ever even touching a hunting gun, did not even look at my manuscript. "Tarar sahib I will publish it but drop this Tarar thing from your name, nobody will take you seriously with this tongue twister name."

"I don't want to be a writer if I am not a Tarar."

"As you wish Mr Mustansar Hussain Tarar," he was all smiles. "I hope you wont add a Chaudhry in the beginning!"

So began my career; Talmiz had pushed me into the quagmire of literature.

After retiring as a director public relations Wapda, he voluntarily worked with an organization for a few years and then finally landed in Canada where his only son was serving as a senior banker. He had some ailments while he was here, but Canada's loneliness and aloof society was too much for him. He was an extremely social animal who loved Lahore and his many friends who adored his sincerity, which bordered on insanity. A lost soul in Canada, he used to wander through its malls, looking for somebody to talk to and most of the days he didn't find anybody.

At times he would talk to my daughter, Annie, settled in Orlando, USA, for hours remembering me and Lahore. Of course he knew her since she was a toddler. It was not that his son ignored him or anything, on the contrary his obedience was exemplary and he provided his father with all the amenities of a luxurious life. But at the same time, he and his wife were a working couple and they could not provide him with what he needed most; friends and Lahore.

Then as luck would have it the son was offered a better deal by an international bank in Pakistan so the whole family packed and left Canada, its winters and its loneliness and came to Lahore.

Although I knew that his sugar level was high, his blood pressure soaring and his heart erratic, still I was not prepared for what I saw. He was totally bedridden because he had broken his hipbone in the bargain too; he was in pain but smiled all the time because he was back in Lahore. He narrated stories of his ailments and how he fainted on the plane on his way to Pakistan and was treated in Alaska with snow bears peeping through the windows. After a while, when it was just the two of us in the room, he whispered, "Mustansar sahib, can you see something on the other side of this glass window?" In front of us was only a blank wall. "Which glass window Talmiz?"

"Don't tell me you can't see it either," he was slightly cross with me.

"Just a blank wall Talmiz, there is no window I assure you." "Everybody keeps telling me that," he sighed. "But at times I see people across this window; they smile and wave their hands. As a matter of fact one of them even came into my washroom and hid there. Do you believe me?"

"Yes Talmiz, I believe you. I am sure when your hipbone is operated upon and you can walk around Lahore with friends, these people will disappear."

"Yes, when they will put curtains on this glass window, they won't be seen, I am sure."

Was he hallucinating or was it that four and half years of solitary confinement were having their effect?

It is said that no matter how many offsprings, friends or relatives you have around you, it is in your fate, especially a man's, that eventually you will face utter loneliness. I remember that in his last days my beloved father was bedridden. Although most of his three daughters and three sons, including myself, were always nearby, it was well nigh impossible that all of us should leave the battle of bread and butter procurement and the family, to sit beside him for twenty-four hours, although one of us was always taking care of his needs.

My mother had passed away a few months earlier and her departure completely shattered this magnificent man. At times I would enter his room and he would just be sitting there, on his bed, staring at a wall unaware that I was there.

It was a beautiful spring morning, bubbling with life, when I with great difficulty placed this big hunk of man on a wheelchair. He hated this exercise. Only a year back he could carry his six feet frame with dignity and could walk for ten or fifteen kilometres with ease and leisure. Now he had to be helped and carried and he hated it; his blue eyes brimming with tears of helplessness and sadness.

As we came out in our small lawn he saw the dahlias blooming and said, "Hum sehra main hain aur ghar main bahar aye hai" (we are in the desert and there's Spring in the house). He advised me not to over water the dahlias. I wheeled him away to the nearby market; there was great hustle bustle all around him, children running, cars honking, people shouting and he smiled happily, "The world is so beautiful."

"Abbaji is there anything your heart desires right now?" "I would like to have some juice," he replied.

With trembling fingers he held the straw, placed its end in his mouth and sipped the juice happily.

"Would you like to have a cigarette abbaji?" I asked. He had been a regular smoker throughout his life. At home he had a huqqa which he prepared himself and out in the world, when in a three-piece or a safari-suit, he would smoke his favourite cigarette. Then, a few months back, some stupid doctor imposed the prohibition: "Chaudhry sahib, no more cigarettes, your age your health...". There was a marked change in his behaviour after this ban, he felt morose and did not know what to do with his fingers.

"Yes I would," he said sheepishly.

I lit his favourite cigarette and placed it between his shaking fingers. I had never seen him so happy and smiling.

A few days afterwards he whispered: "Mustansar you should lock the doors properly for the night, there are certain people who come during the night and roam around my bed, harassing me."

"Yes abbaji."

"Don't you believe me?" he asked angrily.

"I do abbaji," my eyes filling with tears for my beloved. "Rest assured, I will lock all the doors properly tonight." It was the final loneliness and desolation.

My pretty and doll like mother-in-law, when nearing ninety, faced the same predicament. She had nine children in all, numerous grandchildren and even when her son Aftab, who worshipped her, was with her, she felt utterly alone. At times she would ring up my wife and order her to leave everything and come to her immediately. Mamoona would rush to her mother, bathe her feet, which she loved to do and then after hours when she would get up to go my mother-in-law would say: "You are all alike, abandoning me for your children and home, you don't love me."

At times she too would raise an alarm that there are people who roam around her bed during the night. Her sons and daughters would gather around her, stay the night with her and she did not see anything. However, the very next day, there was the same complaint; there are people who come and go.

I know Talmiz is not that old and he will be much better when he can walk around, but it worries me. Is it man's fate to face desolate loneliness eventually?

When a death shocks you, when you see somebody's mental faculties declining and you are hurt and when you witness the last loneliness and you feel a fear, it is not only the milk of human kindness which generates these feelings, it is your death which shocks, you are afraid that you also might reach the same stage and will be engulfed in the final loneliness and despair.

Since I met Talmiz, it seems that I am also seeing things from a different perspective and at times I hear voices, which I am sure do not exist. I may be imagining it but the other day while admiring some potted dahlias and renancculuses I positively saw two look alike figures hardly the size of a small finger rollicking in the petals. Perhaps they were twins and they were talking to each other in English. If I am not mistaken one of them was Yajuj and the other was called Majuj. They were smartly attired in three-piece suits with matching ties, wearing joggers to jog on the flower petals. They were conversing on all sorts of local and international topics and if I see them again I have a mind to note down their conversation and report it to you.

You do believe that there are these two Lilliputians residing in my dahlias and renanculuses don't you? If you don't then I won't tell you what they converse about.

Happy New Year.

Dubai chalo

ALMOST a quarter of a century ago, a TV series titled Ek Haqeeqat Ek Fasana was launched from Lahore in which I was cast as a golden hearted Edhi-sque journalist whose life is dedicated to the service of humanity. In fact the dramas were based upon real life stories provided by the late Riaz Batalvi.

One of the stories was about a young rustic and innocent man who came along and sells all his valuables and goes to Dubai to fulfil his dreams of a better life. When he reaches Dubai he is arrested because of the forged papers provided by the agent and comes back empty handed, his Dubai dream shattered. Ali Ijaz played the role of this half-witted young man, admirably, and sky rocketed to fame. The drama was called Dubai Chalo which became a national slogan in those days, as Dubai was the dream city of all desires. So when I announced my forthcoming Dubai visit I immediately became the target of all sorts of jokes and insults.

"Good heavens Tarar, don't tell us that you have not been to Dubai as yet! Every Tom, Dick and perhaps Harry also has been to Dubai repeatedly. And you call yourself a vagabond, shame on you".

So it was with a heavy heart and a sense of shame that I boarded the plane for Dubai. I was going there to record a TV show. My co-host, Aliya Shah, who was accompanying me, was vastly excited by the prospect of shopping in Dubai, especially its famed festival and chirped about it incessantly. The cabin crew was a cocktail of all nationalities and we were informed by the British pilot that we could communicate with them in eleven languages, including Mangolian. As it happens my Mongolian is rather elementary i.e.; Ulan Bator or Changez Khan etc., hence I refrained from communicating.

The Dubai airport was palatial, vast and so well lit that one wondered that, our Arab brethren, who can buy anything on Earth, might have bought a minor sun from some galaxy to brighten Dubai airport. I was not shocked, but deeply amused when I saw "The Irish Village" bar and restaurant offering all types of Irish brews and fresh pork chops, and right opposite to it was a mosque where you could offer your prayers. "Rind ke rind rahe hath se jannat na gai."

This was Dubai where the devils and angels reside side by side, so you have a choice and can be the guest of any one of them, or better still both of them.

The Dubai Duty Free Shop is another vast complex stacked with such enchantments which are hard to resist; gold, cameras, chocolates, electrical appliances and what not. This "what not" is the variety of bottled waters which are supposed to cheer the soul.

Finally after covering at least one kilometre within the airport complex, we reached an area where hundreds of passengers were queuing up for God knows what. We were also required to join them because here your eyes were to be photographed for security reasons. However, for the next 30 minutes, the queue hadn't moved. It was disclosed that the eye machine was out of order; a mechanic had been sent for and the possibility was that we will spend the night on the airport. So I approached a burly airport officer, "Sir, we are here to record a television show and our crew is waiting outside, is it possible if you could kindly let us go because the eye machine is out of order?"

"Is it your first visit to Dubai?"

"Yes sir," I said gleefully.

"Then you cannot go without your eyes being photographed, you may be a terrorist."

"Well sir, my eyes are brown, you can peep into them and the eyes of this lady are the colour of the lenses which she is wearing presently, please?"

He peeped into Aliya's eyes instead rather enthusiastically and the female charm worked, "You can go."

Here I must declare a geographical ignorance of mine, I could never differentiate between Dubai and Abu Dhabi, at times I thought they were one and the same thing. However, a tourist brochure enlightened me and I found out that UAE actually comprises of seven independent states i.e. Dubai, Abu Dhabi, Sharja, Ajmam, Umm Al Quwain, Ras Al Khaimah and Fujairah which were ruled by their respective sultans.

In Dubai, we rarely came across a genuine Dubaian; there were hordes of Europeans, scantily clad hopping from one shopping mall to another, loaded with heavy shopping bags, Iranians gobbling Chillu kababs, Indians running their restaurants and stores, Filipinos, Egyptians, Palestinians and of course Pakistanis, mostly taxi drivers. During my whole stay I hardly spotted a few Arab women clad in black shawls, otherwise the national dress of Dubai for the females was tight jeans and shrinking blouses.

The central Asian women were also very visible especially after the sunset, visibility of their contours left nothing to imagination. I was informed that the locals hardly amount to 15 per cent of the total population that is why we hardly saw any locals. The apartment hotel where we were lodged had an Indian manager, the waiters were from Goa, the receptionist was a stern Chinese lady, the housekeeping staff was from the Philippines, the drivers from Pakistan and the electrician was a burly Sikh gentleman.

At times an Arab in flowing robes just strolled in, smiled and said Salam to everybody and after exactly five minutes disappeared for the day, he was the owner. In the meantime the rest of the crew also appeared including, Mr Abdul Rauf of Pacchas Minute fame. We decided to spend our first evening in the pursuit of unnecessary shopping because it is such a pleasure to spend your hard earned money on items that are totally useless.

The world renowned Dubai Shopping Festival was on, we counted our dollars and dirhams and headed for the City Centre which is the craze in Dubai. It was so huge that we promptly lost ourselves in the labyrinth of thousands of stores, restaurants, cinemas, coffee bars, designer's showrooms and what not. Our one and only female companion, Aliya was starry eyed, excited beyond limits gazing at the vast array of goodies displayed in showcases and because of the festival, available at reduced prices.

She would disappear in some huge store; emerge after about an hour or so clutching a pair of shoes declaring triumphantly, "Look Tarar Sahib only ten dirhams!" She would again get lost and this time holding a small dainty handkerchief inform gleefully "Look Tarar sahib, only three dirhams." However, I was not loosening the strings of my purse because the dollar supply was meagre and I intended to buy a camera and some designer suits.

As I came out of a French shopping mall, naturally without buying even a hairpin, the security guard stopped me, "Why you do not pay for things you take from the store?" He was a thin Filipino whose uniform was hanging from his hanger frame.

"I do not pay because I have not bought anything."

"The security alarm beeped when you come out of store, why?"

"Because I have a magnetic personality," I smiled back at his sternness.

"Go back and come out again."

So I obliged him by going back into the store and then coming out; he was right, the alarm beeped like mad, I was alarmed. Maybe I had put something in my pocket absentmindedly. The guard went through all my pockets and then again asked me to repeat the procedure of going back and then coming out.

The damn alarm again shrieked.

"Please come into this room, you have something."

He took me to a small room where he searched me thoroughly, my cigarettes, a lighter, wallet and some tissue papers.

"You have nothing," he was clearly disappointed.

"I told you so."

"Then tell me why the alarm goes beep beep?"

"I told you I have a magnetic personality," this time I did not smile because I had enough. "There is something wrong with your bloody alarm mister, why don't you get it right?"

"No the alarm cannot be wrong, we have very modern security system," he insisted. "Look here little man," I felt like grabbing him from his neck and wringing it good and proper, "You want to search me again? I am going to your security head and lodge a complaint against you, you have harassed me without any proof and I am going to get you fired."

The little man was terrified by my empty threat and smiled for the first time, "No, you are right, you have a magnetic personality, thank you, goodbye."

That evening in the food court of the City Centre, over a bowl of Chinese soup I met one of the most amazing personalities in UAE, Mr Suhail Zarooni, whose name is mentioned in The Guinness Book of World Records.

An Arab with a Pakistani soul

THAT evening, in the Food Court, at the City Centre, over a bowl of soup I met one of UAE's most amazing personalities; Mr Suhail Al Zarooni whose name is mentioned in the Guinness Book of Records.

Suhail is fluent in Urdu and Pushto, has an imposing figure and when he walks in his flowing Arab robes, he looks like a character straight out of Alf Laila, speaks haltingly with the innocence of a child, rather shy but confident. One cannot imagine that this simple soul runs a vast business empire beside being an enthusiastic collector of stamps, coins, watches and cars of all sorts. His eloquence in Urdu and Pushto is from his mother's side who is a Pathan lady and his father is an Arab connected with the Royal family.

Educated in Atchison and at heart he is still a pucca Lahori relishing nihari, siri payas and Gowalmandi's fish. Although affluent even by Dubai's standards, he is very humble and almost obedient at times.

The very next evening he invited the whole crew for dinner at his, needless to say, palatial house. We were promptly told that Benazir Bhutto lived nearby in an equally humble abode.

As the huge iron gates swung open we thought we had entered a car showroom instead of a residence; the only difference was that the cars displayed were not brand new. These were actually vintage cars collected by Suhail including two Rolls Royces and half a dozen Land Cruisers. The car, which took my breath away, was a red sports car. If I recall correctly, it was a Bugatti from Italy.

"There are at this moment only seventy sports cars of this make in the whole world and only three in the Middle East, would you like to see the interior?" he raised the door and it went up like a huge red wing. I admit that I am not a connoisseur of cars and they have never fascinated me as such. But this Bugatti was entirely a different cup of tea and I know I could ever afford it and this likelihood is rather remote as the cost is in millions. So I have to be content for the time being with my ten-year-old Toyota.

The leather interior was fabulous to say the least and one could smell the millions which were a prerequisite to its ownership. All the servants who hovered over us in spotless dresses were Pashtuns because the lady of the house was a Pashtun and they were delighted to receive Pakistani guests as they recognized some of the faces from the television screen. The endless drawing and dinning room was decorated with stuffed wild animals including a lion and dozens of deer whose sad eyes looked alive. Abdul Rauf who had once upon a time served with the WWF in Geneva, looked disturbed. "Suhail I believe in the conservation of wildlife and hunting and stuffing such animals for your personal pleasure is distasteful to me."

Suhail was as cool as ever, "I also believe in the conservation of wild animals because I love them and I personally contribute to some of the organizations who are trying to save the precious animal species. But these stuffed deer you see around here are an exception. You see some of the African countries raise these deer in huge farms and then an exact number is released into the wild. You obtain a hunting licence, pay a very large sum and only then are you permitted to hunt one animal. The money generated through this procedure is entirely spent on the conservation."

Suhail had a point because in the Northern areas of Pakistan this method of conservation was also applied officially with the backing of conservation experts. When the animals exceed a certain number, especially the Marco Polo sheep, a couple of hunting licenses are issued at a rate, which is not easily affordable. The money thus generated is spent on the well being of local residents and the animals in wild.

The Pathans and the Arabs, both are known for their extravagant hospitality and if they are wedded together you can well imagine what the end result will be; an endless table laden with food which looked like a food festival of sorts. "We normally have Pakistani food in our house because once you develop a taste for it, it is well nigh impossible to appreciate any other food," Suhail told us. "The cook is a Bengali gentleman who has been with us for the last many years, he is a chef par excellence but on one point he loses his temper.

"If you praise anybody else's cooking, for instance if you casually remark that once upon a time in Karachi I tasted a better pillau he will lose his temper."

"What does he do when he loses his temper?" Aliya looked really frightened.

"Well he will go back to the kitchen, prepare another dish of pillau and will make you eat it till such time that you admit that he is the best pillau chef in the whole world."

After dinner we were served the typical Arab qhahva, which tasted more like Joshanda but it helped to digest all we had gobbled. The comment which really gladdened our hearts that evening was from Suhail when he said, "You know when I go abroad and people ask me what my nationality is, I always say that I am an Arab with a Pakistani soul."

Suhail is known as King of model cars and his name has been added to the Guinness Book of Records for the biggest model car collection. His car assortment includes the John F. Kennedy limousine in which he was assassinated, Hitler's cars, Russian presidents, the British Queen and James bond cars. At present he has more than 5500 model cars that is estimated to be valued at more than $5 million.

At the end of the evening, Suhail ordered his two chauffeurs to drop us at our hotel in his limousine, which to my middle-class looked like three cars welded together, one after the other. I hesitated to get in, because ten years ago I had a ten-minute ride in such a machine and my outlook on life changed for the next ten days; then I recovered. I was returning from a wedding and the only car available was this limo. It was a strange experience, sitting all alone in a small room complete with a bar and music system, cruising quietly while through the tinted windows even the dirtiest parts of the city looked romantic, the driver nowhere to be seen. After two minutes the humanity outside seemed, as if they were insects, ants that did not have a right to walk in the vicinity of "MY" limousine. Five minutes passed in that secluded luxury and I thought these insects had no right to live either. After the ride, when I entered my home, it looked shabby and poverty stricken, even my wife seemed rather decadent. This short ride made me realize that if ten minutes in such a luxury can change a person's outlook, then how can the people who are born with such unparalleled comforts realize the agony of the masses, if they treat them like insects, which comes natural to them.

However, this second half-an-hour's drive in Suhail's limousine did not have the same effect as it was crowded with our crew including Abdul Rauf and Aliya, middle class like myself; so it had a sobering effect. However, when the hotel people saw us emerge from this grand white limousine, they immediately started respecting us, and bowed at times, for the rest of our stay in Dubai.

I will always remember the evening spent in the company of Suhail Al Zarooni who was an Arab with a Pakistani soul.

Saving Gandhara treasures

ONCE upon a time, naturally in Greece, the great Plato claimed that all Greeks were made of gold, the Mediterranean of silver and rest of the humanity of iron. His disciples were amazed and asked humbly as to who would accept such a ridiculous thesis. The great teacher replied, "The present generation will laugh at it, the next generation will start doubting it and the third generation will accept it as the ultimate truth."

I suppose that is how historical misconceptions take root and we Pakistanis are the champions of such distorted misconceptions. Some "Plato" of ours floated the idea that Pakistan is the castle of Islam and we have been parroting it for the last half-century or so with total conviction without ever bothering to analyze this ridiculous statement.

If there has to be a some sort of castle of Islam why not Saudi Arabia, or for that matter the largest Muslim country in the world Indonesia? Although Turkey and Iran could be close contenders but it has to be Pakistan because once upon a time some "Plato" said so. We thrive upon another great misconception that Pakistan will last till the Day of Judgment without ever realizing that geographical boundaries change over the course of centuries; nothing remains the same, countries, ideologies and even holy convictions. As a matter of fact our day of judgment came on 16th of December 1971, the original Pakistan lasted only till then.

Now I would like to draw your attention to another historical misconception which is very prevalent in the official and art circles; the so called smuggling of Gandhara sculpture and artifacts is a great loss to the cultural heritage of Pakistan. Recently the New York customs authorities confiscated a consignment of Gandhara antiques booked from an Arab country. Immediately Pakistan laid claim to it and demanded that these antiques be returned to the rightful owner, as these were the cultural heritage of our country.

Numerous editorials and letters to the editor mourned the loss of such priceless objects and demanded their immediate return to Pakistan. However the American customs did not co-operate and asked us to furnish solid proof of their ownership in the form of museum catalogues in which these stolen artifacts were listed, as was required under the law. How could we provide any proof of ownership, as there was none? These artifacts did not belong to any museum; I think they were mostly bought from the supermarkets of Gandhara pieces in Swat and NWFP and shipped abroad to the rightful owners. I don't think it will be out of place if we take stock of our attitude at the national level towards all art forms, especially sculpture. We are mortally afraid of all forms of sculpture and detest its presence anywhere in our homes or cities. Hence we find horrid missiles and Chaghi replicas littered all over the place, being depicted as our real cultural heritage.

Recently in Lahore's Defence Housing Authority, a mere relief depicting Pakistani soldiers was vandalized on the pretext that it portrayed human beings, which was sacrilegious. And on top of it, the hooligans who were responsible for this violence, were obliged by the authorities by removing the same and today there's nondescript garbage in its place.

A sculpture of beautifully designed white horses on a city crossing is also under threat, again it is a replica of a living thing hence a grave danger to the Islamic Republic of Pakistan.

My own mother-in-law, whenever she visited us, always complained, "Mustansar, where do I offer my prayers? Your house is full of these ungodly statues."

And jokingly I would say, "Ammijee, when you are offering prayers in the nearness of a statue, does that statue attract you and you are tempted to bow before him?" Naturally she scolded me in return.

I am afraid that it is the still breathing Hindu in us and just to deny that he is not there anymore, we oppose all sculptural forms vehemently. Whenever I offer my Fajar prayers in my house, I assure you my small collection of Gandhara sculptures does not bother me a bit, they absolutely do not tempt me to bow before them instead of the Almighty. It is only we Pakistanis who are terrified of any sculptural form, the rest of the Muslim world does not feel threatened by these infidel images be it Syria, Indonesia, Turkey or Morocco. Saudi Arabia, however, is an exception. Saudis will adorn their cities with monstrous bicycles, ships, pots and pans, but will not touch anything, which vaguely resembles a living form, even images and photographs are taboo. However, they do not uphold such strict moral code while displaying provocative ladies under garments on headless busty mannequins, easily the sexiest I have ever set my eyes upon.

The mannequins are headless because the face is again a taboo. Besides the Saudis believe that a woman does not have a head, hence they cannot drive or own property etc. The Pakistani hatred of sculpture was also transmitted to Taliban who were trained and educated in Pakistani seminaries and they displayed it by destroying the most magnificent Buddha statues of Bamiyan, an act of unparalleled madness.

The Afghans for many centuries prized their cultural heritage Even. Mahmud of Ghazna, the idol destroyer, did not think of destroying the Bamiyan masterpieces; it was the singular honour of the Pakistani educated Taliban. During the so-called Jihad of Afghanistan, the Mujahideens looted the Jalalabad and Kabul museums, but they did not destroy sculptures which were thousands of years old. They were not that stupid. Instead they smuggled these ancient treasures to Pakistan and made millions.

I have had the opportunity of viewing some of these magnificent pieces, which were later smuggled out of the country. Please do not ask me to pinpoint the location or the name of the gentleman who offered me such a rare opportunity.

I remember that in times of Zia-Ul-Haq, Ayaz Mir rightly commented that we were not that bad a nation to deserve a Zia-Ul-Haq. Pakistan Television was told to make a documentary on Gandhara art for foreign consumption. However, the showing of any sculpture in this documentary was strictly forbidden. I also remember that some high-ups very passionately defended the decision claiming that showing statues on TV was also un-Islamic. It was like making a documentary on Everest without showing the Everest or asking a player to play tennis without a tennis racket.

After the destruction of the Bamiyan Buddhas there was a lobby in this country, which suggested that all the statues on display in our museums be removed, and there was a rumour that the famous classic of Gandhara ,the fasting Buddha could become a target for the purification of land of pure.

How can such a society claim that artifacts and sculptures smuggled out of the country are our cultural heritage and demand its return? I have visited most of the Gandhara sites in Pakistan and they are in bad shape. There are numerous villages in Swat whose inhabitants deal in Gandhara objects although most of them are homemade. These people really know the value of these antiques and hide them from the Mullas roaming around, hell-bent on finding them and destroying them. Thanks to the local and foreign buyers, these poverty stricken areas make a decent, although from the government point of view, illegal living. In bargain these objects either land in some collector's drawing room or are shifted abroad. In both cases they are at least saved from an idol destroying society.

Am I advocating the so-called smuggling of Gandhara antiques? In a way I am, what would a villager do if he finds a rare Gandhara piece while digging his land or a nearby site? Throw it away or destroy it. Once an old man from these areas approached me, he had two fabulous Gandhara pieces wrapped in a blanket, I sent him to a Lahore museum official. The official regretted that the museum could not buy these pieces because already there are hundreds of such sculptures lying around in a cellar for the lack of space to exhibit them. Now what could that patriotic old man do, naturally sell it to the first private buyer who approaches him.

Let the Gandhara sculpture be smuggled out of the country so that it is safely kept in some foreign collection or in some museum so that when a time comes, if it comes at all, when we realize the importance of our cultural heritage, at least we can take pride that it is still intact somewhere in the world.

If you ask me, I would suggest that the Fasting Buddha should also be dispatched to Japan or America for safekeeping.

Back from the Yellow Devil

"THANK GOD, I have returned to my civilized world from that uncivilized world." These were the very first words that my dear and departed wife uttered — departed for Pakistan from the United States of America after a period of more than four months — while coming out of the exit of the International Lounge.

My wife had left for the US, after obtaining her delayed visa. As soon as the visa materialized, my wife packed her bags and a few pots filled with local herbs and oils, which were to be administrated to young Noffel, my grandson, during his infancy.

I do admit that initially I had enjoyed my newfound freedom; it was the first time in my life during our thirty-four years of blissful, or blisterful, marriage that we parted from each other, for such a long period of time. And not with tears but with smiles.

I was all alone in the house and could do whatever my heart desired, could watch the navels of half-clad Indian damsels on television with glee; invite all those friends whom my wife despised; order the housemaid to prepare all those foods which my wife had forbidden me to gobble; parathas, fried eggs and toasts roasted in desi ghee etc. But the real freedom was to chat freely on phone with all my male and female friends with immunity. My wife has an uncanny sense of immediately being aware that, this husband of mine is not talking to any female fan or acquaintance, but on the other side there is somebody who is taking undue interest in him. So much so, that if I am conversing with a male friend and in due course use the expression, "darling", she will immediately look at me and growl, "And who is this darling of yours you were talking to on the phone?"

"Oh, come on Muna, it is an old college fellow and a male for heavens sake," I would try to explain.

"Then why were you calling him darling, repeatedly?"

"It was just a manner of speech like sweetheart and beautiful etc."

"You never call me a darling, sweetheart or beautiful," she would say sarcastically and how sarcastic she can get, only I know.

So initially I did enjoy her absence. But with the passage of time I had my fill of all unwanted friends and amorous phone calls and the food prepared by the housemaid became monotonous. I could not read or write at ease because the doorbell kept ringing; the milkman got on my nerves. Even the Indian navel-shakes started looking like routine exercises. And then there was this influx of relatives who came in hordes to inquire about my mental state in my wife's absence. They were sympathetic and looked at me mournfully as if, God forbid, I had become a widower and showered me with food gifts and books like Marne ke baad mot ka manzar.

The refrigerator could not be shut properly because of the vast quantity of food stacked in it, donated naturally by my well wishers. But trying to consume it I put on an extra five kilos on my already bulging bulge. I really started missing my wife for the first time in my wedded life!

Before I proceed any further, I should inform you that my wife has a very different notion of our culture. For instance she would always declare very proudly that thank God we still adhere to our Rajput traditions and have not followed in the footsteps of those Arabs whose moral values are very dubious. Naturally I would be shocked by her statement and ask her to kindly elaborate.

"Don't you remember when a cousin of mine was in Libya with her family where her husband held an important post in an oil company? Well she had three very pretty daughters in their teens and you know people started approaching her and offering her money for them, most of them wanted them as their second or third wife. When my cousin refused these offers, the locals were shocked; it is the local custom and there is no harm if your daughter is chosen to be the third or fourth wife, the more the merrier. Finally my cousin and her husband had to leave the place. There are many Pakistani families in Saudi Arabia and the Gulf states who have had to face the same problem. Can we follow this tradition? I will murder the first person who makes such a shameful offer for my daughter. We'd rather stick to our old Rajput tradition of marrying our daughters, giving them their share of dowry and advise them to stick with their husband for the rest of their lives no matter what."

Besides these strange notions she also believes that Pakistan is the very best country in the world. Once returning from Saudi Arabia, where she lived with our diplomat son for a few months, she remarked as soon as she stepped out of the airport, "Oh, this is beautiful, children playing in the streets, girls walking around and people laughing heartily; Saudi Arabia is so glum that nobody laughs, you don't see any children playing or girls smiling. Even their potatoes and plums are tasteless."

I was sure that after spending more than four months in the land of opportunity, the great Americas, she would have been reformed. But that was not to be. So, her very first comment after emerging from Lahore airport was, "Thank God, I am back in my civilized world from that uncivilized world."

As soon as we reached home I took her to task. "What a sacrilegious comment Muna, don't tell me you did not like even America and you still consider Pakistan the best country in the world."

"I liked America because my son and daughter are there; but it is not a civilized and a happy society."

"How come?"

"Once you gave me a book by Maxim Gorky, City of the Yellow Devil which he had penned after a brief visit to New York. Gorky says the Americans in their pursuit of the Yellow Devil i.e. gold, have abandoned all sorts of human emotions and have turned into robots, running day and night after dollars, earning them and then spending them on such consumer goods and pleasures which one can do without very easily. He felt that every morning millions of people stream out of their abodes and there is this huge money tree shadowing the whole city. Its branches blossoming with dollar notes and the whole day this mass of humanity jumps and strives to snatch the maximum dollars from this tree. They come back with their pockets full and the very same evening they spend all that money in bars, restaurants and superstores in pursuit of what they think is happiness and go back home empty handed. The next day the same vicious process starts all over again."

"Remember Gorky was a communist and ideologically opposed to capitalism."

"Maybe, but no one has depicted New York any better."

"How was your visit to the 9/11 site?"

"I felt sorry for the innocent people killed there, it was a senseless act, I also felt sorry for the thousands of Iraqi and Afghan civilians who were killed in another equally senseless act."

"What about the great Statue of Liberty?"

"I thought it was all white but it turned out to be greenish in colour."

"And the Empire State Building?"

"You had to pay $10 to go to the top, so I refrained."

"Begum their health services are one of the best in the world."

"You know when I arrived in Orlando, our grandson was a month-old, strictly under the doctor's supervision and he cried day and night. The first thing I did was to give him a massage with desi sarson ka tel and then bathed him daily. I also gave him a small dose of pure honey and the child was up and kicking in a few days. When the doctor found out that he was being fed honey, he was shocked and he forbade us to feed him anymore, took a lot of tests to find out the negative effects of honey on the child and in the end found none. For this he charged a hefty bill. That is their health service."

"In short you did not like America."

"I loved America," she beamed. "I was surprised that the average American has almost the same moral values as us. I did not see any immoral acts being performed everywhere as we are led to believe by the American movies. In Orlando, Annie's neighbours are much friendlier and helpful than in Pakistan. They shower you with gifts and food parcels every other day. When Annie was expecting the whole neighbourhood inquired about the forthcoming baby and her health continuously. I did not face any colour prejudice at all. Much is reported about the mistreatment of Muslims on the airports but I did not encounter any problem. The immigration people were extra nice to me, although everywhere I shouted at the top of my voice that I am a Pakistani. If a child wants to cross a road jam-packed with traffic, every vehicle stops at once like he is a prince. I liked their variety of food, which is of very high standards and very cheap also. Oh, yes I loved America."

"So you would like to go back again?"

She pondered for a while and then smiled, "Yes, I would, but presently I would like to enjoy my civilized world first and then I will think about it. You know Pakistan is still the best country in the world."

Yajuj and Majuj in India

Yajuj and Majuj have come back from India after watching the cricket extravaganza, smelling of dals and vegetables as they could not find any halal karhai gosht or roast chicken anywhere and they were hankering for meat. So I invited them for a sumptuous meaty meal.

I was very keen to share their travel experiences in India and while their tiny mouths were full of chicken botis, I asked, "How the devil did you manage to cross over into India, without a passport or valid documents?"

"It was easy," they chuckled. "We told them that we were politicians and intellectuals of Pakistan and they let us go."

"But you are midgets, Lilliputians for heavens sake."

"Exactly, that is why they believed us."

"Enough of the wisecracks," I almost lost my temper at their insolence. "So somehow or the other, you crossed into India, but how did you manage to get into the stadiums? The tickets are hard to come by."

"That was also easy, we hid ourselves in some buxom lady's blouse or jumped into her handbag and along with her we were transported into the stadium. In Delhi it was easier. Yajuj hid in Manmohan Singh's turban and although it was slightly risky, I took refuge in Pervez Musharraf's bushy hair. It was risky because the gentleman has the habit of repeatedly brushing his hair with his hand, like Dilip Kumar and I tell you he was no less than a filmi hero, ask the ladies of Delhi."

"Look Majuj ..."

"I am Yajuj."

"Whoever you are, I am not interested in the amorous looks of our President, although I now have some interest in parties, I am only interested in the cricket matches you have watched directly."

"Did you not watch them on TV?"

"I did, like most of the Pakistanis I wasted full 21 days glued to the TV screen."

"But that cannot be," both of them smiled. "There was no match that lasted for 21 days."

"Ah, after all you are Lilliputians and your brain is no bigger than a dot, wisecracking about our esteemed politicians and intellectuals, 21 days is the total duration of three Test matches and six One-Day fixtures you stupid."

"We stand corrected," they again smiled but rather maliciously this time. "We hope your politicians and intellectuals also had the courage to admit they are just like us."

"Enough is enough," I removed the chicken karhai from the table. "You cannot keep on insulting me and my countrymen and gobble my chicken at the same time."

"We can you know," they replied in chorus. "Because we are in the karhai ourself, I am clinging to a leg-piece and Majuj is having fun with the breast." The hateful Lilliputians were right; I could not possibly grab them with my fingers because they had become slippery with the gravy so grudgingly I let them have fun.

They burped for a while in unison and then most probably it was Majuj who spoke, "We are really grateful for the chicken karhai because in India even if you eat meat, it tastes like cabbage, we had koftas once and they were made of sag and cabbage; just imagine!"

"I will if you permit me imagine it later, but first the details of good old cricket."

"First of all, despite all the hullagulla of Pak-India friendship the crowd reaction was rather unfriendly, only in Mohali, our boys were cheered a little, otherwise in Bangalore or in New Delhi there was a deafening silence whenever a Pakistani batsman scored a six or a four. The same silence was observed as in mourning when any of the Indian batsman lost his wicket. The positive advantage of this silence benefited the blind "spectators"; they immediately knew if a Pakistani batsman was on a rampage or an Indian is leaving the crease. For an Indian their cricketers are mini-gods and they cannot tolerate their ungodly failures whereas we Pakistanis are at times pleased with the failure of our team so that we can proudly claim that we told you so, the team is good for nothing."

"And what was this good for nothing team like, any comments?"

"Very frankly most of them were totally unfamiliar, at times we thought that this lethargic young fellow roaming around is an ice-candy man or some bearer, and the very next moment he was bowling and smashing the wickets of Tendulkar or Ganguly. Then there was this little kid, keeping the wickets and we were amazed that a Vietnamese was hired for the job by our cricket board. He kept on smiling and chirping all the time, "Shabash Danish", "Well-bowled Rana" etc. and I tell you he was a real pain in the, you know where. But he did his job splendidly. Do you know his name?" "I am afraid I don't but I thought he was an Indonesian!"

"Oh yes, I forgot this Rana somebody who was declared the Man of the Series, never saw the fellow before but we think he needs a hair transplant to improve his image. Then there was this tall elderly fellow, perhaps Arshad Khan who looked totally bored while bowling and his boredom affected the Indian batsmen and they got bowled. There were a lot of beards around in the Pakistani camp and at times it looked more like a gathering in Raiwind than a cricket match."

"What were the most perplexing moments during these matches?"

"When Irfan Pathan, Mohammad Kaif and Zaheer Khan faced Danish Kinaria's bowling."

"What was so perplexing in it?"

"Well, don't you see, a Hindu bowling to sons of our Umma, the Muslims, it was difficult to decide whom to cheer, if we cheered the Muslim players as was our duty as good Muslims then Pakistan suffered and if we sided with Kaneria and supported Pakistan, but then we were up against our Muslim brethren."

"So how did you resolve this tricky problem?"

"We asked Allah to forgive us and decided, Pakistan first. Although we are not supporters of Musharraf, even though some of his colleagues are from our creed, sort of Lilliputians."

"You know that Kaneria went to the Kali Devi temple in Calcutta for blessings?"

"We know he did and that is why he did so well, Kali Devi, it seems, has a soft corner for Pakistanis and we should be gracious enough to thank her by saying 'Kali Mata ki Jai'."

"What were the most entertaining moments during these matches?"

"When at the end of a match, our rolypoly Inzi spoke in English."

"Look here, English is not our mother tongue, Ronaldo, Maradonna, Zidane and Ch. Shujaat don't speak a word of it. But they are great guys in their respective fields."

"Well, you asked me what were the most entertaining moments and I don't mind a bit if the whole team is devoid of the English language."

"Now that you have mentioned it, what was so entertaining about it?"

"The commentator, Ravi Shastri asked Inzi, 'Well you are victorious Inzamam, when did you realize that you are going to win this game?' and Inzi replied 'The boys work hard, they do good, very good because the boys worked hard'. And then Shastri would enquire 'What was your game plan?' and Inzi spoke like a cool cucumber 'The boys work very hard, good game because the boys work hard, thank you'. However, Rana Naveed did better he said 'I will speak in Urdu so that people may understand what I am saying'."

"So it is your opinion that Pakistan was a better side and the Indians were rotten?"

"No, not at all. The Indians were a great side and still are and the Pakistanis were raw and inexperienced but some time a little David overpowers a Goliath and that is what happened."

"You are mean Lilliputians the two of you, who make fun of our heroes and criticize their English after gobbling a chicken karhai at my expense? By the way the last of the Dahlias have withered away and there isn't a single flower around, so where are you going to live?"

"We have a game plan. We are going to the President house and we are sure there will be some place for two more Lilliputians. Goodbye."

City of the golden owl

How could I at that moment know that a special angel in the garb of Vinod Dua had descended upon me from the skies of the city of Djinns?

I accepted his invitation of a drink, soft if I wished, and we entered the ever-favourite bar cum restaurant of India International Centre. Vinod had recently visited Pakistan with a team of journalists and had garlanded the President of Pakistan with a tri-coloured muffler, much to the discomfort of the president I presume. During his stay in Lahore he paid a visit to the Food Street and was all praise for the niharis and sri payas etc; however, it was his pilgrimage to Hira Mandi, which he cherished the most as according to him he witnessed the finest mujra in the subcontinent.

Vinod was, as far as aesthetics were concerned, more of a Muslim than a Hindu. In fact I later found out that he was not much of a Hindu either. His taste for Urdu poetry is superb and he quoted Ghalib or Mir or Bulleh Shah whenever the occasion arose; and a ferocious meat eater on top of that! Besides all these idiosyncrasies he is a music maniac, can sing in a husky voice the ghazals of Mehdi Hasan and Pakistani milli naghmas including Sathio Mujahido Jag Uttha Hai Sara Watan without going out of sur.

Upon his return from Pakistan he was carrying a bag full of music cassettes of Pakistani singers weighing exactly sixteen kilos and it was not due to the inclusion of Abida Parveen or Nusrat Fateh Ali Khan!

As if the surprises were not enough, in walked Saddam Hussein, dressed in a Multani-Kurta and pyjama! Vinod, noticing my amazement, introduced me, "Meet Malik Sahib, a very dear friend of mine, we did plan to hand him over to the Americans and earn a cool twenty-five million because as you can see he is ditto copy of Saddam Hussein. But unfortunately the real Saddam did not co-operate and made himself available to the Americans while we were in our planning stages."

Throughout the evening I suspected that the Americans had the wrong Saddam in their custody while the real Saddam was sitting next to me gulping numerous olives and cups that cheer.

In the meantime an elderly gentleman, lost in thought, brooding, oblivious to the surroundings entered the bar and seated himself in the corner; a waiter hurriedly came over with his already prepared drink, placed it in front of him and withdrew respectfully. The gentleman, oblivious to his surroundings, took a sip from his drink and was submerged in his thoughts. "Tarar Sahib do you know this gentleman?" Vinod whispered.

"He looks familiar; maybe a disgruntled retired bureaucrat."

"He is Ramu Gandhi, grandson of Mahatma Gandhi, an intellectual of great repute, lives in a small servant quarter nearby." I was amazed, a grandson of Bapu of modern India living in a servant quarter? What an unfortunate man. If he had been the grandson of some minor politician in Pakistan, he would have been living in a palace with a Texas ranch for the rainy days. "He does not like company, sits in his particular corner and after having a couple of drinks, leaves."

"My younger son Sumair has entrusted me with his autograph book with the instructions that if I find anybody worthwhile in India I should obtain his autograph. I think Mr Gandhi is worthwhile."

We approached him, Vinod knew him during some travels in India. He introduced me as a Pakistani writer and he immediately showed interest but that interest turned into coldness when I made a request for the autograph: "I don't give autographs."

"As you please sir but it was indeed an honour to meet you," I extended my hand smilingly. "The autograph request came from my son, I will just tell him that junior Ghandhiji simply refused." He smiled in return and took the autograph book from me: "What is his name?"

"Sumair."

"Sumair? What does it mean?"

"One who narrates stories, a Dastaango."

"And what is your profession?"

"I write stories."

Half rising from his seat he shook my hand warmly: "Well, that is a good combination; father writes and the son narrates the stories." I could see I had won him over with my comment. He signed "To Sumair with love, Ramu Gandhi" and handed over the autograph book. Then he immediately got disinterested and we came back to our table. The local Saddam Hussain was in an advanced stage of exuberance.

"Tarar Sahib where do you plan to have your dinner tonight?" Vinod asked.

"The whole lot of Saarc writers are going to 'Chor Bazaar' for dinner and I plan to accompany them."

"I have a proposal, my Madrasi wife, Nikki is waiting for me to collect her and then we are proceeding to a 20th wedding anniversary party of a doctor couple who are Nikki's colleagues and great friends of mine; they will be overjoyed to have a guest from Lahore. Please!"

Vinod did not have to plead because I had already made up my mind to meet normal Indians in their normal homes having had enough of writers and intellectuals for the evening.

On our way to his flat Vinod reduced the speed of his car and pointed towards an old rundown structure of perhaps Mughal period and said: "Here lives the golden owl of Delhi."

"A golden owl? You must be joking. Owls are, as a rule grey, black or white but never golden."

"This one is golden I assure you and I have seen it. Nobody knows for how long he has been residing in the middle of Delhi in this ancient ruin. I can show you if you wish."

"Right now?" Suddenly I felt that my life was worthless if I did not set eyes upon a golden owl.

"It is night time Tarar sahib and owls have their nights out, perhaps he is out with a she-owl to paint the town red; we will revisit the place during the day sometime."

I wondered if the owl's date was a blonde i.e. a golden she-owl or was he having fun with a brunette?

Vinod's wife was an attractive brunette with the salty charms of Madras and we proceeded towards the flat of the celebrating doctor couple who were easily the most handsome pair I had seen in Delhi so far. It was my first time in a typical Hindu household and to me the statues of different deities, pictures of major and minor gods and the decor was like a museum. Most of the guests were doctors and Vinod was right, they were overjoyed to see me amongst them. Like everywhere else in Delhi "Lahore" was the magic word which opened all doors. Almost everyone sang, danced or played some musical instrument; I was the only exception.

When the celebrating couple insisted that I should join the crowd I regretfully declined fearing for my old bones and my aching back, although there was no dearth of medical assistance if the need arose. Nikki surprised me by singing some Punjabi tappas in her melodious voice; Vinod had turned this Madrasan into a typical Punjaban. In the end Vinod rendered some verses of Bulleh Shah with deep emotion.

It was almost three in the morning while cruising towards my abode Vinod asked, "Have you visited the tomb of our great saint Hazrat Nizamuddin Aulia?"

"No, I am afraid not as yet."

"You are in Delhi and you have not offered Fatiha at the shrine of Sultanji?" Vinod was slightly upset, being a devout disciple of the saint. "We can drop in right now if you want?"

"At this time of the night?"

"This is the time."

The area in which we entered hardly looked like a part of New Delhi; filthy narrow lanes littered with the bodies of poverty stricken sleeping humanity, open gutters, rundown houses and the air loaded with stink. The shrine rested right in the middle of this mess. There was a small gate on the side of a glittering door, going inside through a labyrinth carpeted with sleeping beggars, men, women and children in all, avoiding stepping upon them, we finally reached the burial place of the saint.

Vinod with a covered head immediately bowed and went into a sajda. There was hardly anybody around at this time of the night except a young bearded dervish resting his head on a door, praying. Next to the shrine of Sultanji rested Hazrat Amir Khusro, the faithful disciple who was away from Delhi when his Murshid died and upon his return he lay beside the grave of his beloved Chal Khusro Ghar Apne and died there and then.

"Vinod my murshid, an uncle of mine, is also buried somewhere around here, is it possible to visit his grave?"

A few dingy and dark streets away in a small compound was the final resting place of the man who more than anyone else shared my sorrows, failures, heartaches, happiness and quest for spiritual elation, a man who despite being a drunkard was a Wali; Mirza Ghalib.

Upon our return in the slow moving car in the dead of the night, Vinod's sentimental voice rose, "Dile Nadan Tujhe Hua Kia Hai" and Nikki sitting beside me sang the next verse, "Aakhir Es Dard Ki Dawa Kia Hai".

My heart was filled with strange emotions; Ghalib still ruled the soul of Delhi.

If the golden owl had returned to his ruins, maybe he was also humming Ghalib — Hum Biaban main hain aur Ghar main bahar aai hai.

(To be continued)

A tear on the cheek of eternity

We were on our way to the Taj Mahal. The suburbs of New Delhi stretched on and on and it took us almost one hour to manoeuvre through them. We stopped at a roadside stall to quench our thirst, as the day was rather hot. A nondescript town sprawled around us aimlessly. "What is the name of this town?" I asked the driver.

"Mathura," he said without any enthusiasm.

"Mathura?" I exclaimed excitedly. "Mathura of Pairas and Pandas," I exclaimed as I gave a hearty slap on the shoulders of yawning Asghar Nadeem Syed. "Shahji do you know there are lot of Pandas in Mathra?"

Shahji was rather lethargic due to a last night binge, twirled his graying moustaches and looked at me as I had gone senile.

"Chaudhry Sahib are you out of your mind? Pandas are only found in China."

"I tell you pandas are around here somewhere, big fat bulging pandas gorging enormous quantities of sweet Pairas."

"And I tell you Pandas only eat bamboo shoots."

"Well these pandas of Mathura eat sweets, I know."

During the long winter nights we would gather around our Abbaji and he would narrate strange stories of his travels in India before partition, the Bankas of Lucknow, Chinioti Sheikhs of Calcutta, elephants of Sylhet, tigers of the Sunderbans but our favourite was Pandas of Mathura and it went on something like this."

"There is this holy town of Mathura near Delhi littered with temples. Devout Hindus will go there to get rid of their sins. There they will hire a panda, a sumo wrestler type holy man or pandit and will squat in front of him with a tray loaded with the famous Mathura Pairas. The panda will open his large mouth and the devotee will start feeding him. It was their firm belief that according to the numbers of pairas devoured by the panda their sins in equal number would be wiped out. A time would come when the panda was fully loaded with the famous sweet almost bursting from the seams, his mouth stuffed and he would refuse to eat anymore and this was the crucial point. The devotee would beg him to eat just a few more pairas and will offer him a lot of money in return. The panda very much tempted would agree and the devotee would force a few more pairas in his mouth until the poor panda, sweets oozing out of his nostrils and ears, would collapse, but not before collecting his fortune from the devotee."

Prior to my departure for Agra I had made enquiries about the "Pandas of Mathura" and was told that the number has dwindled and if I probe around in Mathura I might find a Panda or two. But we did not have the time to probe; it was either Taj Mahal or a panda. So I left Mathura with a heavy heart. Would I feed a panda to get rid of my sins? No, because just one panda won't do, the number of my sins is such that at least a dozen pandas would have to be engaged for the job.

On our left, a road branched off for Aligarh, the city of the famed Muslim University some thirty kilometres away. Two magnificent Gurudawaras emerged from the green landscape built entirely with white marble, perhaps an indication that Taj Mahal was not far off. Upon entering the great Mughal city of Agra we saw on our left the river Yamuna, not much of a river at this time of the year but there was enough water for the numerous buffaloes that rested their black bulks in it. An iron bridge again packed with buffaloes and cows spanned the holy Yamuna.

In Agra you do not have to ask where is the Taj Mahal, you just follow the numerous buses, tourist wagons and coaches and you are there. But when we were there, there was no Taj Mahal, just a huge parking lot as it is forbidden for any vehicle to go beyond this point to protect the Taj from petrol or diesel fumes. From the parking lot either you walk, which is not recommended because it is at least a kilometre away and the heat that day was unbearable. Or you hire a good old tonga, a cycle rickshaw or a battery run vehicle, all of them pollution free. We opted for a rickety tonga and were amused to hear the tongawala coaxing his skinny horse in pure U.P. Urdu, "Abay chalta hai ya doon jhanpar, mian chal do" etc. I forgot to mention the hordes of young tourist guides who storm every tourist, pleading, almost begging to be hired, nearly abducting the harassed tourists. One of them forcibly entered our tonga and we had to push him away!

The entrance much to our dismay was packed with humanity, school children, scantily clad skinny women, families, tourists and naturally Sikhs. Perhaps it was because it was a Sunday. There were endless queues all over. The entry ticket was 20 Indian rupees for the locals and a mere $20/- for the foreigners. But then, who said we were foreigners? Shahji was the spitting image of a Mahant gone astray amongst the Devdasis and my features resembled the high priest of Kali Mata's temple. So we were locals for once and bought 20 rupee tickets without any remorse. Another endless queue underneath the burning sun, the ticket checker and then the short tempered security man who rummaged through my shoulder bag and shouted, "No cigarettes, no lighters allowed inside, deposit in the luggage room outside."

"I will just throw them here if you please."

"No littering, get out," and he pushed me so hard that I crashed on at least three innocent sightseers who abused me profusely. Thank God I did not understand their language. I was not used to being pushed around, except by my wife and I felt humiliated but not enough to abandon my visit to the Taj. So I rushed out, threw the objectionable items under a bush and came back and the security man let me pass.

"I am grateful sir," I said humbly.

"You should be grateful and you know why!" he thundered.

Initially I failed to understand his retort but then it dawned upon me that while rummaging through my bag he had noticed my green passport and the Pakistani brand of cigarettes realizing that I was not a local but a bloody foreigner who was skipping through with a twenty-rupee ticket; indeed I had to be grateful.

All this excitement and the heat was affecting me and I had a feeling that I may collapse the very next moment due to dehydration. Those who knew that there was no water available inside the premises had brought their personal water bottles and I was waterless so to speak. I requested the Almighty to please delay that collapse till my first glimpse of the Taj Mahal. The inner compound was teeming with tourists, guides and dozens of photographers and the whole lot was heading towards a huge and impressive red stone gate; the entrance to the Taj and we were part of this enthusiastic crowd.

A very high arch came into view and it was totally filled with a mass of dazzling light, the pure glistening whiteness was unbearable. And then the whole of Taj Mahal, recently descended from the heavens, was placed before us. I felt as though the pure and dazzling whiteness flowed into my eyes, filling my whole body and turning it into marble. Now I was seeing the marble miracle with marble eyes. Do I exaggerate? No sir. I do not even posses the vocabulary even to do justice to narrate it very ordinarily.

I had come with total reservations, ready to condemn the Taj at the slightest pretext, I was sick of its stories of splendour, and beauty, the most beautiful structure on earth and all that sentimental hotchpotch, wonder of the world indeed. But its first sight bowled me over; it razed my body structure, brick by brick and then rebuilt it with dazzling marble that is why I was looking at it with marble eyes. Seeing it was not believing because it was not real.

"Shahji, we have been hoodwinked, it's a fake, a model, a film set, its not the real thing." Shahji looked aghast, thinking that the dehydration was having its effect. "Because real things are built by human hands, always, somewhere in the construction, design or symmetry the human touch is there, a slight flaw which makes it real. I am afraid it will presently disappear right in front of our eyes. If at all it is created by human hands it surpasses all that the creations created and if a human after creating it declares that 'Anaulhuq I am the truth, I am God' then can you blame him?"

The Taj Mahal, a tear on the cheek of eternity? Rather poetic I agree but a total misrepresentation because there isn't a speck of sorrow or gloom or tragedy for that matter in its visual, on the contrary it is a celebration of life, a breath of eternal happiness, justification of human existence and a reason to live on.

It is chiselled from the virgin snows of Shah Gori the K2 and entices you to a kiss before dying.

A huge bird, grey and red in complexion rose from the depths of Jumana, prominent against the simmering blue sky, came down and lazily flew in front of the Taj, the bird lost its colours and turning white, became a part of Taj so much so that despite my constant gaze I could not spot him anywhere and finally when he flew out of its range of white dazzle it regained its colours. I remembered a famous line of Punjabi poet Hafiz Barkhurdar.

"Last night the moonlight was so white that when a crow flew into it, its blackness turned in to a tuft of pure cotton."

So this was Taj Mahal, I am sure if any crows lived by, they will be of dazzling white colour.

Lost in Rajasthan

A trip to the Taj also deserves a must mention of the most sought after and the luckiest marble bench in the world. For it is continuously polished by the eager bottoms of newly married couples and at times by an old foggy, like myself, who want to be photographed with the best view of Taj.

After the visit to the Taj, when one sees this memorable photo, it seems that you are sitting on a bench with the Taj looming large and hardly anybody in sight, smiling in your romantic loneliness. However, the ground reality is totally different. There are hundreds of people waiting for their turn and dozens of photographers making sure that nobody jumps the queue. The experienced photographers instruct the couple to be romantic, the newly wed bride reclining on the bench with her head in the lap of lucky, or unlucky, bridegroom. Thereafter both gaze into each other's eyes with eternal love and with the Taj in the background. As soon as the camera clicks the couple is almost pushed away to make room for the next candidate.

In the olden days there used to be a flock of photographers beside Mayo Hospital, Lahore, with black hooded strange boxes and for the background crudely painted curtains depicting either Shalimar Gardens or Taj Mahal. Whenever I expressed a desire to be photographed with the Taj, my father would take me to the "Egyptian photographer" on Nisbet Road because that was the proper thing to do. Gentlemen never sat on a footpath to be photographed. However, now after almost sixty years I could fulfil that childhood desire and pose in front of the real Taj for a bargain.

I was not fortunate enough to have a pretty damsel leaning on my shoulders and looking at me with adoring eyes. Instead it was the bulk of hairy and moustached Shahji smiling like a love stricken Himalayan bear. We intentionally did not look at each other with adoring eyes lest we were dubbed gays.

After the photo session we walked towards the Taj, sizzling in the heat of the day. It was a strenuous ordeal to enter into the main building as there were thousands of people pushing and cajoling through a single door. I fear there were some women who fainted due to the heat and lack of air inside the Taj. It was just impossible to offer Fatiha or to observe the exquisite tombs closely. Children crying, women shouting and some hooligans laughing. Most of them were touching or slapping the inlay work with their sweaty hands. The harsh voices and shouts, I am sure, hurt the delicate dome and those two buried underneath.

In Florence you cannot touch the David of Michelangelo or can you imagine sweaty hands being wiped on the lips of Mona Lisa? A work of art is meant to be viewed not to be desecrated with hands. Absolutely nobody should be allowed to go inside the Taj Mahal let those poor things rest in peace.

By now I felt that if I do not immediately quench my thirst I will be resting in peace along Shahjehan and Mumtaz Mahal. So we hurried out.

A mere two hours visit is an insult to the Taj; one should have at least two days to view it from all four sides and from across the Jumna, experience its mornings and sunsets. And if lucky, view it during the full moon, "Kal chaudwein ka chand tha shab bhar raha churcha tira sort of thing".

On our way back, our chauffeur driven car, courtesy Vinod Dua, passed underneath the great citadel of Agra. Perched on a high plateau we saw the magnificent spectacle of white palaces and red fortification. In it somewhere was the room in which Shahjehan was imprisoned by his son Aurengzeb. And in there was that historical window framing the distant Taj for the eyes of dethroned emperor. According to Ibne-i-Insha: "Auregzeb was so pious that throughout his life he never left a namaz or a brother".

We had to make a quick decision, do we turn left and visit the great fort of Agra or proceed straight for Fatehpur Sekri, the red stone capital of the great Mughal Akbar? We did not have enough energy and especially time to visit both. We opted for Fatehpur Sekri and drove straight on. We were still on the outskirts of Agra when we passed a road sign that read "Emperor Akbar's Mausoleum". How could we ignore the grave of Mughal-e-Azam?

The delicate and impressive three storied structure of the mausoleum was designed by Akbar himself, intricate but simple in its grandeur. A low-roof tunnel lead to the grave of the great Mughal and there he lay underneath a plain marble slab without any decorations or epitaph underneath a huge windowless dome. It was a lonely and gloomy abode, even the lightest whisper resonated not finding any opening to escape and came back in a loud melancholy form. Shahji and myself were totally alone and we felt, as if we were entombed alive in the burial chamber of some Egyptian Pharaoh. Suddenly I remembered a dialogue from the film Mughl-e-Azam, delivered by the inimitable Prithivi Raj when on top of an elephant he orders his armies to march on against his Anarkali-struck son Prince Salim. I don't know what got into me but I uttered it loudly with a theatrical flourish: "Yalghar ho Maan Singh."

Shahji almost jumped with fright as the dome of the tomb reverberated with a series of Yalghar Ho Yalghar Ho. It was a good thing that the great Mughal was in no position to protest otherwise he would have ordered me to be trampled underneath his own personal elephant!

A few kilometres outside Agra, a road turned right towards Fatehpur Sekri. It was supposed to be a mere forty kilometres away but we travelled on and on through dirty little villages and uninteresting landscape with no Fatehpur Sekri in sight. It was late afternoon and we had to be back in Delhi before nightfall. Just then a milestone gave us a fright for it said that we were headed towards Ajmer. Another fright was in store for us when a high arch welcomed us into Rajasthan. Where in the name of Dickens were we heading for? The final nail in our coffin, so to speak, was another milestone which gleefully informed us that we were on our way to Jaisalmer. In one day we had traversed through the capital territory Delhi, then into Haryana and Uttar Pardesh and finally we were in Rajasthan.

We heaved a sigh of relief when eventually we entered Fatehpur Sekri. I had visualized ruins of a vast city as far as the eye can see. But there perched on a hilltop was a palace complex in brand new condition and the magnificent Bulund Darwaza Mosque, housing the remains of Saint Salim Chishti. We did not have enough time to ponder over the intricacies of red stone wonders. So we rushed through a palace which according to our guide was of Jodhabai, the mother of Jehangir. But at the same time, a notice declared that it had nothing to do with Jodhabai! We also hurried through the vast Bulund Darwaza Mosque which looked fabulous and it was vast. The shrine of Salim Chishti was indeed a jewel of architecture but the caretakers were not too happy with us because we did not offer a nazrana. A bearded caretaker was selling pieces of strings to foreign tourists for Rs10 each. "Tie a string with the jali of Saint and you will get your wish." It was not a bad bargain but I refrained. Actually one should visit Fatehpur Sekri first and then proceed towards Agra because after seeing the Taj every other building pales in comparison. Perhaps that was the reason of our slight disappointment. There was one consolation though; while we were distancing ourselves from Fatehpur Sekri, we looked back towards the red city perched on a hillock and it turned rose red, courtesy of the setting sun.

The driver sensing our urgency for reaching Delhi as soon as possible suggested that instead of going back to Agra we can take a short cut through

Bharatpur. We readily agreed without inquiring from the good man whether he had ever driven through this route previously or not. He had not.

Bharatpur was the domain of some ferocious Jat tribes who during the decline of Mughal Empire invaded Delhi and on their return brought with them two huge Mughal guns. These rusty guns are still the pride of Bharatpur resting on a hillock outside the town.

Although a slight drizzle had started while we were leaving Fatehpur Sekri, it had now turned into a heavy downpour. Sheets of stormy water descended from the heavens and despite full lights it was hazardous to drive on a bumpy road. All around us was black desolation and the road was totally deserted when the driver decided to give us the happy news; we were lost. We were somewhere in Rajasthan but, only the pouring heavens and the pitch-dark night around us knew where. At that particular moment of desperation I realized that our passports carried a visa for Agra only and we had no business to be in Fatehpur Sekri. And on top of it we were wandering in some part of India rather illegally. We could be arrested if checked on some road block as enemy spies. I conveyed this information to Shahji who was equally terrified. The rains came down in torrents. A milestone on the edge of the road appeared that read that we were approaching a place called Peeli Bheet.

"Shahji in my childhood I had read a book called Dacoits of Peeli Bheet. Maybe it is the same place and may be it is still infested with dacoits."

"Chaudhry sahib why don't you shut up?" he growled. "Don't talk to me till we reach Mathura, if we reach Mathura."

Farewell to New Delhi

So it was my last day in Delhi, the city of Djinns and the golden owl and I laughed and laughed like a madman as the five hundred years old Lodhi tombs, wet in morning dew, towered above me.

It was only last night when I was lost in Rajasthan and the rains came down in torrents and Shahji had forbidden me to utter anything untill we reach Mathura and finally in the dead of the night we did manage to reach Mathura and eventually Delhi. I had my last laugh in Lodhi gardens and then returned to my abode in India International Centre where good old Vinod was waiting for me to show me the sights, which I had missed so far. We went past the residence of the golden owl of Delhi who I am sure was having a nap after prowling the Mughal ruins throughout the night.

During my stay in Delhi I had noticed that photographs of a saintly figure dressed in a single robe with a long white beard appeared on the back of the three wheelers, taxis and in some shops. When I inquired, I was simply told that this saint is, "Sain Baba." As always, Vinod came to my rescue.

"Sain Baba was a devout Muslim, praying five times a day and during the night very few people saw him resting; he was always in sajda. He spent his whole life in a single chadar, blessing whosoever came to him. The Hindus revered him as a great saint. When his devotees became numerous and he wanted to be left in peace, he went to Orissa and settled there. When he died in 1922 his followers built a huge temple on his grave and erected his statue there. He is still worshipped throughout India and people believe that even in death, he is capable of showering his blessings on those who visit the Sain Baba mandir."

"You Hindus are a strange lot Vinod, you own everybody who comes your way."

"Not everybody Tarar Sahib, if a person is full of love for humanity without any prejudice of cast and creed what is the harm in owning him even if he is a devout Muslim? You know that I revere Nizamuddin Aulia and Salim Chishti, we have even adopted your national poet Iqbal because for all practical purposes. Sare Jahan se accha Hindustan Hamara is our national anthem. So much so that we own the great Bulleh Shah to such an extent that he is buried near Mussoorie."

"Now that is the limit Vinod," I laughed. "It amounts to body snatching, Bulleh Shah is buried in Qasur for heaven's sake."

"Well he is in Mussoorie also," Vinod said in earnest. "You know I have a house in Mussoorie; year before last while going there I saw a sign board near a small village which read 'Mazar Bulleh Shah'. Naturally I knew that Bulleh Shah is buried near Lahore in Qasur so I was intrigued. I stopped the car and went inside a small tomb. An old man was the caretaker and I asked him 'Baba whose grave is it?' and he replied, 'Bulleh Shah'.

"I asked which Bulleh Shah and he replied Enayat Qadri wala Bulleh Shah."

Now this information was amazing as Bulleh Shah's murshid was indeed Shah Enayat Qadri.

Vinod continued: "According to the old man, once upon a time a king of Afghanistan came to Mussoorie and fell seriously ill. So much so that he was almost on his deathbed, he requested somebody to inform Bulleh Shah of Qasur about his illness as the king considered him to be his murshid. Bulleh Shah then came to Mussoorie, prayed for the health of the Afghan king who recovered miraculously and then Bulleh Shah decided to stay here. Here he died and a mazar was built over his grave. Every year his Urs is held and people come from distant lands to pay tribute to this great Punjabi saint."

Is there any shred of evidence that Bulleh Shah ever visited Mussoorie? If not then who is buried there? Perhaps Shafqat Tanvir Mirza of Punjabi themes can solve this riddle.

We were going round the old walls of Tughlaqabad but did not enter the citadel as we were heading towards Mehrauli to visit the Qutab Minar. Like the Taj, no photograph or description can do justice to the mighty Qutab Minar and its magnificent red stone carvings of the Holy Quran. In its grandeur it is no less than the Taj, only its awesome beauty has a different shade. Vinod was unaware of the fact that Qutubuddin Aibak, the builder of this Minar, lies buried near Anarkali in Lahore where he had fallen from his horse while playing polo.

In my childhood days Aibak's grave was located in a dingy and dirty street and I remember that through its old roof seeped dirty water from the houses built on top of it and fell on the unkempt grave. Then some history conscience people took notice, cleared the street, demolished the houses and let the great Sultan breathe. The mausoleum was decorated with red stone carvings similar to Qutab Minar. The calligraphic portion was executed by the master calligraphist Hafiz Yusuf Saddidi and it is a treat for the eyes.

Underneath the Qutab Minar there is this small courtyard of Masjide Quwatul Islam, built mainly from material confiscated from Hindu and Jain temples. Suddenly one of the carved pillars of a temple drew my attention; many years ago I had seen a photograph of a stunningly beautiful woman leaning against this very pillar, I could never decide who was more beautiful, the exquisitely carved pillar or the perfectly proportioned contours of that woman? Standing there she looked like a demigoddess, this was the very pillar which was once touched by the magic of a beautiful woman.

One of the main attractions in the courtyard is that amazing mythical iron pillar of Prithviraj Chuhan, which according to the legend, was placed here to crush the brother of a snake king so that Chuhan's empire may not disintegrate. But it did anyway.

We had to rush back to the Centre as we had to pack our bags and catch the evening flight. That is why we just passed near the tombs of Altamash and then Humayun, although with a heavy heart that I did not have enough time to visit them. I had also planned to pay my regards, in person, to three of my favourite Delhi personalitites. I missed Annie Apa's invitation because that very same day I was going to Agra. Mr Khushwant Singh had very kindly invited me to have dinner with him tonight, but regretfully I was leaving in the evening. So I planned to see Amrita Pritam at least on my way to the airport. In the meantime I told Vinod that if ever I have the chance of going to Mumbai I would like to meet Dilip Kumar, Naseeruddin Shah, Gulzar and A.R. Rehman in the same order. And guess who I spotted, during my lunch at the Centre, sitting near a window of the dining room with his white beard glistening in the sunshine? Naseeruddin Shah!

Vinod approached him and introduced me and I had the pleasure of listening to his magical Ghalib voice for a few moments. He was in Delhi for a theatre performance and he invited me to watch his play as his personal guest — tonight! I remembered Napoleon's words: "Not tonight Josephine, not tonight." It was indeed a misfortune to miss Khushwant Singh and Naseeruddin Shah because I was leaving — tonight. I sent my regards to Gulzar through the good offices of Naseeruddin Shah and asked him the eternal question as to what he was doing these days. He told me that he was trying to make a film for the past two years but the finances were hard to come by.

"Even Naseeruddin Shah has to try to finance a personal film?" I asked.

"Tararji, anybody who wants to do some creative work has to try, even Naseeruddin Shah," and he laughed.

I asked Ahmad Faraz to accompany us in Vinod's car to the airport as he was also leaving on the same flight. On our way I told Faraz that en route, we will call upon Amrita Pritam and then proceed towards the airport.

"Tarar you have never met the lady before, I suggest that you do not meet hernow, her mental state is such that she does not recognize anybody, is totally bed ridden and lost. You will be pained to see the great poetess in such a state of misery, why spoil the image you have of Amrita?" So with a sense of great loss and remorse I dropped the idea.

Finally when we boarded the PIA plane it was like homecoming. Sare Jahan se accha Pakistan hamara. Delhi was great, true, but Lahore is Lahore!

Go, camel kids, go!

Yajuj and Majuj almost evaporated in the recent heat wave sweeping the country. I am sure you remember these little fellows who once upon a time resided in my dahlias and when these flowers withered away, they shifted their abode, God only knows where. Recently though, they re-appeared.

It was during a power breakdown when I was drenched with sweat and frustration, squatting on the floor to save my precious sofa and bed sheets from getting stained, that these two identical Lilliputians, dressed as usual in matching suits and ties, appeared out of nowhere.

I was horrified to see their attire in these scorching circumstances. But they were the type of those bygone Victorian gentlemen who always dressed properly in Scottish tweed and went out in the midday sun where they were in the gracious company of mad dogs.

Although their suits were really bothersome I was really happy to see them after such a long time. They could at least keep me company while I waited for my ceiling fan, that hung above my head, motionless like a stunned mourner, to start.

The two seated themselves right in front of me, cross-legged like two miniature Buddhas. "Tarar sahib we need your help." Perhaps it was Yajuj who addressed me, or maybe it was Majuj! They were identical.

"We have been unemployed for a long time, we have no money to feed ourselves. So much so that we haven't changed our ties for quite sometime."

"What sort of employment would you have in your mind?"

"Well you know in Pakistan most of the top jobs are in the hands of Lilliputians, so you could exert your influence on our behalf and procure such a job for us."

"Well my dear Yajuj, or are you Majuj? Whichever, if I had an iota of influence don't you think I would in the first place procure such a prestigious job for myself instead of writing senseless columns and hosting ludicrous television shows?" I said irritably wiping my streams of sweat with the third towel of the day which like the previous two was again drenched in my perspiration.

"If you could lower your standards a bit and come out with a suggestion of an ordinary job, then perhaps I could be of help."

"We want to be camel kids," they cried in unison.

"Camel kids?" I was horrified. "You want to become camel kids of your own accord?"

"And why not, it is better than starving, having no roof over your head, no opportunities of education, no medical facilities. The only opportunities for most of the kids in this country are either to become a 'Chota' in some workshop or a wayside Chai khana, working almost 24 hours without any respite, mostly in the midday sun, earning, if at all, 10 or 20 rupees daily, and in the fear of being molested by the owner or some frustrated customer."

"You are a pair of simpletons for sure. You are not aware of the rights of a child. You are so ignorant that you have never heard of UNICEF protecting every child in the world, except the Palestinians and Iraqi children who are terrorists. I am sure you are stupid enough not to realize the efforts of some NGOs who are killing themselves to safeguard your rights. Rights of a child are to be protected at all cost even the rights of starvation and molestation."

"We are an ignorant pair we confess. But have you read some of the statements by those camel kids who were 'rescued' from UAE? They seemed to be regretting their so-called rescue. One of them stated to the press and I quote 'The UAE was a good place as we were earning a handsome amount of money. Our future is uncertain here. We used to earn between 800 and 2000 dirhams a month, besides receiving another 50 to 100 for winning a race'. Another camel kid stated, 'I am happy that we have contributed to our family to ease the financial burden on our parents and I have no regrets in losing my childhood to camel sports'. You must bear in mind that most of these camel kids are not exactly kids and they are between the ages of thirteen to fifteen years which is a normal age for a Pakistani kid to earn a living and help his family while doing so. I have heard that organizations that arrange such rescues are flooded with donations afterwards for their selfless humanitarian efforts."

"Well what should they do, they have to live also and you know the rising cost of living, specially maintaining the airconditioned offices, Nissan Patrols, arranging walks, creating awareness and then finally reporting in details their humanitarian efforts to the kind-hearted souls in the West who cannot sleep at nights worrying to death about the plight of poor camel kids and how magnanimous of them if they loosen the strings of their overburdened kitty for the sake of humanity. By the way Yajuj-Majuj, your reporting is selective just to prove that camel kids were really having fun in the distant deserts and they were forcibly rescued. For instance a camel kid Shaukat Ali stated and I also quote, 'After imparting one and a half months training on how to ride a camel, our owner started using us in the races. We woke up at 4am daily and used to feed and clean the camels. The race usually started at 9am and continued for two hours. They gave us only two meals a day to maintain our weight less than 35 kilograms which is considered ideal for the job. After taking our evening meals we used to watch cartoons and Indian movies before going to bed at 10pm. We were given 2000 dirhams per month, and the money was collected by our father'. Now what do you say to these atrocities?"

"What atrocities?" they again cried in unison. "To us these seem to be ideal working conditions what with watching cartoons and Indian films and 2000 dirhams per month on top of it." "You are miserable wretches both of you," I lost my temper. "Giving only two meals a day to these innocent souls to maintain their weight, isn't it shameful?"

"It is better than having no meals at all. Besides all professionals keep their weight in check and normally skip meals. What about the horse kids... the normal race jockeys in our country, they also maintain their weight. What is good for horses is good for the camels also. Even the disc jockey ladies you see on the music shows starve themselves to death to look sexy. The same goes for actresses and athletes. They also watch their weight, at times athletes can also be actors and most of the actresses are athletes to be sure. So why don't you rescue all these poor things from their professions also?"

These Lilliputians were incorrigible, their brains were not larger than a pea so it was useless to argue with them. So before giving up I asked, "So you think that these camel kids have been rescued by force?"

"Yes the same way an old man was taken across the road."

"Which old man for heavens sake?"

"A school kid came very late in the class and when the teacher admonished him he said, 'Sir you always advised us to do good deeds, for instance if an old man is standing on the footpath we should help him cross the road and that is exactly what I was doing.' The teacher was rather pleased but asked, 'It takes less than five minutes to help an old man cross a road but you took more than half an hour, why?' The kind-hearted kid replied, 'Sir, the old man did not want to cross the road that is why it took me so long.'"

"Very funny Yajuj Majuj," I smiled sarcastically.

"The funny thing is that these camel kids are rescued and duly sent back to their native villages where once again they start living in abject poverty and misery. Why can't the government, NGOs or the Unicef or whosoever brings them back, give them a better life instead, arrange for their education, boarding and lodging, their daily expenses and support their families. Then the rescue operation will be justified otherwise they are that old man who was forcibly taken across the road and left there to rot."

"Look here Yajuj and Majuj. Are you here to prove this noble rescue as a cruel act or you yourself want to adopt this profession?"

"All we want is to become camel kids because we are unemployed, hungry and shelterless, can you help us?"

"No, I am afraid even if I want to I cannot. To start with there are these new rules according to which one must be over sixteen years of age to become a camel kid and you are so tiny and little."

"We are actually as old as this world but we do not look it so age limit is no problem."

"But how can you ride a camel being so tiny, so small, less than an inch tall? How would you manage to coax the camel to run?"

"Though we are quite confident that the camel will be rather overjoyed to have us on the top because we hardly have any weight and he can win the races by lengths, but if we have any problem we have a plan."

"What kind of plan?"

"We will descend into his long ear and whisper, 'camel darling if you don't run, we will import a humorous poet from Pakistan to recite to you some of his "humorous" poetry'. We are sure he will be frightened out of his wits and will run for his life."

"What if this threat does not work?"

"Then we will be very mean and tell him that we are inviting a Pakistani politician to ride him and we assure you he will run like mad."

"In short you are bent upon becoming camel kids?"

"Yes, we are"

"You don't care about rights of a child, child labour and the Unicef charter?"

"No we don't. We believe in food, shelter, dirhams, cartoons and Indian films."

"What is your final message to the Pakistani masses?"

"Either provide every kid in Pakistan with education, medical facilities, food, shelter and a monthly income to support his family or let the kids go."

Believing in reincarnation

I AM a Muslim, devout or otherwise, although I do not believe in stabbing somebody to earn a berth in Paradise, especially in a foreign country, which is kind enough to accept me and gives me the right to a decent living and education. I also do not believe in burning half of my city just to protest against an insult or plan to blow up the underground rail of my adopted country or destroy the giant Buddhas of Bamiyan to prove my credentials as a Muslim. Well, am I a fit candidate to be kicked out of the circle of Islam?

Anyway despite being a Muslim, good or bad I truly believe in reincarnation. Now that should raise some pious eyebrows because the belief in reincarnation is held sacred only by infidel Hindus and Jains. If you do good deeds in this life then in your next life you could be a king or a saint and if you are a bad boy, well, be prepared to be born again as an insect or a dog. Naturally I do not believe this interpretation of reincarnation otherwise I am sure to be reborn as an insect or a dog considering my deeds.

I believe that you have just one life on this planet earth and you are not going to be born again and again. But during this one lifespan you are, for sure, born again and again and on every birth you are a different man altogether. Your firm beliefs, your nature and your general attitude towards life takes drastic turns. When for the very first time you see a human being totally crushed by a truck, a part of his arm still twitching, when your mother dies or when for the first time you are insulted, after each of these and many more such experiences you are born again, you are a different person with a totally reshaped perspective towards life.

Well, why be so morose and philosophical about this reincarnation business, why not look at it from a different and more pleasant angle. For instance, once upon a time I almost hated children, I avoided these little brutes like the plague, and I could not understand those people who kissed and cuddled these dirty brutes, saying all sorts of silly things to extract a smile from them. I also avoided my married friends with kids. I could not even force myself to declare that their babies were so cute and lovely, especially when their noses were running profusely.

Finally, like most human beings, I too was trapped in marriage and I accepted it as an inevitable hand of fate, but as far as kids were concerned, I was still in neutral gear. One of these married friends was dear old Nawazish, who was very late for a certain luncheon appointment and when admonished, he said apologetically, "Yaar, I went to bed very late this morning, 3.30am to be precise, so I got up very late hence this delay."

"What kept you awake till 3.30 am?" "Well, during the night my little son got up and insisted that he wanted to see a parrot. Although I tried to convince him that at this time of night all respectable parrots are fast sleep but he kept on howling for a parrot. So to prove my point, I took him to the zoo which was closed naturally, and told him, 'Look sonny, no parrots around here like I said they are all sleeping.'

"Nawazish you must be out of your senses, you knew that the zoo was closed at that hour and even then you got up in the middle of the night in search of a parrot?"

"What could I do? The kid wanted to see a parrot."

"You could have been a little stern with him, maybe a slap would have done the trick."

Nawazish grinned broadly, "Yaar Mustansar, when a kid insists that he wants to see a parrot you cannot slap him, you have to show him a parrot or at least prove to him that the damn bird is sleeping. When you have kids only then you will understand."

"I assure you I will never be that stupid, I will raise my kids in a way that they never demand to see a parrot in the middle of the night. And if they do I will thrash them good and proper."

"We will see," these were the last and golden words of my friend Nawazish.

I always wondered how could he foresee what was to happen in future, because exactly that happened only three years later. My son, Seljuk, started howling in the middle of night, "Abbu elephant, one elephant!"

And Abbu immediately gets up, places him on the petrol tank of his Honda 175 and rushes to the local zoo and then curses the authorities because it was closed. Didn't they have the common sense to know that a kid may want to see an elephant in the middle of the night? Heartless people! At that moment, I wanted to present all the famous elephants of history to my little kid.

Now what about my utter dislike for the little brutes? Well, there was this pleasant evening with my little kid, firmly placed on my head, I am casually walking on the Mall when I feel that a watery substance, rather warm, is running down my cheeks. Then I realise its source and even then I do not disturb the process lest the kid is frightened. What would you call this total change in my attitude, nothing else but a rebirth, a reincarnation? Now even the dirtiest, and not much to look at, plain kids become the royal breed for me. They were the princes of my re-birth. I wanted to hug and kiss every kid who came my way. Now my kids are grown up and even have kids of their own.

Once upon a time Madam Noorjehan told my wife that she had strictly forbidden her grandchildren to call her "Dadi" or "Nani" because it gives her the creeps and she has instructed them to call her "Ammi" or "Apa" instead. I agreed with her philosophy wholeheartedly, because I also shivered at the thought of being called a "Dada" and specially a "Nana". This "Nana Jan" thing immediately conjured up visions of Nana Farnavis and Nana Patekar in my mind and I was not too keen to join their ranks.

Then my daughter Annie, who resides in Florida, came to attend the marriage of her brother Sumair along with her little kid Noffel. I thanked God that this kid of hers, my grandson was still muttering "Bla Bla" and did not utter a single proper word, but then one fine morning he came to me and, lo and behold!, he uttered his very first word and it was what I feared. He grabbed my arm and casually said "Nana", and — can you believe it — that it was the most beautiful word I had ever heard. Now I follow him wherever he goes, hoping that he will once again call me "Nana" and when he obliges me, my eyes start brimming. Reincarnation it is.

The only negative aspect of being a "Nanajan" is the realisation that now I am married to a woman who is a "Nanijan". How awful!

Dreamland and wasteland

The motorway route to Islamabad has made life easier for frequent travellers. It is smooth and less hazardous compared to the classical GT Road. However, after a certain period of blissful calmness the landscape around you becomes monotonous and dreary. It seems as if you are travelling in a tunnel and that too in a movie — a movie which moves at a constant speed of 120kms per hour. All sensations leave you and you become a puppet driving a toy car. These are the moments when you yearn for the good old GT Road with its bumps and bounces, the buffaloes and the tractor trolleys and the death merchants on wheels. Most of all, you miss roadside truck hotels where the most delicious food this side of Suez is served along with the intoxicating doodh patti — perhaps with a dash of bhang leaves.

So, during my last visit to Islamabad I opted for this intoxicating and hazardous route dreaming about the freshly baked tanduri parathas and daal at Mianji's hotel near Lalamusa, which at one time had the dubious reputation of reproducing famous international products proudly branded as "made in LalamUSA". And who could object to bifurcating Lalamusa a little? The GT Road had also improved considerably since my last visit; however, the toll plaza extracted a handsome sum for this improvement.

Just about a quarter of a century ago when I was a frequent traveller, beyond Kalashah Kaku lay an amazing dreamscape. On both sides of the road sprawled vast ponds brimming with monsoon waters covered with white and pink lotus flowers. These moss green ponds were a favourite haunt of migratory birds. For most of them it was just a night stop, but some of them would stay on. They swam amongst hordes of lotuses while hundreds of cranes stood motionless on the banks like white meditating Buddhas. But the bulrushes surrounding these ponds were teeming with Kalashah Kaku's famous paddy snakes whose poison could only be compared with a turncoat politician. Whenever I passed through this watery wilderness I would park my motorcycle or car beside the road, go down towards the banks of these ponds and smoke a cigarette admiring the view, feeling the luckiest man on earth.

But now that breathtaking beauty is no more. Like the Sassi Punoon legend camel riders have departed and Sassi weeps in the desert for her beloved. According to Mian Mohammad, the nightingale does not sing for ever in the gardens and the spring is not here for ever. The chemical complexes in Kalashah Kaku have polluted the entire area. Nullah Dek, which had more fish than water, is a chemical waste drain and the dreamland of lotuses has become a wasteland. One day while passing through that area, suddenly a small lotus pond appeared in the middle of that wasteland simmering in the sun. A lonely crane stood motionless like a guard. Was it hallucination? Like Rebecca I was dreaming of Manderlay? I parked my car on the edge of the road and approached this pond which had somehow survived the onslaught of industrialisation — it was no dream. Its water was stagnant and smelled strongly of acid waste. There were only four or five lotuses struggling to breathe in the acidic and polluted water of the pond. I placed myself on a small mound by the bank and lit a cigarette in memory of the days gone by. The motionless crane was perhaps allergic to nicotine. He turned his head away to show his displeasure. I was about to depart after stubbing out my cigarette when somebody sneezed near the place which once teemed with snakes. Soon another muffled sneeze was heard. It could not be a snake because snakes are not known to sneeze. So out of curiosity I went into the bulrushes. It was a bird, his beady eyes were watery and his beak was wet. He would flutter his wings as if to fly away and then sneeze just like a human being, grab a tissue from a nearby tissue box, wipe his eyes and beak and then again sneeze. In the muddle of a yet another sneeze he spotted me amongst the bulrushes and said "sorry".

"Who are you?" feeling sorry for him I asked.

"Can't you see that I am a bird," he was irritated by my question and sneezed again.

"What kind of bird are you?"

"Have I asked you as to what kind of human being are you? I am just a bird."

"Please do not get offended, I just wanted to know whether you are one of the birds from Attar's 'Conference of the bird' in search of the Simurgh, the ultimate truth."

"No, I am not that mythical and spiritual."

"Perhaps you are a cuckoo and if one flies over your nest you go bonkers, or you are the bird that inspired the birdman of Alcatraz in his solitary cell."

"You have displayed your scanty knowledge of Hollywood films, but I am not one of those either."

"How come you are here in such a hostile environment in a wasteland."

"Well my whole tribe lives along the banks of lake Baikal and there is a legend narrated by one of our ancestors that during winter migration on our way to the lakes of Sindh there comes under your wings a vast paradise of water and lotuses which is birds' heaven; nobody believed it but I decided to investigate and taking leave from my mates I descended here. That is how I am here. Now I feel that it was a very unwise decision on my part because there is no heaven around here just this little pond full of mud and a wasteland surrounding it. It was just a myth or our ancestor was a liar."

"My dear bird I assure you it is not a myth. Your ancestor was speaking the truth. I am witness to that lotus heaven which has been engulfed by the acidic fumes of industrialisation. Why are you still hanging around, why don't you fly away?"

"Because I am stricken with bird flu, you stupid and a bird cannot fly and sneeze at the same time."

"But as far as my knowledge goes only chickens get affected by bird flu."

"You really are stupid, it is not chicken flu; it is bird flu and I am a bird, get it?"

"Yes wise guy, I got it, but have you done anything about it?"

"Yes I have had a little joshanda but to no avail; my tissues are also running out perhaps I need a towel to wipe my beak."

"But why are you hiding yourself in these bulrushes?"

"I am hanging on to my dear life. Your government officials are killing thousands of chickens even if it hears a human being sneeze. It might kill me too, although I am not a chicken but your stupid government would not know the difference."

"You insolent little bird how dare you call our benevolent government stupid?"

"What would you call a government which through its negligence and incompetence has destroyed a billion dollar poultry industry? Your health ministry assures you through newspaper ads that eating chickens and eggs is totally safe and on the same page appears a news item that chickens and eggs are totally banned at the banquets of the president and the prime minister's house because they are hazardous to health!"

"It's just a precaution because we cannot afford to lose our PM and president at the same time. Where would we get such a pair?"

"Well, if you don't mind you can import another PM and you still have hundreds of generals who are not presidents as yet."

"You son of a bird, if you don't go away I will shoot you as a suspected terrorist."

"I will go away despite my flu, but first get me a box of tissues if you don't mind, a towel will also help and please don't let anybody know about my hideout otherwise I will be destroyed by your flu squads."

The gates of Babylon

THE Literaturwerk-statt Berlin is a place where authors from all over the world can come to meet their audience from Berlin and Germany. It promotes German literature abroad and in turn brings foreign language literature into German-speaking countries.

Over 100 organized events a year are a testament not only to not only the productivity of this work, but also to that of literary life itself. It is an interface between text and author, but also publicity, media and international exchange producing projects with a variety of media.

A typical evening consists of a workshop-style conversation with authors about the stories that lie behind their words, what the words mean and how they were aesthetically combined to produce the resulting artwork.

The first such evening was reserved for Urdu poetry with a special reference to the partition. Iftikhar Arif from Pakistan and Nida Fazali from India adorned the stage. Nida is a seasoned "mushaira looter" whose dramatic and emotional style was well received, whereas Iftikhar's poetry in his usual Shakespearean rendering moved the audience on a philosophical level. The moderator of this evening was Ulrike Draesner, a poetess in her own right and a strikingly handsome woman.

Soraya Khan and Urvashi Butalia from India were the stars of the next such evening. Soraya read some extracts from her novel Noor in her typical sing song style whereas Urvashi spoke verbally about the plight of women during the partition days. Afterwards a dinner was arranged for the participants in an Indian hotel which echoed with the mystical songs of our very own Abida Parveen.

During dinner a dashing blond German gentleman addressed me in halting Urdu, "From the numerous works I have read, only Undlus Main Ajnabi which fascinated me and these days I have your Snow Lake under my pillow."

I was flattered naturally. Ghaine's passion is Urdu language, which he learned in Delhi during his stay there. I suggested that he should visit Lahore also to be aware of the latest trends in Urdu which are prevalent in the contemporary literature.

Berlin has a large population of Turks and their cultural and culinary impact on the city is obvious to say the least, specially their donor kebab cafes are at every nook and corner. The food is comparatively inexpensive and for us a safe bet because they serve only halal meat, so I was a frequent visitor there.

On one of these occasions a Pakistani approached the Turk owner and asked, "Do you serve halal meat?"

"Alhamdulila, it is halal," he replied.

"Then give me a donor kebab and a beer," the Pakistani placed his order.

"Well," the Turk smiled mischievously, "Brother, I will give you the beer but it is not halal."

The Pakistani brother fumed with anger, "Why don't you mind your own business. Did I ask you whether the beer is halal or not?" He had a point.

The next day a beaming Dr Christina Ostenheldt arrived from Heidelberg where she heads the department of South East Asian studies. She did a doctorate on Quratulain Hyder's novel in German and is an old friend of mine. About 20 years back when she arrived in Lahore for her research, she was such a stunning beauty that half of Lahore fell in love with her, the other half had not seen her. Some time ago she was requested by Columbia University, New York, to read a paper on a representative South East Asian novel and she was kind enough to choose my novel Rakh for the occasion. She also travelled all the way to Doha to read another paper about my novels when the Doha International award was bestowed upon me.

"Well, Tarar sahib at last you are in my city, and how is Memuna and your tall son Sumair whom you still call 'Baby'. But first of all tell me frankly what would you like to see in Berlin?"

"Christina I have always dreamed of seeing the gates of Babylon."

The Pergamon Museum is like an ancient dream, where the Ishter gate of Babylon in its blue splendour appears like a miracle from the past. I was stunned to see it, all the structures created by human hands, besides the Taj Mahal, pale beside it. Beside the Ishter gate, the Pergamon Altar from I70BC is also a breathtaking marvel, from Babylon to ancient Greece is the path of unrivalled beauty. However, this path of beauty leads us to the museum of Islamic art where I was amazed to see perhaps the oldest Islamic structure in existence, portal façade of a palace of Caliph Al-Walid built in 743AD.

The climax of Literaturwerkstatt Berlin was the third and last workshop reserved for the Pakistani and Indian fiction which dealt with the subject of partition. I was going to share the stage with Mr M.J. Akbar, a prominent Indian journalist, an ex-MP and a close associate of different Indian prime ministers with an amazing regularity. Initially the famous novelist Kamleshwar was to represent Indian literature but somehow or the other he could not make it and Mr M.J. Akbar made it. Dr Christina conducted this function with a flawless mixture of English and, of course, German. She spoke at length about my novel Rakh and other writings.

I was asked to read some portions of the novel which were later rendered by Dr Christiane Lange in German in an impressive dramatic stance. Unfortunately, the name of the German translator has escaped my mind. During Dr Lange's German rendering, the audience at times showed their approval by clapping and I desperately wanted to know which portion of my writing had appealed to them but it was not to be.

Then Mr Akbar's autobiographical novel The Blood Brothers came under discussion and while talking about his novel he deviated a little and started discussing Hijab and Osama bin Ladin and at times harped about the "tragedy" of the partition. His sermon on the occasion reflected that he was more of a politician than a writer.

I did not want to cross swords with this mighty foe so I presented my point of view very humbly, simply stating, "How could we have a fruitful dialogue about peace between our two countries when you do not accept my credentials? doubt my identity. The partition was the dream of millions of Muslims for a separate homeland, if that dream is turning sour it is not the fault of the dream. In the massacres during the partition, mostly Muslims lost their lives and if you keep on calling the present frontiers as 'Line of blood', then kindly work out the percentage of Muslim blood also.

"As a conscientious writer I have narrated the cruelties done to the Hindu population of Lahore during partition, I hope that writers of India will also describe the mass murder of Muslims of East Punjab. Please accept our Pakistani identity and we will again become 'blood brothers'."

At the end of the function Mr Akbar and I parted as friends and he gracefully accepted my point of view with some reservations, of course.

I left Berlin with some very pleasant memories and dreams and in these dreams the towering blue gate of Babylon still haunts me. Who knows that Alexander the great also passed through this gate to enter Babylon and then died there.

Literary wanderings

For once I had absolutely nothing to do — no deadlines to meet, no TV recordings, no dictatorship and no democracy. A bald headed eagle flew over the lush green golf course and disappeared in the nearby marshy forest.

In the mornings I packed my obnoxiously disproportioned figure in a jogging suit and started walking lazily beside the thick forest from where strange animal sounds emerged along with the morning symphony of the birds. At times a couple of deer would suddenly appear in front of me, gaze at me with their beautiful eyes for a while and then head back to the jungle.

The very first morning of this walk I was surprised to see a very aesthetically laid out flower and coloured plants bed at the end of the track which was not there last year. In the midst of this arrangement was a plaque bearing a smiling photograph of a very young and attractive girl. She had died in an accident about eight weeks back and her loved ones had erected this flower monument in her memory. What a way to remember the dear and departed.

Every morning I stood there for a while and prayed for her soul. I felt a strange affinity with her, the first rays of the sun illuminated her dust into a smiling face wet with the morning dew.

I was once again in Orlando, Florida, visiting my daughter Annie, her husband Bilal and my first grandson Noffel whose second birthday was the occasion which attracted me towards this far away land of America. On one of these days of leisure and contentment, I received an unexpected call from Berlin. On line was a certain German lady Claudia Kramatschek who, after exchanging pleasantries, scolded me for being in Orlando instead of staying put in Lahore because she had a certain amount of difficulty in tracing me."Mr Tarar, I represent a German literary organization called Literatur-Werkstatt Berlin. It is our desire that you should participate in a literary event being held at the end of September to represent Pakistani fiction which reflects the Partition of India and Pakistan. Your novel Raakh has been shortlisted as a representative creation, certain portions of your novel will be translated into German for the benefit of the local intelligentsia. Needless to say, we will provide you with the return air fare and you will receive a certain amount of royalty for the translation of your work."

The invitation was very prestigious to because in the past Intizar Hussain and Quratulain Hyder were also invited in this forum and the best part was that it was also very lucrative and beneficial. But there were certain hurdles in the way, I did not possess a German visa which, as luck would have it, could be issued to Pakistanis in Islamabad only, my literary engagements in Canada could not be postponed and, above all, I was too lethargic to radically change my future schedule.

But the indomitable Claudia K surmounted all these hurdles and in the next 20 days she bombarded me with dozens of e-mails and telephonic instructions. So by the time I landed in Toronto, I had two pieces of luggage instead of one. The extra bag was stuffed with Claudia K's e-mails, instructions, air tickets, health insurance, hotel bookings, etc. The German foreign office had intervened perhaps and the German Consul General in Toronto was requested to issue me the desired visa which was promptly, but miserly, issued as it was valid for only five days. I could be arrested by the German police if somehow or the other I failed to leave the country in time. delayed flight could lead me to a dungeon.

When I arrived in Berlin via Frankfurt, utterly exhausted and hungry after an 11-hour flight from Calgary, Canada, there was no one to receive me at the airport. After America and Canada, I was feeling slightly uncomfortable in Germany as most of the males and females were dressed very formally, a stark contrast to the casuals I was used to. I felt as if everyone was going to a funeral because they were dressed so neatly.

After about an hour's wait, I noticed that a lean and sparsely bearded German was hovering around me, I let him hover for a while and then asked, "Can I do anything for you?"

He adjusted his rimless glasses, brought out a small diary from his pocket, consulted it and said, "Are you Soraya Khan?"

"I hope not, at this age I cannot afford to be a woman by the name of Soraya."

"Well then," he beamed, "You are Mr Nida Fazali, the poet from India."

I don't mind being mistaken for a woman but a poet, now that was hitting me below the belt, "No, Do I look like a poet?"

He consulted his diary again and then said sheepishly, "You could only be Mr Tarar from Pakistan. The Literatur-Werkstatt people gave me the names of three people whom I had to receive from the airport so how would I know who is who?"

This bearded young man Lium was as student of arts in the local university and was temporarily attached with the literary organization mentioned above. While he was placing my suitcase in the car he noticed a piece of paper attached to the windscreen and gave a howl, "Oh shit, Oh f——! Oh I have been given a ticket. Oh shit!"

I tried to console him but to no avail he kept on muttering his "Oh shit" and "Oh f—-" laments. After a while he recovered and again leafed through his diary "Oh, Soraya Khan is due on next flight so we will wait a while."

Finally Soraya Khan arrived from New York and then finally we headed for the hotel. Soraya Khan is somehow of Pakistani origin but was born in Vienna, lives in New York and, to further complicate the matters, is a Dutch national, author of a well received novel Noor with a backdrop of East Pakistan debacle.

Berlin and I were not exactly strangers to each other. After attending the World Youth festival in Moscow as a British delegate in 1958, we stayed in East Berlin as the guests of the then communist regime. Parts of the city were still in ruins devastated by the allied bombings during World War II where war-worn Germans still wandered like lost ghosts.

Then in 1969, Mike Miller an American of dubious credentials, along with three Australian girls whom he called ducks due to their plain looks, coaxed me in to accompanying him to Berlin in his sports car. All of us stayed in the Hilton Hotel in a single room with a little bit of doubtful manoeuvring by Mike. The Berlin wall had not divided the city as yet.

On our way to the hotel, Lium informed me that Iftikhar Arif was also in town and the Pakistani Ambassador had invited both of us the same afternoon for a little chit chat. Our ambassador in Germany H.E. Asif Azdi, turned out to be very amicable gentleman and matters of "mutual interest" came under discussion. He had on his table the latest clippings from the Berlin Press which gave details of the event in which we were to participate.

As the main theme of the event was the Partition of India as depicted in the literature of both countries, he was slightly apprehensive of the fact that the papers were slightly biased as to the creation of Pakistan and this event may reflect the same sentiments. However, our discussion was not very "fruitful" — the long table in front of us remained deserted. There was no sign of a lavish diplomatic lunch. The only reason which my starving mind came up with was that the good Ambassador has been serving in this country for the last five years showing his diplomatic competency, so his entertainment funds have been exhausted in the meantime.

By the way, I forgot to mention Mr Ubaid Niazamani, the first secretary at the mission, who is so pleasant that his long beard also smiles. He is a close friend of my diplomat son, Seljuk and we had performed Haj together so I whispered to him "Ubaid, aren't you going to offer us a cup of tea at least."

His beard stopped smiling, "Uncle, its Ramazan, aren't you fasting?"

How could I tell him that I was coming straight from Alaska and was completely unaware of the advent of Ramazan.

The politicians of New York

OUTSIDE the Metropolitan Museum of Art while the shadows of looming skyscrapers were lengthening, a trio of Afro-Americans was dancing, singing and somersaulting on the wide pavement situated between the museum stairs and Sixteenth Avenue. While the huge doors of the museum were closing for the day I came out in the open air, still breathing the ancient airs of Egypt and Babylon. It was such a respite to see these carefree gentlemen performing on the pavement. So, along with the rest of the spectators, I also seated myself on the Roman stairs of the museum to watch the show.

New York is one big open air stage where dancers, jugglers and musicians display their talents and earn a meager living from the amused passersbys. However, not all of them are street performers. Some of them are professionals and they just perform there to test their ability to perform in front of a crowd. I enjoyed a rare violin performance by a very neatly dressed woman who was a teacher in a music school of some repute. She was not there for money but for the pleasure of performing in the open air, however, she did not mind an offering of a dollar or two to boost her pocket money.

The performers, Frankie, Morgan and big boy were attired in baggy T-shirts large enough to accommodate a willing female and their shorts were flirting with their ankles. They definitely had the gift of the gab and their sense of humor was typical of their race, at times slightly vulgar but hilarious all the same. One of them approached an unsuspecting jean clad girl resting her tired body on the stairs and said "Hey lady! Do you know why everyone is fighting to get a place right behind you?"

The girl looked back and true to his words, the stair right behind her was totally packed, "No, I do not." she smiled sheepishly.

"They are there for a better view, the view of your most beautiful butt crack in town."

The girl hastily got up, adjusted her jean and did not resume her seat lest there is another wise crack about her certain crack.

I am sure if these witty and spontaneous gentlemen decide to perform in Lahore's stage dramas, our local comedians will be out of business in no time. Finally, when they were satisfied that their dancing, somersaulting, singing and wise cracking had gathered enough crowd, one of them addressed his companion, "Hey Morgan! These white folks always complain that we people are not educated. Why aren't we educated?"

"Well, Frankie we are too poor to afford education, if we had the opportunity, we are talented enough to drive all the white folks from their executive jobs."

"Perhaps that is the reason white folks don't want us to be educated but there are good white folks and bad white folks, and here I can see that all folks are good."

"So Morgan you want to be educated."

"Yeh, I am dying to be educated."

"I am a witness to that Morgan, last year you actually died and then a college book was placed on your coffin and you sprang to life again, you love education so much."

"What are we to do? Education is more expensive than a mug of beer."

"Can you afford a mug of beer?"

"No, I cannot."

"Then how can you and all three of us afford education and even then we are dying to be educated, to become millionaires."

"What is the first thing you will do when you become a millionaire?"

"I will buy myself a mug of beer."

"How mean of you! Won't you buy me one also?"

"You will also become a millionaire and then buy your own bloody beer."

"But first of all we have to be educated, there are so many good and kind hearted people gathered around us that they will help us to be educated if they are born legally."

Morgan steps toward the crowd and collects some dollars in a plastic bag, then he sniffs the money and says "Frankie, I don't smell any wealth, we can't even buy a college bag with this amount."

"I have an idea," Frankie says philosophically. "Folks, just to prove that we are bent upon being educated we will perform an impossible task risking our lives right in front of you. However we need three volunteers from the crowd to help us, their lives won't be at a risk because they are educated. Now who will volunteer?"

They pick amongst the willing spectators a tall German tourist, an American girl and a Japanese tourist and ask them to stand in a queue. They naturally oblige smilingly. The Japanese girl places her handbag on the pavement before joining the queue and big brother pounces at her bag and starts running. The Japanese girl, frightened out of her wits, dashes after him, but he suddenly stops, grins and says "Lady, you are not in Tokyo, this is New York. Never leave your bag unattended."

Now all three of them in unison announce to the crowd, "Ladies and gentlemen, you are going to witness a world record. As we told you, we might die in the attempt so if you are faint hearted please leave immediately, otherwise the police will only arrest us blacks for the homicide. All three of us in one go will come running and jump over the heads of three volunteers and then immediately do a back somersault and land on the same spot from we started, Can you believe that?"

"I can't believe that," Frankie says.

"I can't believe that either," says big brother.

"You don't believe that because you have never done it before," announces Morgan and then turns towards the crowd "Shall we do it?"

"Do it! Do it!" the crowd shouts.

They prepare to perform the impossible task and then Frankie addresses the crowd, "You know, we are black but we are not stupid, once we do it you will just get up and go home. So please help us to pay our college fees and then we swear upon our mothers' graves that we will perform the act."

All three of them go in to the crowd which is very spirited and willing and collect a handsome amount, then oblivious to the plight of three volunteers who are still standing in a queue they count the money and big brother says, "Not enough for a college education. Let us give the money back to these misers."

"No, big brother, if we do that they will be hurt, instead let us go to a bar and drink beer and thank God that we are not as stupid as these spectators."

"Why are they stupid Morgan?"

"Because nobody in his right mind can believe that such an impossible jump is possible. If we were such super sportsmen we will be Olympic gold medalists instead of begging in the streets of New York. Let us go and drink man."

"But big brother we swore by our mothers' graves that we will do it."

"How could we swear by our mothers' graves if the ladies are still alive." Big brother grins, "Let us go and get drunk man."

They pack up their gadgets and leave the pavement dancing and somersaulting. The crowd instead of feeling cheated gives them a standing ovation and scatters.

Perhaps I was the only person in that multitude who was not amused but depressed because the whole performance was very familiar. I knew exactly what was going to be the climax and was dead sure that they are not going to perform the promised act although they have sworn to do so by the graves of their mothers. They will promise the moon, befool the masses, collect their pound of flesh and leave. I knew it. This khel tamasha I had witnessed many a times in my own country. Does it ring a bell?"

Of mice and men

HE was the most innocent and playful mouse that ever lived on New York's Broadway Street. He was not even a regular mouse, because he was so tiny that you could trample him under your feet without realizing that you have trampled something.

He was sharing a flat with my son, Seljuk, and his wife, Rabia, without ever bothering to share the rent which was considerable. He roamed around in this flat with such immunity as if he was strolling in the Central Park. He was generally found perched upon Seljuk's bookshelf, which was his favourite resting place. Edward Said's Orientalism was his favourite book and whenever he was in a sombre mood, he would nibble at its pages and was extremely thoughtful for the rest of the day.

He was not like our desi rats, ungainly and ugly. Far from that. He was very sleek and smart, and rather charming looking. I am sure in rat world he could have been a super model, beating Noamy in grace and proportion by yards. The only reason the rat world abhors modelling is that they are terrified of the cats, so how can they catwalk.

Just because of him my daughter-in-law Rabia was plunged into deep gloom for days with her green eyes brimming with tears all the time.

Although Columbia University, where Seljuk was doing his masters in International Affairs, had a sprawling complex of student hostels on the main campus, due to the large number of foreign students the administration had acquired some adjacent buildings on Broadway Street for the same purpose. Seljuk's flat was on the tenth floor of such a building, with a very large glass window which framed the New York skyline like a painting. At times I saw an aeroplane slowly floating over the tall buildings and this sight always filled me with unknown fears. For days I could not pinpoint the reason of this strange fear and then finally it dawned upon me that I had in my home watched exactly the same view on my television one September day. A plane slowly moving towards the World Trade Centre, it was the same image.

It was a studio flat consisting of a large room, kitchen and bathroom. Although the rent was rather on the high side and Seljuk could easily procure a better and cheaper accommodation outside Manhattan, the daily shuttling between the distant flat and the university would have been costly and time consuming. So cutting down on some of his other expenses of daily life, he preferred to stay on in this expensive abode.

In these flats cleanliness was the rule of the day and if a resident chanced upon a foreign object crawling or flying in his flat, he would immediately report this happening to the University authorities who take immediate action to wipe out the unwanted intruder. Normally a notice was pasted near the elevators at first floor which declared as follows.

"Termination Black Warant:

It has been brought to the notice of Columbia University's administration that there are certain unwanted species crawling in certain flats, the detail is as follows:

1. Flat No: 6 — second floor — a cockroach was spotted in the kitchen.
2. Flat No: 10 — second floor — a large black insect crawling in the washroom.
3. Flat No: 2 — fourth floor — something in the flat but has not been named.
4. Flat No: 7 — fourth floor — a suspected mouse but could be anything unspecified.
5. Flat No: 9 — seventh floor — a small lizard residing behind the curtains.
6. Flat No: 3 — ninth Floor — some large winged flies.

It is hereby brought to the notice of all and sundry that a black warant has been issued to terminate these unwanted insects and animals. The terminators are in action and can knock at your door anytime to rid you of these nuisances, kindly be at hand so that nothing else is terminated instead. Thank you."

Seljuk and Rabia did not have the heart to hand over such a cute mouse to the heartless terminators, hence they refrained from reporting his presence. For this reason he was not mentioned in the black warant list.

Then it so happened that the cute thing became rather insolent. He became so fearless that during the evenings he would surface from his hideout and make himself cozy and comfortable on the sofa staring at the television screen. And at times when the cartoon channel was changed, he showed his displeasure by nibbling at the cushions and looking at the other occupants of his flat with accusing eyes. At times he was found sniffing the karahi chicken being cooked in the kitchen and approved the aroma of it with great rat relish.

He was tolerated but a night came when he signed his own death warant by nibbling at the toes of the fast asleep Rabia, who immediately screamed and screamed and woke up Seljuk. The insolent mouse even then did not blink an eye and kept on nibbling at the toe of Rabia who was frozen with terror.

From this eventful night onwards, Rabia not only sat on the sofa or bed on her toes all the time but even hesitated to walk around the flat for essential household chores. Because she was totally out of action, Seljuk had to do her part of cooking and cleaning. She refused to budge from her defensive position. Finally, he decided that enough is enough, there is a limit to kindness to animals. The mouse had to vacate the flat forcibly if necessary. Even then he refrained from reporting his presence to the authorities because he was so attached to the cute companion and could not tolerate seeing him being killed violently by the terminator crowd. Instead, he decided to do the job himself, bought an adhesive designed for the purpose of trapping rats. The saleswoman assured him that the mouse will be lured by its smell of poison and will die immediately without any pain. The tape was rather expensive.

With a heavy heart, Seljuk and Rabia laid-out the trap. The mouse sniffing the fumes of poison, came out of his hideout, walked up to the adhesive tape, mesmerized, and was then glued to the trap laid-out for him. Unfortunately, he did not die easily and suffered, looking at Rabia in particular with accusing eyes. From the day the mouse died, Rabia was plunged into gloom and depression, and I tried to bring her out of it assuring her that they did no wrong, he had to be removed but she could not be consoled.

"Uncle, I feel terribly guilty. It is not his death which worries me but the way we trapped him. You see he trusted us completely and we betrayed his trust, we deceived him. He thought we were friends and no harm will ever come to him from us that is why he looked at me so accusingly while dying, saying, 'Look what you have done to me. I am dying a horrible death because I trusted you, I will never forgive you'."

Rabia is young yet and does not know that we human beings also treat fellow humans just like this innocent mouse. We apparently love them, flatter them and when a feeling of mutual trust is established, we lay traps for them to achieve our ignoble goals in life. They fall into it because they trust us completely. But again, what can one do? If you do not betray their trust, they will betray yours at the first opportunity. So better to betray than to be betrayed. However, we humans do have a choice to kill others before they kill us but a mouse does not. So better to be a human than to be a mouse.

Our dogs and their dogs

So amongst the august American royalty, besides the children and handicapped persons, dogs have the bluest blood of them all. Kindly do not even dare to compare them with ordinary Pakistani dogs loafing around and being kicked around by all and sundry. They are simply a superior species because they are American.

A friend of mine while driving almost collided with a stray dog, and trying to avoid him hit the pavement damaging his car considerably. He came out of his car fuming and addressed the dog: "Look here, what can I say to you? You are already a son of a bitch."

In America I have seen posters calling the President a SOB, but you cannot dare to call a dog a son of a bitch. You do that and the owner of the dog will sue you in the court for hurting his animal's finer sensibilities. You may abhor kissing a human being but kissing a dog is an honour and a national pastime. If you have any doubts, just watch closely the dogs taken for a walk in Central Park or Fifth Avenue and you will notice the smudges of finest lipstick on their snouts, wishing you were in their place and the lipstick was on your collar reminding you of Connie Fancis's famous song. In America you cannot give a dog a bad name so hanging him is out of question, although every dog has his day, starting with kisses and hugs.

Special beauty salons and baths for dogs are a thing of the past. Now you can consult a special psychiatrist if your dog is acting queer and barks at the wrong tree. For instance, if your dog one fine morning looks morose and disinterested in life because it has dawned upon him that he is leading a dog's life, and no matter how much you kiss or cuddle him, he does not recover from his depression, then what a heartless person you will be if you don't take him to a dog's psychiatrist immediately. And if your bitch, while passing near a very handsome dog, does not even raise her tail in appreciation, surely this case is also to be referred. Bulleh Shah in his famous Kafi about dogs says:

"Staying up all night, praying,

Dogs stay awake at night,

More than your stature their height" (Translation: Muzaffar A. Ghaffar)

Bulleh Shah declaring that the dogs are superior to human beings must have had American dogs in mind. But Faiz sahib definitely had only Pakistani dogs when he said:

"These stray and useless dogs roaming the streets,

Who were blessed with taste of begging,

All they own is the contempt of times,

All they have earned is the curses of the world.

During nights they have no comforts,

And during day no pleasures, Living in filth and residing in gutters."

Perhaps you may assume that I am a dog hater. Far from it, I have had my share of dogs, I have not led an entirely dogless life. There was this little English dog who was not much of dog, an apology for a dog to be sure, being so tiny and utterly without charm which explains the absence of bitch friends in his life. He was the darling of a recently acquired landlady of mine, Mrs Gibson, who adored him naturally.

The very first day when I sat down for breakfast, this Darling, that was his name, also jumped into my lap, sniffed at my fried eggs and then started licking my cheeks with great relish, highly approving the aftershave lotion which I had sprinkled on them. I did not want to lose the accommodation, which was to my liking, the very first day by pushing away this damn thing. However, Mrs Gibson was ecstatic: "Oh, Mr Tarar you are so lucky. Darling does not like very many people and he seems to be in love with you."

Mr Tarar, camouflaging his utter disgust, forced a smile and said: "Oh, Mrs Gibson. I could never dream of a day when a darling would lick my freshly shaved cheeks during breakfast." Although I had a different "Darling" in mind, but boy lick away...

These morning licking sessions continued without any respite for some days and then came the Saturday night. I was all dressed up in my Austin Reed suit with a Christian Dior white silk tie to attend a gala ball at the Palladium. This Darling appeared from nowhere, jumped with joy and clenched my blue coat in his teeth thereby practically hanging with my attire. When I pushed him away smiling and lovingly because Mrs Gibson was around, my Austin Reed coat was torn properly and my Saturday night and any chances of a night out were also torn. The next day when Mrs Gibson was away shopping I lured this Darling into my room, locked the door and then with a stick beat him good and proper and for quite some time. The next day while I was having my breakfast, this Darling entered the dining room and as soon as he saw me yelped and yelped with fright and then ran away.

"Whatever has happened to this cute thing," Mrs Gibson said, very upset.

"God knows Mrs Gibson, to tell you the truth I am not enjoying my breakfast without his licking."

Needless to say that from then onwards, Darling always stayed away from me at a safe distance.

Then there was this German shepherd, with a jet black coat and grey eyes, he was prettier than most of my friend's kids and we named him Sherry. He looked so ferocious that when a friend of mine from Jhang, Mr Samiullah Qureshi, came to his visit me one evening, Sherry, sitting in a dark corner, raised himself to full height and growled. Mr Qureshi beat a hasty retreat and the next morning he complained to me on phone: "Tarar sahib, last evening I called on you and was almost torn apart by the wolf you are keeping."

"Qureshi sahib," I started laughing, "How could I possibly keep a wolf in my house, it was my dog Sherry."

Qureshi sahib simply refused to believe me. "Tarar sahib I am not that simple. I know the difference between a dog and a wolf. It was a wolf which I saw last evening."

Now this wolf of mine was so brave that even if a small fire cracker exploded somewhere in the suburbs of Lahore, he would immediately hide himself under the double bed for the next two hours, shivering and looking at us with frightened eyes, refusing to come out.

Once a posh Begum asked my rustic Begum, "You know, I also have a German Shepherd and I feed him on special imported dog feed and vitamins. What do you feed him?"

"I feed him on the left overs — roti, salan, anything. And if he does not behave himself I feed him with my sandals."

Thank goodness my Begum does not live in America otherwise she would have been arrested under some cruelty to animal Act. At times I wish she was in America.

Presently there is an organization in the States which is demanding a complete ban on the practice of eating dogs in Korea and China, etc. They strongly object to serving Bull terrier steakes, Alsatian roast legs, and instead of noodle soup, serving poodle soup.

In Greenwich village I saw a dog shop which sells exclusive designer sweaters for darling dogs and you could see the variety in the showcase where dog mannequins wore the expensive attire. However, it does not imply that dogs in America are not mistreated and abused. A case in question was a dog placed on the footpath of Times Square, a placard announcing his plight.

"Folks, this poor dog was found in a rubbish bin, mistreated and hungry, some evil and heartless person had left him there to die. The dog was rescued, fed properly and given medical treatment but the poor thing is still in a state of shock and has not barked since. This was a natural outcome of his shocking experience and now needs the help of a psychiatrist which costs a lot of money. Please help otherwise he will never forgive humanity."

And the humanity, I was a witness to it, with misty eyes was showering him with dollars while the kind gentleman who placed him there was sitting in a corner enjoying a beer.

A strange thought crossed my mind. What if an Iraqi kid who has lost all his limbs in the war is placed here on the Times Square footpath, how would the placard describe his plight and will he be showered with the dollars also or he would have to pay the price of being a human and not a dog?

Hangman's noose

Was Shakespeare thinking of the London bombings when he wrote "Murder shall breed murder till the end of history always in the name of justice?"

Do we have to wait till the end of history for this game of murder dominos to collapse finally or is it in our power to break this chain of bloodshed? Perhaps we could wait patiently if we had any idea as to when the end of history is to come. But again, the end of history will only come when the end of the world comes, that is a fatal wait which we cannot afford. Naturally, I cannot suggest any remedies but I will narrate a story which may or may not help to understand the present situation as it did not develop overnight.

A distant relative of mine, settled in England for the last 30 years or so made sure that his children visited the country of his birth every summer so that they may not forget from where their Daddy dear originally came from. These children were born and bred in Britain and the annual visit to their ancestral land was a torturous trial for them, what with the heat and dirt and so on, but they tolerated this forced exile from their country to please the old man. They forced themselves to hug their grandmother lovingly at least twice, once when they arrived and the second time when they were departing cheerfully. Naturally they bathed themselves properly after every hug as the grandma had a smell of sarson ka tel and desi soap all over her. The eldest daughter was at that time about 17, a thorough British teenager with jeans and a strong taste for hard rock. She was a cheerful kid, confident and intelligent, securing A grades most of the times. She did not mix with the boys or anything but enjoyed life thoroughly. Suddenly the "change" came, a drastic unimaginable change. On her next visit to Pakistan, she was clad in a hijab and a long coat and her face expression had become very severe and forbidding, she admonished all and sundry for not following the true Islam, considered almost every second thing as haram and almost every male as a namehram. She even considered giving up her studies because the teachers and fellow male students were namehram.

Her father, a decent and honest soul was worried because she also criticized his lack of enthusiasm for the tenets of Islam. When she came to visit me she refused to use the foreign brand toothpaste, soaps and shampoo. During a discussion, she said that although I was her uncle but not being the real uncle I was also a Namehram. Hence she could not sit with me all alone in a room. This observation totally shocked me but the worst was to come. She declared that even if a single hair of a female is visible she will surely burn in hell.

"Your grandmother who covers her head with a dupatta but some of her 70 years old white hair is visible. What would become of her?" I asked jokingly.

"She will burn in hell for sure even if she is 70 years old and I told her so," she said, dead serious.

"And what about all your ancestors whose hair was maybe visible sometimes under stress or need?"

"Hell is their abode."

"And who told you all this?"

"The Maulana who comes regularly to deliver lectures on Islam from Pakistan, I have also studied some pamphlets printed by some local Islamic organizations."

I have lost touch with that family and do not know the final outcome of this "change".

Unfortunately, this change phenomenon has become rather common recently. I met some young men who were born and educated in Europe but their concept of religion was frightening. They were totally critical of the Pakistani society where, according to them, tenets of Islam were not being followed rigidly. Who is responsible for this "healthy change"?

Way back in the 50s, the onslaught of immigrants from Mirpur and rural Punjab ensued, and they were mainly concentrated in the Midland industrial areas where they could easily find factory jobs as the WWII had taken the toll of British men. Although most of them were totally illiterate, they were an honest and hard working lot and they prospered. They managed to buy rundown properties on hire purchase and turned them into "Day Night Hostels" with at least ten sleeping places per dingy room, where the night shift people will return from their labours in the morning and wake the occupant of the bed who was to proceed to the day shift and make themselves comfortable till the evening came and the day people returned.

They specialized in the door to door business of selling ladies stockings and underwear. The gentleman carrying a huge trunk on his head full of ladies stockings etc would knock at some door and as soon as the lady of the house opened it to peep outside, the gentleman would put his right foot in the door so that it was impossible to shut it on his face. The lady at times willingly and most of the times unwillingly would buy a stocking just to shut the door and rest in peace, the gentleman prospered. Then these immigrants were joined by their families, mostly rustic wives who had stepped out of their villages for the first time in life and then landed straightaway in Birmingham, Manchester, Nottingham or Bradford.

With them they brought their limited mindset and prejudices of their native villages. Even these days you will find in the local Urdu newspapers the advertisements of hakims, specialists of black magic and jinnat, pirs whose tawiz gunda has the power to enslave your husband or produce a male baby, magicians and all types of nefarious characters who do roaring business in these little Pakistans. These immigrants generally stayed away from the main stream of British culture unlike other immigrants from Jamaica, Africa and Poland. You will hardly find anybody worth his name in any sports or creative activity at the national level.

Recently, young Amer Khan by winning the silver medal in Olympics has made up to a certain extent. Naturally, the best doctors in Britain were Pakistanis and some engineers too, but they hardly had any interaction with their compatriots for obvious reasons. Then the second generation came and things started changing, this thoroughly British lot was totally frustrated. Amongst their class fellows and co-workers they were in the present times but as soon as they came home they were thrown back into a mediaeval atmosphere and they could not reconcile with this duality. Along with magicians and hakims came the so called Ulema, mostly village maulvis who took over mosques and introduced their own very limited intellect in the name of Islam, preaching that only their particular sect was the path of righteousness and rest were kafirs.

Then the American sponsored Jihad of Afghanistan surfaced and you know the rest of the story. The younger generation, disillusioned by the limited intellect of their elders, without any identity in the land of their birth, found solace in religion. I do not claim to be an authority on Islam and thank goodness for that, but I do claim that Islam amongst all the religions is the most balanced and normal faith. Its liberality is far beyond the corrupted liberal concepts of West, and that is why even in these troubled days European and Americans are converting to this faith more than any other creed. So where did the British Muslims go wrong, we have to search our souls, souls which were corrupted by hate preachers and limited intellect.

There is going to be a backlash after the London bombings. It has already started and thousands of Pakistanis for the first time in their life are thinking of going back to their native land. Unfortunately, we Pakistanis are not in a position to complain because we are also experts in backlashing and at times without rhyme or reason. If a Christian sweeper on the orders of his Begum burns some newspapers, and some kids detect that there are some Arabic pages which they presume to be part of the Holy Book, the sweeper is chased. The police takes him into protective custody and declares him innocent, but a large crowd gathers outside the police station demanding that the man be handed over to them for lynching as was done in a similar case some time ago.

The West is bent upon proving their farfetched and ridiculous theses of clash of civilizations, and right now we are at the receiving end — thanks also to our bigoted approach towards religion. They believe in their idiom that give a dog a bad name and hang him. They are trying their dishonest best to give us a bad name. The question is, how do we avoid the hangman's noose?

The city of the yellow devil

The immigration officer at JFK airport entombed in his glass cubical, apparently oblivious to my presence, was gazing suspiciously into his crystal ball which was flashing my identity, my past and my present, what was my purpose of visit to America, my profession, my political leanings — in short my whole life.

"How old are you?" he finally shifted his gaze from the computer screen and addressed me. I stated my age.

"You don't look it. Which media company are you associated with?" The profession column in my passport indicated that I was a TV compere and writer.

"I am a freelance writer, journalist and a media person, self-employed if you like."

"What is the purpose of your visit?" the inevitable question.

"To see my first grandson, Noffel, and to participate in his first birthday party, to hug his mom, my daughter Dr Annie, who resides in Orlando, Florida, and to visit my son Seljuk who is at Columbia University doing his masters in International Relations."

"Nothing else?"

"Nothing else when my kids are around, but I have plans."

"Do you plan to give any lectures in United States?"

"I am not qualified for such prestigious activities."

"What kind of books do you write?"

While I was elaborating what kind, a PIA staffer spotted me and embraced me in the typical warm Pakistani style. The immigration office did not approve of this spontaneous interruption. "Are you famous?"

"Kind of."

"Do you know Pawaize Musaroff?"

Now this was a tricky one, this Musaroff was some Russian Czar or a cocktail, so how could I know him or it. "I beg your pardon, but I don't understand."

"Pawaize Musaroff, your president, do you know him."

"He knows me."

"How come?"

"Well, only a few weeks back he invited me to the President House for an exclusive dinner."

The officer looked doubtful, although my statement was based on pure facts. However, I conveniently forgot to mention that there were, beside myself, more than 300 "intellectuals" in this mass dinner party. Why go into details?

"Why did he invite you to the President House specially?"

"Well, he wanted to discuss the Pakistan-India rapprochement, and war on terror, etc," I said casually, this statement was also partially correct because the president, while addressing the 300 "intellectuals", was also addressing me, although from the other end of the room.

"Where do you plan to stay in New York?"

"With my son, somewhere on Broadway"

"Which street?"

"I don't really know, he will be outside the airport and he should know."

"Are you sure he will be there?"

"Yes, he is my son, he will be there."

The immigration officer stamped my passport and handed it over to me and said: "Enjoy your stay in the USA." I was granted an indefinite stay on my I-94, about four years that is as long as my visa was valid.

"Is that all?"

"Yeh."

How could that be all, the interview took hardly a couple of minutes, I was not grilled, so to speak. I was not bodily searched or humiliated or forced to take off my shoes, etc. I was rather disappointed, how could I relate the American atrocities at the airports if I was treated so properly. I had heard that some of our ministers and generals were bodily searched and were made to take off their shoes and boots. Well, maybe I looked like a gentleman.

After collecting my luggage, I was expecting and hoping that the custom officials will rip apart my suitcases. But, alas, there was another heartbreak, the opulent black lady just waved me off. Pushing my luggage trolley, I stepped out of the JFK terminal into "The city of the yellow devil".

Maxim Gorky, whom a very literate friend of mine always pronounced Maximum Gorky, author of a classic novel like Mother, visited New York in 1906 and stayed in America for some months. He wrote a small comparatively unknown book The City of the Yellow Devil about his impressions of a New York one hundred years ago. The book also contains some of his interviews and letters to his friends in Russia and Paris. Gorky was a staunch socialist and viewed this Capitalistic city with pessimistic and prejudiced eyes, however, his creative genius cannot be doubted. It is possible that the picture he has painted of New York was true to its colours a hundred years ago. Let us view this city of yellow devil through Gorky's eyes.

"They have again started reviling me in the newspapers. I published an article about New York in one of the local magazines and entitled it 'The city of the yellow devil', they did not like it. I imagine I will be kicked out in the end. Still, I will get my money."

"Over earth and ocean hangs a fog well mixed with smoke, and a fine slow rain is falling over the dark building of the city and the muddy waters of the roadstead. 'Who is that?' a polish immigrant girl asks softly, staring in wonder at the Statue of Liberty."

"The American god," someone replies.

"The massive figure of the bronze woman is covered from head to foot with verdigris. The cold face stares blindly through the fog, out to the vast ocean, as though the bronze is waiting for the sun to bring sight to its sightless eyes.

"This is New York. Twenty storied houses, dark soundless skyscrapers, stand on the shore. Square, lacking in any desire to be beautiful, the bulky, ponderous buildings tower gloomily and drearily. A haughty pride in its height and its ugliness is felt in each house. There are no flowers on the windows and no children to be seen....

"Everything is running, hurrying, vibrating tensely. And everything — iron, stone, water and wood — seems to be protesting against a life without sunlight, without songs and happiness, in captivity to exhausting toil.

"The people's faces wear an expression of immobile calm, not one of them apparently is aware of his misfortune in being the slave of life, nourishment for the city monster. They think they are free, it is the freedom of blind tools in the hands of the yellow devil — gold.

"English culture is an extremely interesting thing. What amazes me in it is that political freedom exists along side utter slavery. Corpses are the breath of life to them, and they worship authority like savages.

"An American will never refuse to accept a dollar even if he has been dead for two days.

"Asleep and muttering deliriously in its sleep is the lurid city of the yellow devil."

Gorky was paid a very handsome amount of five thousand dollars for his writings on New York, a princely sum, with which a hundred years ago he could buy at least two mansions I am sure, talk of an American accepting a dollar even if he was dead for two days.

The American royalty

THE Americans have achieved almost everything under the sun, what they could not achieve they procured and if there was anything beyond their achievement or procurement, they simply grabbed it by force in the name of freedom and democracy. Even then they are a frustrated lot because they have not been able to own a royalty, a superfluous distinction which even a minor principality like Monaco can boast of.

Their frustration is such that they start worshipping even Jacqueline Kennedy as a queen — a famished and undernourished lady of ordinary looks whose thin body could only serve as a hanger for all the designer clothes which she wore without any grace. Even Jack Kennedy had achieved the status of an unofficial king.

So the Americans are all the time desperate to have some sort of royalty. When they can't find it, they create it. Sports legends, actors, singers, fashion models, television hosts, millionaires, chefs, firefighters, and even Nike shoes are their royalty. Billboards, newspapers and magazines are plastered with the images of these queens and kings but a real royalty does exist in America. There are genuine kings and queens i.e., old and handicapped people, children and dogs. Amongst this royalty the dogs have the bluest blood of them all.

A handicapped person is a real VIP around here, enjoying such privileges which even the president can't dream of, although some of the presidents could easily apply for these privileges without any fear of being rejected. They have special seats in the public transport and reserved spaces in the parking lots. Upon seeing a wheelchair or a person with crutches, the bus driver will immediately leave his seat and practically carry the person and his or her wheelchair lovingly in the bus. A wheelchair on the streets of New York is like a president's cavalcade (our president's), on all kind of traffic stops, people give way and the traffic lights hold their breath. It is a wonder that Al-Qaida never thought of it, instead of blowing up the twin towers and losing two whole countries in the bargain, they, all the 19 hijackers, could with impunity cruise into the Pentagon or White house on wheelchairs and do the needful. If a handicapped person feels that he cannot travel far on a bus or a wheelchair, he can request for a special van and it will be on his door step in no time with a smiling driver. I personally know two handicapped gentlemen, staunch diehard revolutionaries of the old guard who went to America and were converted to capitalism. According to one of them, they were not shunned by the public as lula langras and apahaj like at home in Pakistan, but were treated for the first time in their life as human beings, and privileged ones at that. Then there is the royalty of children. No matter how insolent and unbearable brutes they are, you cannot even touch them, if you do that and your neighbours report this brutality to the police, you can be arrested and even the children can be snatched away from you because you are not fit enough to raise them.

If on a busy street without rhyme or reason the traffic starts slowing down and then comes to a sudden halt, it must be the children going to or leaving school. The kids, in general devoid of any manners, cycling, on skates, chewing gum, listening to their MP3 players, can be seen bullying around like princes. If you run over the President of United States, you may get away with it but if the bumper of your car even touches a kid, then only God can help you.

In this regard, I would like to narrate an incident which recently took place on the tarmac of Karachi airport. An international flight arrived from New York, amongst the passengers were a father and son. The father, a bearded and docile gentleman, and the son, a teenager, in swanky and trendy clothes chewing gum. A soon as they alighted from the plane and stepped on Pakistani soil, the bearded father grabbed his darling son and started beating him, the son totally shocked by this sudden attack tried to escape the wrath of his father but the father would let go shouting all the time "You scum of the earth, you nalaiq bum, now call the police and have me arrested, I will see who comes to help you here. We are in Pakistan."

When the amused public finally rescued the trembling teenager from the clutches of his father, who had tears in his eyes the story was unfolded by the grieved party, the father. "You know we live in America and like a good father I use to pull his ears or slap him once in a while just to build his character and one day he called the police, and I was arrested and locked up. Afterwards he always chided me 'Abbaji, won't you like to slap me please'. Well I was waiting for my chance, this is just the beginning, he will know what a real father is like in Pakistan."

On my way to Liberty Island to pay homage to the American god, the Statue of Liberty, I came across a harrassed gentleman who was chasing his kids all the time. One was about eight years old and he was making the life of every passenger on the ferry miserable by running around, grabbing their legs or just pushing them to make way. The other wild one was a 12-year-old girl who was sulking all the time, or pulling violently the tie of her miserable father who, with a forced smile, was trying to humour her without any success.

I could see that the gentleman was trying his best to control his anger, whispering in her ears perhaps some threat but to no avail instead the girl gave a loud shriek and started crying. This attracted the attention of some passengers who glared threateningly at this monster of a father who was responsible for the misery of this poor child. The girl, so encouraged, banged her foot on the toe of this poor wretch who in turn shrieked louder than his daughter. But his howl was received very approvingly by the ferry passengers as he deserved it. I believe that a light slap or two would have produced amazing results but this was America.

It so happened in Orlando that my daughter left me near her car to look after my grandson Noffel while she could shop with ease and serenity in a mall. Noffel was fast sleep in the back seat of the car and while standing away at some distance I lit a cigarette to smoke away the time. In the meantime an Afro-American lady of gigantic proportions parked her truck nearby, came out of it with considerable labour, looked at me puffing away then peeped into Annie car and said, "That baby there is yours?"

"Yes." I said proudly, "That there is my grandson."

"You are a horrible man, smoking near the baby, you should be ashamed of yourself, you are jeopardising the health of this cute thing."

I believe she would have attacked me if I had not extinguished the cigarette immediately.

"That's like a good grandpa," she smiled approvingly and walked away like a faulty road roller.

The houses of my dream

Most readers must have gone through a short story by Leo Tolstoy, which I consider to be one of the best short stories ever written. The title eludes me but most likely it is How Much Land a Man Needs. A man is offered all the land which he can cover by foot from sunrise to sunset, he walks briskly, at time starts running to cover as much land as possible. Possessed with the greed of acquiring just a few more meters of land, he stretches himself to the utmost limits and finally collapses with exhaustion and dies while the sun is setting. He is buried on the exact spot where he dies because that is all the land a man really needs.

We can, in the same sense, wonder as to how many houses a man needs. Basically, he needs only one house and, to be precise, he needs only that space where he sleeps as a house. But the greed for more never subsidizes and a man wants more — another house in a better locality, then in a better city and then maybe in a better country, in Islamabad, London, New York, and somewhere in Thailand perhaps. Recently, I met a once-upon-a-time-a-very-close-friend at a wedding and he owns flats and houses all over the world. But he is still unhappy. "Tarar yar, I read somewhere that Marlon Brando bought a whole island and built the house of his dreams on it. Now I am a man of limited resources but I do deserve a house away from it all on a deserted island where only once a week a small launch comes to deliver the mail or household provisions."

"Yes, yar a man of limited means like yourself deserves a small island retreat, it is not much to ask."

I am personally in no position to condemn such a person who hankers for more abodes all the time because I am sailing in the same boat. My greed for more houses and huts is limitless. Every year I build a new house for myself, although I am also a man of limited means. The greed, mind you, is a very noble passion as even Waris Shah admits: "Although I have reached the end of my life, even then my nature is not free of greed".

I have so far built dozens of abodes for myself. And all of them are in Pakistan, the northern area of Pakistan to be precise. By the way, I have laboured day and night to build these houses, risked my dear life for them, walking through the largest ice mass in the world, gasping for breath on snowy heights, crossing deadly mountain streams, almost drowning myself to look for the sights where I can build these houses while the whole world laughed at my madness. It has not been easy, I assure you.

Most of these abodes consist of a single room built with logs or mud bricks, and I am sorry but there are no bathroom facilities — one has to go out in the forest to do the essential needful. The porch for a car is also missing because even the four wheelers fail to reach those spots. I have been so busy in building them that I have not been able to spend a single night in them so far. I am just waiting for the day when I will have enough money stacked in the bank vaults to retire from the drudgery of writing books and appearing on the idiot box for my daily bread and butter. When these golden days will be here, I will shift into one of these houses. But amongst the dozens, which house or log cabin will I choose? Now that is the problem, perhaps you can help me out if I narrate the location of some of them.

Perhaps I will opt for that log cabin facing the killer mountain Nanga Parbat on the highest spot in the fairy meadows, where on my first visit to this heavenly spot I pitched my tent. I did not face much hardship while building this log cabin. There was plenty of deadwood lying around in the nearby fairy meadows jungle. Everyday I loaded my donkey with the trunks of pines and brought them to the top of the hillock and then just placed them on top of each other. There is a layer of "bhoj puttar" on the roof of this cabin which is waterproof to the extent that the worst rains and snows have not seeped through. This ancient organic form of paper is also easily available in the fairy meadows forest, one has just to peel it off the trunks of trees.

This cabin of mine has only one window. As a matter of fact, a full wall is in the form of a window, facing the snows of Nanga Parbat. In the coming days when I will be its only occupant, I will not need an alarm clock to wake me up because the reflection of the first golden rays of the rising sun from the eternal snows of this magical mountain will enter through my window and will illuminate my aging face, and I will know it is morning. However, there will be some nights when the roar of avalanches descending from the glaciers of Nanga Parbat will disturb my sleep, but I will get used to them in time.

Another one-room cottage of mine is in the valley of Phunder, which is situated on the Gilgit-Shandur Pass dirt road. The trekkers call it the little Kashmir because of its beauty and serenity. My cottage is right on the bank of the river meandering through the lush green valley like a silver snake. I have built a wooden corridor in front of the cottage door so that I will just sit there and try my hand at fishing for the silver trout. I hear that only a few fish remain in these waters due to over fishing. But this does not worry me — I am in my own cottage and can try again next morning while reciting the poetry of my uncle Ghalib loudly. If a fish has an iota of aesthetics it will willingly jump out of the water, landing right in front of me and saying, "Wah", before going into my frying pan.

Another of my log cabins is in the valley of Sokhtar Abad, underneath the Pamir mountains which change colours during the day and turn a fiery red at sunset. I am sure while this cabin is empty, the snow tigers from Pamir descend into the valley and putting their wet snouts over the window panes, peep inside to see whether that Tarar fellow has arrived or not.

Another house of mine, which, compared with my other abodes, is nearest to so-called civilization, is in Khaplu, overlooking river Shayuk. It is built with mulberry branches and mud bricks, with four exquisitely carved pillars supporting the roof. The courtyard in front has cherry, mulberry and apricot trees laden with fruit. A mountain stream passes through this lawn of mine and when the red cherries fall into its icy waters, they turn into glittering rubies.

Did I mention my single room abode in the Tarshing village, which is surrounded by the eternal snows of Nanga Parbat massif? Tarshing is on the other side of this Himalayan giant and I consider it to be the most enchanting village in the whole of Pakistan. To reach the valley of Rupal, all you have to do is to cross the Tarshing glacier, a valley which is littered with alpine flowers and its inhabitants still wear ancient dresses and caps which reflect the colours of these flowers. The locals believe that the mountain of many faces, Shallmukhi, is the abode of the snow queen and in her snow palace live frogs and snakes, also made of snow and at times they come down to the Rupal valley. That is why I built my cabin in Tarshing instead of Rupal, could not take the risk of having snow frogs and snakes disturbing my solitude.

My snow lake hut is rather problematic, due to heavy snows it collapses every year and I have to rebuild it. I have numerous other huts and cabins. In Nagar valley, underneath the snows of Rakaposhi, on the banks of lake Cromber and Ratti gali, in Askole and on top of Deosai, in Kalash and in Koghzi in Chitral, etc.

Whenever I mention any of these houses to my wife, she smiles knowingly, and when she keeps on smiling without saying a word I get furious because I know she does not believe me. She thinks I have gone soft in the head and these huts and cabins are just a fantasy of my immature imagination. Well, she will regret it one day when I will just pack my little rucksack and head for one of these huts. I will never invite her there because she is a disbeliever and does not deserve my paradise.

Sometimes, I wonder as to how many abodes a man needs? Only one. And this house he does not build himself but it is dug by other people for him where he can rest in peace forever.

In defence of Pakistani films

Once upon a time a term "Paki Bashing" was coined by white raciest shaven-headed youths who terrorized the Asians settled in United kingdom. They targeted old men and girls in particular, beating them up and at times killing them and no matter what the nationality of the victim, Indian, Bangladeshi or even Chinese they called this sport "Paki bashing".

However, the Pakistanis are invovled in "Paki bashing" now. Pakistanis love to "Paki bash", ridicule, degrade and almost hate anything which is Pakistani, be it politics, literature, language or local products. But their favourite target these days is Pakistani films, the actors, directors, script writers, singers and everyone connected with films is ridiculed.

This condemnation started with the advent of cable television when the Indian channels bombarded us with cheap soap operas and Bollywood films. The Indian "navel" invasion was on, with the rest of the of the body parts chipping in. Now it is almost sacrilegious to praise or mention a Pakistani film, a height of bad taste so to speak and against all norms of aesthetics. This is yet another symptom of a sick and insecure society.

True that recently our films have degenerated and their quality at times is pathetic to say the least, but how can you condemn Pakistani films totally when in the last 57 years the industry has produced dozens of memorable classics along with scores which even the Indians could never match? And kindly consider that this art form along with other creative art forms are an anathema to Pakistani society in general. Basically it is an anti-art society which does not tolerate any creative activity, the actors are called miraasis and anybody remotely connected with showbiz is looked down upon.

An actor friend of mine, and mind you, one of the top most actors of today, although a Syed, highly educated, belonging to a scholarly family has problem marrying off his sons because he is in showbiz. About ten years back I asked the ghazal maestro, Ghulam Ali as to why he so frequently visits India, is it the money?

"Nahin Tarar sahib," he said "there is enough money in Pakistan, I go to India for a little bit of izzat which is not available in Pakistan." It is said the Ustad Bare Ghulam Ali Khan used to reside in a dingy abode inside the old city of Lahore. Some thieves broke into his house and carried away whatever little possessions he had. Therefore the Ustad went to the nearest police station to report the theft. The thanedar, however, had better things to do, so he told him to wait outside for a while. The Ustad sat there underneath the scorching sun for about two hours, sweating profusely. In the meantime, as his complexion was rather on the dark side, he again requested the thanedar to oblige him. The thanedar seeing this great hulk of darkness sweating in the sun called his assistant and said, "Oi, take the report of this buffalo's "Kutta" he is in a hurry".

Although Ustad had numerous offers from India in the past, he preferred the poverty and indignity of his own soil to the riches and dignity of a foreign land. But this incident shattered him completely and the very next day he left for India and it is said that the provincial governor there, was there to receive him at the airport and touch his feet. So in such a callous art hating society, if certain individuals still pursue the notorious arts of acting, singing, dancing and making films they are exceptionally brave and committed. Under such circumstances producing those film gems is no less than a miracle. Most of these films had amazing musical scores; the compositions were magical to say the least. And what else do you expect when the likes of Khurshid Anwar were around, a close associate of martyr Bhaghat Singh, a college fellow of Faiz sahib, a philosophy master and a composer unparalleled in the subcontinent. I honestly believe that some of his pieces had a mystical element and could melt your earthly existence and transport it into worlds unknown, otherwise how can you explain the flute interludes of Sun Wanjhali di mithri tan and Kabhi hum main tum main bhi piyar tha?

Not only Khurshid Anwar but the presence of greats like Master Ghulam Hyder (remember "Gulnar") Master Enayat Hussain, Master Abdullah and Rashid Attre. They all graced an era with their exceptional musical talents. The legends of Noorjehan and Mehdi Hasan owe their prominence and fame to Pakistani films.

Sometime back, famed TV producer Shoaib Mansur came up with a programme of Pakistani compositions which were directly pirated by the Indian film Industry; even the famous Choli Ke peeche kia hai was borrowed from us. Why forget Reshman's Wai main chori chori which was copied unashamedly by Lata Mangeshkar Yara seeli seeli or most of Nusrat Fateh Ali Khan's compositions. Even today, the Indians are overawed by our pop singers and borrow their tunes freely.

I feel the present decline in the film industry started when the import of Indian films was totally banned after the "Jal" agitation. Since there was no competition the industry thought it could churn out any garbage and people will per force see it. Some producers regularly churned out ditto copies of Indian films. The Ziaul Haq era throttled it good and proper, because the entertainment sector shifted to the religious sector and you know what sort of heavenly entertainment it was including conferences of Ulemas and Mushaikh.

The final nail in the coffin of film industry was good old Sultan Rahi, through no fault of his. The dialogue delivery, dresses, scores and even dances remained the same in hundreds of films and Rahi also remained the same with his flat nose and Attila the Hun wig because it is a fact that public loved it proving that if you administer a regular doze of poison the public will start loving it eventually.

There were times when Pakistani films competed with Indian films rather successfully. When Noorjaan's Dopatta was released in a Calcutta cinema hall, the rest of the cinemas in the city were totally deserted due to its popularity. Then finally the cinema hall was burned in retaliation, ban the Pakistani films to save the Indian film industry was the chant.

Despite the agitation, when Gurudut's Jal was released, an excellent film of Yeh rat yeh chandni phir kahan fame, it did not steal the limelight from Pakistani films. I do agree that we have some colossal self-centred fools in the film industry but aren't we self sufficient in this genre in almost every walk of life?

Recently I read an interview of a film writer who boasted that he is a world record holder as far as the number of film scripts are concerned, he forgot to mention another achievement, he keeps on churning only one story and achieving maximum number of flops. Let us call him Grucho Marx and this Grucho stated very casually and I quote, "India has a population of 800 million, but there is not a single Grucho Mark of my stature in them." Aren't the Indians unlucky? I feel that the present slump and decline in film industry is temporary, the films by Javed Sheikh and especially Ajab Gul are doing roaring business on the box office.

Recently Syed Noor's Churian was a treat to watch. I am just an ardent viewer of Pakistani films and cannot claim to be a film historian so I will be missing a lot of worthy films made in the past. However, please go through the list of following films and do point out if a single one of them is not praiseworthy. Actually most of them can easily be called classics considering the size and sources of our industry. Films like Gulnar, ChunWay, Dopatta, Lare, Phere, Shehri Babu, Pate Khan Phanney Khan and many more perhaps prove my point that despite the present drought of good films we should be proud of the Pakistani film industry and not ridicule it straight away.

If you still have any doubts please try to see Koel, Kartar Singh, Susral, Lakhon Main Ek or Heer Ranjha perhaps you will change your opinion about Pakistani film industry because if you haven't watched these films then you have no right to criticize Pakistani films. Can you name a single film from the subcontinent which surpasses Heer Ranjha in direction, acting, camera craft, poetry and heavenly music?

Dasvidania, Moscow

UPON our arrival in Moscow, a plump but pretty Valentina and her lanky and lean male counterpart, Luna were attached with us as interpreters. Besides being fluent in English, they spoke such pure and classical Urdu that at times we were left high and dry as to what they had just uttered.

For instance when I exhausted my supply of camera films I asked Valentina. "Where can I get films for my camera?" and she replied, with mischief in her eyes "Film? We can visit some cinema house and watch a film there."

"I want to procure film reels for my still camera," I implored knowing fully well that she was pulling my leg

"Hazrat to phir feeta kahiye feeta."

"Ok, where can I get some feeta for my camera?"

"From Gum store which is the biggest store on earth." she said proudly.

Gum was indeed a mini-Moscow. But the services available there were terrible. A simple roll of film was not available. Instead one had to stand in a queue for hours and were given a roll of film without a spool. Then you had to stand in another queue and obtain a spool. Finally, another queue so that you can go into a small darkroom and try to feed this roll into the spool, while the door of the darkroom was battered by other aspirants.

But Gum was not all that primitive either. I saw another queue of people waiting patiently, stretching right into Gorky street. I asked "Valentina, are these people queuing for a piece of meat or a loaf of bread?"

"No Mr Tarar", she replied seriously, "These people are queuing for something much more important, a new edition of Fiydor Doestivisky's novel The Brothers Karamazov."

"You mean none of these Muscovites have read this great novel so far?"

"They know it by heart Mr Tarar, like most of the Russian classics. But if a new edition of any of these classics comes out they simply have to buy it even if they have to miss a meal or two because books are more important than food".

I bear witness to the fact that in 1957 an average Russian would have gone hungry, dress shabbily, in order to save just to be able to buy a new edition of any classic, to procure a ticket to see Swan Lake in the Bolshoi Theatre, or to purchase records of classical music by Beethoven, Wagner and their own Tchaikovsky. I really could not understand this strange phenomenon. An average British would not care two hoots for classical music or literature. Compared with Russians they were totally devoid of any aesthetics, although the British dressed better, had bars and nightclubs, prostitutes and democracy.

One of the most memorable evenings in my life took place when I had the opportunity of watching the heavenly ballet, Swan Lake, performed by one of the greatest ballerinas in the world, the legendary Galena Olanova.

Those were the times when Vladimir Lenin was the only symbol of Russian pride, revered, worshipped and honoured like a mythical god, what with the thousands upon thousands of statutes, photographs littered all over the place. So a visit to the Lenin Museum was a must and then under the walls of Kremlin in Red Square into an underground chamber, seeing the great leader face to face, personally was an historical experience never to be repeated, as the good man is not there anymore.

Again there was a queue more than a kilometre in length outside the mausoleum. But being honoured guests, we were allowed to jump this queue and were in the presence of Lenin within an hour. We also had the pleasure of meeting "The Great Father" Joseph Stalin, for free.

There was a holy hush in the underground chamber where side-by-side in separate glass cases, the two leaders who laid the foundation of world communism, rested in peace, and in war.

Stalin who broke the back of Nazi Germany, was in his uniform, his thick moustaches were still defiant, and his handsome face was pale but impressive. And Lenin, attired in his typical three piece suit, broad tie with a thick knot, bald head, eyes closed, was from waist downwards covered in black. The guards politely requested the awe-struck and, at times weeping visitors to move on.

When a journalist asked Nikita Khrushchev about the maintenance of these bodies he replied, "Oh, every now and then we take the good fellows out of their boxes, polish their faces, clean their insides and put them back."

A few years afterwards Mr Khrushchev simply forgot to put Stalin back in his box. He was cremated and his ashes buried under the Kremlin wall. Later on Lenin met the same fate.

About three years ago, I had the opportunity of seeing the great Mao Tse-tung, in the same state, in Beijing. It remains to be seen as how long his remains remain.

Our hotel, Zolotoikolis, was reasonably comfortable and the food tents served hundreds of different dishes from all the Soviet republics. We always opted for Uzbek and Tajik foods i.e. Polau and Kebabs etc. However, there was one very embarrassing situation that had me worried. The bathrooms were communal.

The very first day when I wanted to take a shower and entered one of these, not knowing that it was reserved for bashful ladies. Upon seeing me, a male, perhaps these bashful ladies, although without any proper or improper attire, did not blink an eye and told me smilingly to go to the men's washroom. Although they did not have any objection if I stayed on, I ran like a rabbit.

In the male section I was the only bather who was having a shower with a towel tied round his waist. In public toilets the Russians provided the same arrangement, rows upon rows of commodes side by side on which perched candidates seeking relief, and in the meantime gossiping and smoking leisurely.

Gradually we became enamoured of Moscow and its simple and friendly inhabitants. The six week "Teach yourself Russian" course, which I had completed prior to coming here helped me a great deal in coming closer to the average Russian.

It was our last evening in Moscow and after the closing ceremony, again in Lenin Stadium, we were invited by the famed Tajik dancer, Tamara Khanum, to her flat on Gorky Street. The great lady who was in her seventies then, cooked us all the typical Tajik dishes herself and served them personally. After dinner she performed for us the folk dances of Tajikistan. Her daughter too was an expert modern dancer.

I remained in touch with Tamara Khanum for many years to come till her death in Tashkent. She spoke and wrote beautiful Urdu.

When we bid Dasvidania, or goodbye to our Russian friends, and our translators, Valentina and Luna, we had tears in our eyes. We thought that our life would not have been complete without a visit to this great country and its lovable people. Now we would not mind if upon our return to Pakistan we were sent packing to the dungeons of Mianwali jail, it was well worth it.

Dancing in the desert

"SAIN TARAR, there is a limit to indecency, may Allah forgive her, look at her closely. She is hardly wearing any thing and the way she is shaking her body, Toba Toba!" the pious Pakistani gentleman squatting next to me touched his ear lobes.

"Sir, it is a great sin to look at half-naked females so do not look," I suggested.

"Sain, I have paid a lot of dirhams to look at her so I have to look."

In the desert night, in front of our tent a belly dancer's slim body convulsed as she was going to have a fit of uncontrollable delight. This was the climax of the famous desert safari, away from the concrete jungle of Dubai. We were also nearing the end of our Dubai trip.

At the end of Dubai's world famous Jumera beach, the concrete sails of the boat-shaped, Burjul Arab loomed large over the ocean, supposedly the only seven-star hotel in the world; two of its floors are under-the-sea! I was told that they offered free pick up facilities to their clients from the airport and you could take your pick from a limousine ride, a motorboat, or if you are in a hurry to utilize the bathroom facilities of the hotel, a helicopter! I was also advised to spend a hundred dirhams, entrance fee for non-residents, and have a look at this marvel for a few moments, have a cup of tea and snack and then get the hell out of it. The idea did not appeal to me. I did not want to roam around a palace like a beggar while the royalty staying there looked at me like I was a kammi kamin.

Abdul Rauf, our guiding and financial spirit decided that the crew deserved a hot cup of coffee and snacks in the most expensive coffee house of Jumera. The coffee house was indeed very posh with an aroma of Italian ambiance and the waitresses were pretty enough to star in movies. In my salad days, in Europe, I always preferred a cappuccino, bubbling with white milky froth with a pinch of brown sugar; I ordered the same here.

The waitress brought me a very small cup which seemed empty at first glance and when I peeped in to it I saw a few drops of thick liquid, resting at the bottom. She also brought a glass of cold water.

"My good lady, I asked for a cappuccino coffee!" I told the waitress.

"This is cappuccino sir," the waitress smiled coyly.

"But the cappuccino I know should have milk and brown sugar," I protested.

"This is cappuccino sir," and this time she did not smile coyly or otherwise.

Naturally she knew better, so I did not argue. Maybe my failing memory was playing tricks with me and it was some other coffee which I used to relish or maybe this is how they make a cappuccino in Dubai.

"And one last question, I did not order a glass of water?"

"It comes with this coffee sir," the waitress again smiled. "When you take a sip of this coffee, may be you will need it," and God be praised, I needed it because when I took a small sip, the coffee was so bitter that to gulp it down my throat, I needed that cold water.

The police in Dubai is not visible, especially the traffic police. They perform their duty through automatic cameras, that photograph an over-speeding vehicle. The next morning, owner of the car is sent the photograph and the heavy fine. A Pathan gentleman, Mr Alam Khan who was our driver, told me ruefully that he has not been able to send any money to his family back home because of the over-speeding fines he has to pay almost daily.

"Why are you not careful, Alam Khan, while driving?" I asked sympathetically.

"I am careful sir, but I love over-speeding. I have been in Dubai for last ten years and I know each and every camera installed by the road to check over-speeding. I normally give my car full throttle and as soon as I approach a camera, I slow down for a while and then speed up again. But at times I get carried away and ignore the camera saying to myself, "come on Alam Khan don't be a coward, be a man; speed on", and the next morning I receive a fine slip. However, on my holidays I really enjoy myself, speeding up to two hundred kilometres per hour but I never get caught."

"How come?" "Sir I remove the number plate at the back of the car and speed on, the cameras flash like mad taking photographs and when the police has the prints, the car is without a number plate so they cannot trace me, simple."

When I asked Alam Khan what he thought of Dubai, his answer was: "Sir, in Dubai a gallon of mineral water is more expensive than a gallon of petrol. Here machines can quench their thirst but human beings remain thirsty."

Coming back to the safari, we started our journey in Dubai and were taken almost forty-kilometres away from Dubai, on the verge of a red-sand desert. There we had a short stop. There I saw powerful three-wheelers available on rent also. So I decided, that if ever I come back, I will opt for one of these and head into the desert all on my own in memory of those days when I use to ride a red Honda-175 in the labyrinth of Lahore's mad traffic.

The safari ride into the red desert was an exciting experience; going up and hurling down the dunes. But for me the vast expanse of red desert was the sight, which freed my soul for some moments. After the hectic and tiring safari we were taken to a large camp in the desert where almost hundreds of local and foreign tourists were squatting on the carpets, eating and drinking freely, too freely I felt.

There was a vast array of different foods and one could have them to his heart's content. Then came the much-awaited belly dancer with Arabian music blaring from the loudspeakers. That was the moment when a Pakistani with thick moustaches was shocked by this show of vulgarity but would not keep his eyes off the dancer simply because he had paid for it! After some time, he asked me, "Tarar Sain tell me, is this dancer a Muslim?"

"Your guess is as good as mine, what if she is?"

"Toba Toba sain, a Muslim girl dancing half-naked is shameful, she should be properly clad."

"I totally agree," I was rather enjoying the company of this interesting gentleman. "Why don't you go up to the lady and cover her with your ajrak?"

"Do you think I should do it?" he became thoughtful.

"It is your duty as a good Muslim," I encouraged him although he did not need any encouragement being so high spirited. "You will be blessed on the day of judgment for this noble act."

He took off his ajrak and held it in front of him like a matador advancing towards a bull. "I would cover her nakedness so help me God," he went towards the belly dancer with resolute determination and when he was face to face with her and everyone was waiting that he will cover her with his ajrak a totally unexpected thing happened; instead of performing his noble duty he threw away the ajrak with a shout of "Ya Allah" and started dancing with her in pure ecstasy!

The next day I was leaving Dubai for Lahore and there in the desert night, a righteous Pakistani was dancing with the belly dancer forgetting that he had gone there to clad her properly.

In the black robes of sorrow

BANO Qudsia and Ashfaq Ahmad were like a pair of royal swans, silently floating on the dark blue lake of creative literature, only making ripples amongst the Urdu and Punjabi readers throughout the world. Last week the pair was separated after the leading swan sang its last song and left its lifetime companion mourning the loss.

Whenever I saw Bano Aapa and Ashfaq sahib together and they were always inseparable I called them a Hanson Ka Jora and they enjoyed my comment.

During his funeral, while thousands of admirers were inconsolable, crying and sobbing, strangely enough I felt unmoved. At peace with myself and at times smiling, sadly, just because I did not feel that he had gone, I felt his presence all around me as I had done for the last fifty years. He did not leave a vacuum which cannot be filled because he had not left. People like him do not leave but hide themselves behind a veil and anyone who visits their written word can see them alive and smiling behind that veil.

While we were burying his mortal remains in the G block Model Town graveyard, where Faiz sahib also rests, there was much talk of his being a Pir or a saint. Pirs and saints are in plenty, but there was only one Ashfaq Ahmad, the writer who was on a much higher pedestal.

However, he was a "Baba Collector". I don't think he ever approved of my crude expression, but then, he never disapproved either. He would go to any lengths to meet a new found "Baba". He would give him the utmost respect, sit at his feet and listen to his utterances with utmost reverence and the moment he realized that the Baba is now repeating himself, has been extracted fully and has nothing new to impart, he would desert him for a better "Baba".

Mostly the "Baba" left behind was influenced by him to such an extent the he would become a little Ashfaq Ahmad for the rest of his life. This was the magnetic charm of his presence.

It is well nigh impossible to sum up and express an association spanning fifty years in a short write up of this nature. Yet, I will try to summarize.

I first heard of the name, Ashfaq Ahmad when I was introduced to a gadget called a tape recorder. Ashfaq sahib had brought it for Professor G.M. Asar, from Rome, and his son Javed was recording his hoarse and vastly out of tune singing voice. When I finally met Ashfaq sahib, he was a picture of manly grace with curly hair, fair complexion and a bewitching smile. After meeting G.M. Asar he would go and meet Saadat Hassan Manto if he was around.

Some years passed and then one winter morning I found him sitting across the table with my father Ch. Rehmat Khan Tarar in our seed-shop near Gowalmandi, discussing his agricultural problems with him. He was a regular visitor and a friend of my father. On certain days he would go to a carpenter inside Mochi Gate to learn his craft, enjoy at least a dozen of Khalifa's heavenly kebabs and then come to our shop for a chat.

Then one day, without any intention, I found myself thrust into the world of acting. And there, at PTV Lahore, he was the king, compering, indirectly directing and of course writing the very first memorable plays that have now become classics. I was pitched against Roohi Bano and Qavi Khan in his series Hairat Kadah. I carried myself slightly with honour and he approved of it. Then came his classic Ek Muhabbat Sau Afsane and I was cast as a father in the very first play Quratulain, which was telecast last week by PTV during the channel's tribute to him. I must admit that at that time I was slightly upset; as a young man I wanted to play a "hero" and here I was whitening my jet black hair playing an old man. But Ashfaq sahib and producer Mohammad Nisar Hussain assured me that it will be a turning point in my acting career and it was.

Initially the play was named Ankh Ki Putli. However, during the recording Ashfaq sahib changed his mind and decided to call it Quratulain. He came up with a very strange logic: "All the plays in this series will carry very laborious and difficult titles so that people will remember only the themes and not the name of plays!" I must also pay tribute to the producer Mohammad Nisar Hussain (MNH to his friends) whose casting and production brought out the spirit and sentiments of the plays in such an artistic way that even Ashfaq sahib was amazed. Although latter on, Saira Kazmi, Mohammad Azim and Arif Waqar also proved to be brilliant. But MNH was the person who blazed the way.

My marriage was another factor that brought me still closer to Ashfaq sahib. My mother-in-law had an inkling that I dabbled in some dubious activities, like writing books etc. So one day she asked me, "Mustansar, do you know this young man Ashfaq?" Naturally I said no ammiji. How was I know that she was referring to Ashfaq sahib? But then she stressed, "Ashfaq, the son of uncle Mohammad Khan Salotri, he also writes something."

Actually my mother-in-law's father and Ashfaq sahib's father were very close friends and belonged to the same town in East Punjab. Uncle Mohammad Khan was a vet; doctor hence the local village term, Salotri. From then on, Ashfaq sahib and Bano Aapa treated me as a relative of some sort. As a matter of fact, whenever I surpassed my limits, he would lodge a complaint with Memoona, my wife. For instance, once Zulifqar Tabish, a common friend and I were discussing his latest short story Dhor Dunger Ki Wapsi and I commented that rarely I have read such a powerful description of cattle returning to the village near sunset, bathed in colours. Truly a moving piece. But, in the end Ashfaq sahib's heroine starts offering Namaz. Why did he have to do it so directly?

To my ill luck, Ashfaq sahib got wind of it and complained to my wife. "Memoona look at this husband of yours. He objects about offering the Namaz in my short story."

A debate ensued during his lifetime as well that Ashfaq sahib should have given more time to his short stories and novels; instead he concentrated more on the media side. He was working on his autobiography, some parts of which I had the occasion to enjoy. A complete novel Khel Tamasha was born out of it. But alas, he could not complete it.

Mumtaz Mufti a very capricious person once admonished me in Islamabad, "Tarar you are also following in the footsteps of Ashfaq. You are basically a writer, why are you wasting your time in media in the pursuit of vulgar fame. Look what it has done to Ashfaq."

Mufti sahib and Ashfaq sahib were the closest possible friends, so how could I evaluate his statement. If Ashfaq sahib was just a run of the mill writer, which he was not, his readership would have been limited. He chose media because he wanted to reach the masses and those masses were there in his funeral procession to thank a man who did not hide himself in the cloak of intellectualism but reached out to them and shared their dreams and sorrows.

In some newspaper interview, I casually declared that a virtuous man cannot be a great writer (Ek sharif adami bara adeeb nahin ho sakta) and the next moment Ashfaq sahib was on the phone, "Oi Tarar, what sort of statement is this? It means that I am not a great writer," and he laughed heartily.

"Sir, you are my ustad and you are a great writer," I said sheepishly.

"But you have stated that a sharif adami cannot be a great writer!"

"Sir, I do not consider you a sharif adami in the usual sense of the word," and he gave another Ashfaqian laugh.

Last time I visited his abode, Dastan Sarai, he was not feeling too well. Even then, he would entertain visitors who flocked around him worried about his health. He was in high spirits, but looked pale, "Tarar these doctors are a strange breed. They have forbidden me to indulge in two things which I love most, talking and eating."

A Persian couplet comes to my mind, which says that a city without a Maikhana is a desolate city. The Maikhana of the city of Lahore is no more and the city is desolate, empty without him. The weaver of dreams and sorrows has abandoned us and a lonely swan is in the black robes of sorrow.